Web Design Principles

A Study of HTML, CSS, and JavaScript

By S. Ken Culp

NEEDLE RAT™ TECH

Needle Rat™ Press, LLC
P.O. Box 801
Goldenrod, FL 32733

Copyright © 2011 by S. Ken Culp

Copy edited by Ed Younskevicius with assistance from Susan Capozza
Cover by Robin Thompson

All rights reserved. No part of this book may be used or reproduced in any manner whatsoever without written permission from the Publisher except in the case of brief quotations embodied in critical articles and reviews or for educational purposes as defined by law.

Printed in the United States of America

Microsoft®, **Windows®**, **Internet Explorer®**, and **Visual Studio®** are registered trademarks of the Microsoft group of companies. Neither Needle Rat Press, LLC nor the author is associated with the Microsoft group of companies and this publication has not been authorized, sponsored, or otherwise approved by the Microsoft group of companies.

JavaScript® is a registered trademark of the Oracle Corporation. Neither Needle Rat Press, LLC nor the author is associated with the Oracle Corporation and this publication has not been authorized, sponsored, or otherwise approved by the Oracle Corporation.

Adobe®, **Photoshop®**, and **Dreamweaver®** are registered trademarks of Adobe Systems Incorporated. Neither Needle Rat Press, LLC nor the author is associated with Adobe Systems Incorporated and this publication has not been authorized, sponsored, or otherwise approved by Adobe Systems Incorporated.

IBM® is a registered trademark of the International Business Machines Corporation. Neither Needle Rat Press, LLC nor the author is associated with the International Business Machines Corporation and this publication has not been authorized, sponsored, or otherwise approved by the International Business Machines Corporation.

W3C® is a registered trademark of the of the World Wide Web Consortium. Neither Needle Rat Press, LLC nor the author is associated with the World Wide Web Consortium and this publication has not been authorized, sponsored, or otherwise approved by the World Wide Web Consortium.

Mozilla® and **Firefox®** are registered trademarks of the Mozilla Foundation. Neither Needle Rat Press, LLC nor the author is associated with the Mozilla Foundation and this publication has not been authorized, sponsored, or otherwise approved by the Mozilla Foundation.

Apple® and **Safari®** are registered trademarks of Apple Inc. Neither Needle Rat Press, LLC nor the author is associated with Apple Inc and this publication has not been authorized, sponsored, or otherwise approved by Apple Inc.

Google Chrome™ is a trademark of Google Inc. Neither Needle Rat Press, LLC nor the author is associated with Google Inc and this publication has not been authorized, sponsored, or otherwise approved by Google Inc.

NMU® is a trademark of Northern Michigan University. Needle Rat Press, LLC is not associated with Northern Michigan University and this publication has not been authorized, sponsored, or otherwise approved by Northern Michigan University.

Publisher's Cataloging-in-Publication Data

Culp, S. Ken.
  Web design principles : a study of HTML, CSS, and JavaScript / by S. Ken Culp.
    p. cm.
  ISBN: 978-1-935715-07-8
  1. Web sites—Design.   2. HTML (Document markup language).   3. Cascading style sheets.   4. JavaScript (Computer program language).   I. Title.
TK5105.888 .C785 2011
006.7—dc2

2011943411

Dedication

I would like to dedicate this book to my Lord and my God who has been a never-ending source of strength and wisdom in my life. His guiding hand has given my life direction and joy and in his providence He has given me the wonderful opportunity to teach and work with young people.

Acknowledgements

This text would not have been possible without a lot of help and encouragement from a variety of people. First, I would like to thank NMU – and in particular the Computer Science Department – for providing such a great work environment and a culture that encourages faculty. I would also like to thank Dr. Andy Poe, without whose mentorship and advice I doubt I would be teaching at NMU. Next, I would like to thank Jeremiah Blanchard for his help in editing this book and making it possible, and also Michael Kowalczyk for his very able technical review. Finally, I would like to thank my wife, Gloria, who put up with my being stuck at the keyboard for hours on end during the summer break.

Table of Contents

Introduction 1
   Book Objectives 1
   Organization 1
   Language Structure 1
   Languages 2
   Choosing an Editor 2
   A Good Backup Strategy 4

Chapter 1 – History and Evolution of the Web 5
   Early Calculations 5
   Early Digital Computations 5
   Hardware Evolution 7
   Development of the Internet 9
   Packet Switching 10
   Internet Protocol Basics – the Post Office Analogy 10
   History of HTML 15
   Review Questions 16

Chapter 2 – HTML Basics 17
   Evolution and Browser Support Issues 17
   Overview of HTML 18
   Headings 23
   Paragraphs and Quotes 24
   Divisions 25
   Line Breaks 25
   Horizontal Rules 26
   Making Text Stand Out 26
   HTML Comments 27
   XHTML Validation 28
   Review Questions 32
   Exercises 33

Chapter 3 – HTML Using Attributes 35
   Attributes 35
   Links 36
   Images 40
   Lists 42
   Tables 46
   Review Questions 50
   Exercises 51

Chapter 4 – Style, Stylesheets, and Colors 53
   Overview 53
   Defining Styles 54
   Inline Styles (Changing One Element) 55
   The Elements `<div>` and `<span>` 57
   Inline versus Block Elements 57
   Stylesheets 58
   Defining Styles in the Stylesheet 61

Internal Stylesheets 66
External Stylesheets 66
Cascading Styles 67
Choosing a Styling Method 68
Folders and Folder References 68
Colors 69
Units for Defining Sizes 70
Box Model (Margins, Borders, Padding, Height, and Width) 71
Positioning Elements 72
Styling Tables 76
Centering Headings with Borders 78
Links as Navigation Buttons 80
CSS Columns 83
Floating Images 85
Styling and Centering Lists 86
Review Questions 87
Exercises 88
Multi-Page Resume Project 89

Chapter 5 – JavaScript 91
Introduction 91
Your First JavaScript Program 92
Adding JavaScript to HTML 93
Fetching User Input with `prompt()` 94
Writing Text to the Screen 96
JavaScript Syntax 98
JavaScript Variables 101
Numbers and Computations 102
Strings 103
Numbers and String Type Conversions 109
Review Questions 115
Exercises 116

Chapter 6 – Conditional Execution and Loops 117
Comparison Operations 117
`if`-Statements Comparing to Whole Numbers 117
`if`-Statements Comparing to Strings 118
Block Statements 119
The `confirm()` Function 119
Complex Conditions 120
Loops 122
Studying Loops 129
Comparing Loops with Numeric Computations 131
Review Questions 134
Exercises 135

Chapter 7 – Functions 137
Value of Functions 137
Function Syntax 139
Standard Script Functions 139
Math Library 140

Defining Your Own Functions 142
The High-Low Game Example 148
Review Questions 151
Exercises 152

Chapter 8 – Forms and Accessing HTML Attributes 153
Defining the Form 153
Form Controls 153
Events 153
Event Handlers 154
Setting Tab Order on Input Controls 158
Accessing Form Content 158
Buttons 159
Text Input and Output with a Form 160
Adding Options to a Form 162
Checkboxes 162
Drop-Down Lists 163
Radio Buttons 164
Accessing Non-control HTML Elements 166
Accessing Style Attributes from within JavaScript 169
Showing and Hiding HTML Elements 169
Input Validation 173
Testing Multiple Input Values and Highlighting Errors 175
Review Questions 181
Exercises 182
Order Form Project 183

Chapter 9 – Advanced JavaScript 185
Objectives 185
The Conditional Operator 185
Additional Replacement Operators 186
Increment/Decrement Operators 187
Classes and Objects 188
Arrays 191
Timing Things and the Date Class 203
Scrolling Image Gallery 210
Obtaining Environmental and Browser Details 211
Review Questions and Exercises 212

CSS Style Guide Appendix 213
Specifying Styles 213
Design Issues 213
Three Ways of Defining Styles in an Internal or External Stylesheet 214
background 215
background-attachment 215
background-color 215
background-image 215
background-position 215
background-repeat 215
border 216
border-bottom 216

vii

border-bottom-color	216
border-bottom-style	216
border-bottom-width	216
border-color	216
border-left	216
border-left-color	216
border-left-style	216
border-left-width	216
border-right	216
border-right-color	216
border-right-style	216
border-right-width	216
border-style	216
border-top	216
border-top-color	216
border-top-style	216
border-top-width	216
border-width	216
outline	216
outline-color	216
outline-style	216
outline-width	216
height	217
max-height	217
max-width	217
min-height	217
min-width	217
width	217
font	217
font-family	217
font-size	217
font-style	217
font-variant	217
font-weight	217
content	217
counter-increment	217
counter-reset	217
quotes	217
list-style	217
list-style-image	217
list-style-position	217
list-style-type	217
margin	217
margin-bottom	217
margin-left	217
margin-right	217
margin-top	217
padding	218
padding-bottom	218

padding-left	218
padding-right	218
padding-top	218
bottom	218
clear	218
clip	218
cursor	218
display	218
float	218
left	218
overflow	218
position	218
right	218
top	218
visibility	218
z-index	218
orphans	218
page-break-after	218
page-break-before	218
page-break-inside	218
widows	218
border-collapse	219
border-spacing	219
caption-side	219
empty-cells	219
table-layout	219
color	219
direction	219
letter-spacing	219
line-height	219
text-align	219
text-decoration	219
text-indent	219
text-transform	219
vertical-align	219
white-space	219
word-spacing	219
:active	219
:after	219
:before	219
:first-child	219
:first-letter	219
:first-line	219
:focus	219
:hover	219
:lang	219
:link	219
:visited	219

INTRODUCTION

Book Objectives

The objective of this book is to give the reader an overview of the various aspects of building web pages using HTML, CSS, and JavaScript®. As an introductory text, this book is more of a survey than a comprehensive treatment, hitting only portions of the much larger base of knowledge that would be part of the repertoire of the professional web developer.

Organization

The book is broken into two sections: chapters 2 through 4 and chapters 5 through 9. (Note that the actual amount of time spent in each section depends on the professor and how he/she teaches the class.) The two parts are:

- Building static Web pages with no interactivity (using HTML and CSS)

- Adding interactivity through the JavaScript scripting language

In addition, some professors may spend a short amount of time covering the basic structure of the World Wide Web and the history of computers contained in chapter 1.

Language Structure

Consider the English language as studied in school. Three of the main parts of English are:

- Vocabulary: words that would be found in a dictionary and would mean approximately the same thing regardless of where the language is spoken (understanding that regional variations do exist).

- Grammar: a set of rules that includes *syntax* for arranging words from that vocabulary. In English, syntax includes parts of speech, word order, and the like.

- Punctuation symbols: periods, commas, quotes, question marks, etc.

> **Secret to Success in Web Development**
>
> To succeed in any class on web development, you must practice creating web pages. You should regularly start with a blank page and write web pages using what you have learned. Practice until it becomes second nature.

English also includes the concept of proper nouns. These are words that refer to a specific person, place, or thing, like "John" or "New York." Proper nouns are chosen by people and are independent of the actual vocabulary of a language. In fact, proper nouns (like John) can be given to multiple people, places, etc.

The languages covered in this class (HTML, CSS, and JavaScript) have the same characteristics. That is, they also have vocabulary, grammar, and punctuation. In this book, you will learn how they work in each of the three languages through practice in creating real web pages. In fact, the only way to be really successful in learning the material is to practice, practice, practice!

Languages

A brief overview of the three languages covered in this text is given below. The material is organized in an easy-to-follow sequence with chapters building upon material in preceding chapters.

HTML

HTML stands for Hyper-Text Markup Language. The operative word is "Markup", which means that it is a formatting tool. HTML consists of both the content of a page and instructions for positioning that content on the page. Detailed formatting of information with HTML is severely limited without also using CSS, as described next. HTML is not a programming language, because data are only formatted with it, not processed. It cannot ask questions or take alternate paths through the source.

CSS

CSS gives the web developer complete control of the formatting of content on a page. This includes fonts, sizes, colors, alignments, positioning, borders, and many other elements. Though it performs a similar function to HTML, CSS has its own vocabulary, grammar, and punctuation. CSS formatting can be embedded within the HTML page or located in its own file.

JavaScript

JavaScript adds interactivity to a web page by providing the basic capabilities of a computer programming language. One example would be validating user input from a web form (like when you purchase something on a website), which would then immediately show a warning when you omit a required piece of information. JavaScript can also be used to modify the format of a page based on complex conditions.

Choosing an Editor

As noted above, students will be creating many web pages and testing their results in the browser of their choice. You should type up web pages, starting with a blank page, using some type of HTML editor (not a word processor). There are a large variety of HTML/CSS editors that you can use and most of these will display your work with special colors to highlight the syntax and vocabulary (see Figure 1, which approximates this using bold/italics). These special colors make it easier for you to correctly type your program and to study your pages for errors. For this reason, choose an editor that properly highlights each of the languages we will be covering: HTML, CSS, and JavaScript.

> **Faculty Note**
>
> Some editors run only under Mac OS and others only under Windows. For this reason, in any given class you will probably find several different editors being used.

The good news (and bad news) is that there are many, many choices available. Furthermore, there is no industry-standard set of rules for highlighting. Therefore, each editor may use a different color scheme from the next. This difference in colors is not important once you have worked with the editor for a while, but it may cause confusion when you see other students or your professor using a different editor. To avoid confusion, you may want to use the same editor as your professor if possible. This way the colors you see on the professor's screen are the colors you see on your screen.

Figure 1 is a complete web document that includes HTML, CSS, and JavaScript. This style and formatting will be used for all of the code samples in this book.

```html
<html>
    <head>
        <title>Area of a Circle Using a Form</title>
        <style type="text/css">
            .inBox
            {
                width: 60;
                border-style: groove;
                border-width: 1;
                border-color: green;
                text-align: right;
            }
        </style>
        <script type="text/javascript">
            function compute()
            {
                var radius = form1.txtRadius.value;    // Get input value from form
                radius = parseFloat(radius);           // Try to make a number
                var area = Math.PI * radius * radius;  // Compute area
                form1.txtArea.value = area.toFixed(2); // Area to 2 decimals
            }
        </script>
    </head>
    <body onload="form1.txtRadius.focus();">
        <form id="form1">
            <table border="1">
                <tr><th colspan="2">Area of Circle</th></tr>
                <tr><th>Radius</th><th>Area</th></tr>
                <tr>
                    <th><input type="text" class="inBox" id="txtRadius" /></th>
                    <th><input type="text" class="inBox" id="txtArea" readonly="readonly" /></th>
                </tr>
                <tr><th colspan="2">
                    <input type="button" value="Compute" onclick="compute();" /></th></tr>
            </table>
        </form>
    </body>
</html>
```

Figure 1. Sample syntax highlightingOnline Source

All of the source examples in this book (including the one above) are available for viewing or download online at http://wdp.needlerat.com. All source files there are organized by chapter. To use the site (see sample picture), first select a chapter number, which will display a list of all source files in that chapter ordered by figure number. To view a particular file in the browser, click the blue, underlined description. Finally, to view the HTML source, click the View button in the HTML column for that figure. If the source has an external stylesheet (see chapter 4), a View button will appear in the CSS column as well. Click that View button to see the CSS source.

A Good Backup Strategy

A good, regular backup process may save you a great deal of pain as you work through this book (and in general). The best approach is to place all your files that you edit for class or personal use under a main folder. This folder would probably best be located at the root of your hard drive and might be named with your name; for example, use `C:\Bill` if your name is Bill. Then, under this folder you can create separate folders for the short name of each class. For example, `C:\Bill\CS101` might have the files for your first computer science class.

Once you have all your files under this folder, you can then move the files to a thumb drive by simply dragging this directory from the C drive to the thumb drive (with copy enabled by pressing the Ctrl key). What about just keeping your files on the thumb drive, you might ask? What happens when the thumb drive goes bad (and they do) or gets lost? It is best to have your files in at least two places. Additional backups offer more security.

With this directory structure, you can also easily create a CD backup. On a Windows-based machine, insert a blank CD and open the writable windows folder. Then drag and drop the main directory to the CD and burn it.

Keep backups in more than one place. Do not keep your thumb drive with your laptop, because if your laptop is stolen or lost in a fire or storm, there goes your data and your backup. Keep a backup in a secure place and update it regularly.

A frequent question is: how often should I make a backup? The answer: often enough so that you would not be caused any extreme pain should you lose everything on your computer. If you are working on a large paper or project, I would recommend a backup every hour or two.

CHAPTER 1 – HISTORY AND EVOLUTION OF THE WEB

Early Calculations

Throughout history, there has always been a need to speed up numerical calculations. Before the invention of numbers, merchants needed ways of counting items, and after they ran out of fingers (and toes?) they started using stones, sticks, or whatever else came to hand. Then the abacus was invented, with the oldest surviving example dating from about 300 BC. The abacus was just a counting device, however, and not a real computational tool, with the user doing the calculations in their head.

This would change in 1642, when Blaise Pascal invented a gear-driven adding machine. In Pascal's day, there were no mass-manufacturing facilities, so instead, Pascal had to hand-make all of his gears, one at a time. Since only Pascal could make them work, his calculator was of little practical value.

In 1674, Gottfried von Leibnitz also made a calculator using a stepped cylindrical gear, creating a machine which he called the "Stepped Reckoner" that could add, subtract, multiply, and divide. (This same stepped-drum design was used about 150 years later in one of the first successful calculators.)

Charles Babbage (1791 – 1871), the so-called "father of the computer," desired to use a computer to solve a real problem in his day. Back then, people generated mathematical tables (like logarithms) by hand through many tedious calculations with pencil and paper. These tables were thus full of human errors, so he designed a "difference engine" which he used to calculate polynomials using the differences method (see Figure 83 for a JavaScript example of the technique). Unfortunately, a lack of automation in its use prevented widespread adoption of his design. However, his concepts were foundational in the early designs of computers.

As governments grew, so did the need to collect and store data. In the US, the Census Bureau was beginning to collect large amounts of information and needed to store that data in a way that allowed it to be viewed in a variety of different ways (by city, age, sex, etc.) For the 1890 census, Herman Hollerith created a "tabulating machine" that used punched cards the size of the old greenback dollar bill. These cards had 80 columns with 12 rows, into which a series of holes could be made. The alphabet, plus digits and some symbols, were encoded into various patterns of holes in each column. Since there were only 80 columns, each card could store up to 80 characters of data.

Part of Hollerith's invention was a keypunch that could be used to type the census data onto cards. The other part of the invention was a sorting machine that could sort the cards progressively on various columns, so the Census Bureau could sort the cards by name, city, etc. His success was significant enough that he started his own company, the Tabulating Machine Company, or TMC. This company then merged with other companies that, in 1924, became International Business Machines, known affectionately as "Big Blue" (for the color of their computers) or IBM.

Early Digital Computations

Early computational systems called *analog systems* were entirely mechanical. Analog systems used gears and other mechanical techniques to solve problems like complex mathematical functions, such as integration. One problem with these systems was friction that distorted the results. In some cases, to reduce friction they literally shook the machine with a vibrator!

Mechanical systems eventually began to give way to electronic machines that were based on large relays, with each relay measured in inches or significant fractions of an inch. Relays were *very* slow. Later, a move was made to vacuum tubes which, although faster, generated large amounts of heat and were notoriously unreliable. One observer has estimated that to make a modern computer using vacuum tubes, the computer would need to be the size of the Empire State Building and would need all the water of Niagara Falls to keep it cool.

During and after World War II, there was a significant effort in developing computers, with names like the ENIAC, the Atanasoff–Berry Computer, and Colossus. These computers used punch cards or paper tape as input and programs were created by switching wires by hand. Clock speeds were in the 10s of milliseconds to 10s of microseconds time range (top CPU speeds are in the 100 picosecond range today).

These hardware efforts were paralleled by many theoretical and architectural design papers. The first of these was a 1936 paper by Alan Turing titled "On Computable Numbers" in which he outlined certain basic limitations that were common to all computers. At the same time, he defined a universal computer for running any program stored on virtual paper tape. All modern computers, like the universal computer, are said to be "Turing-complete"; that is, all modern computers have been shown to be equal in computing power to each other (but only in terms of capability, as the actual speed of calculation between machines can vary immensely).

Computer "Bugs"

Grace Hopper (1906 – 1992) loved to tell the following true story of the first computer bug. Dr. Hopper was a faculty member at Harvard and a Naval Reserve officer well into her old age, reaching the rank of rear admiral before retiring. On September 9, 1947, a test was being made of an early computer called the Mark II Aiken Relay Calculator. As proof of Murphy's Law, when the time came to do demonstrations to the top brass the computer was not working. The engineers traced the problem back to a dead moth lying between the contactors on a relay. The bug was removed and affixed to the engineering log, a log that is still in the Naval Surface Warfare Center Computer Museum at Dahlgren, Virginia. When the engineers removed the bug, the term "debugging" was created.

Von Neumann Architecture

Turing's design was later extended by John von Neumann (a Hungarian-born mathematician). He defined an architecture which used the same memory both to store programs and to store data. His architecture was best described in an article entitled "First Draft of a Report on the EDVAC [1945]," which defined the basic elements of the stored program concept now used throughout the computer industry.

Up to this time, all computers had their programs "hard-wired" into the computer, not programmed in software as we do today. Furthermore, memory (measured in 10s of locations) was only for data. In the earliest models, you had to take the computer apart to make any changes to the program. A little later, computers like the UNIVAC were programmed with a series of jumper wires, which could be plugged into different pairs of holes to produce the program.

Van Neumann's idea was that the computer program would be stored in the same memory as the data, and this program would then be interpreted by a part of the computer called the Central Processing Unit (or CPU) where appropriate actions would be taken based on each instruction that was fetched from memory.

Van Neumann then defined four basic components for the computer (as shown in Figure 2):

1. **Central Processing Unit**. The CPU takes instructions from memory and does computations based on those instructions, modifying data as needed back in memory.

2. **Memory**. Both the program and the data being modified are stored in the same type of memory, just in different places. As far as the memory is concerned, there is no difference between stored data and stored programs. A stored program is just data for the CPU, consisting of a series of machine instructions reduced to binary form.

3. **Input/Output**. The I/O system interfaces with the outside world by connecting the computer to various types of devices, which today could be a hard disk drive, monitor, printer, mouse, keyboard, or CD or DVD drive.

4. **Bus**. The bus is a bunch of wires and electronics that allows the CPU to access memory and the I/O system. Both data and programs are moved on the bus. The I/O system has to understand each specific protocol needed to interface to different devices; for example, disk drives are controlled differently than printers or monitors.

Computer operation would follow a basic pattern: an instruction is fetched from memory, and then based on the instruction, one or more data items would be obtained from memory and used in computation, the result of which would be moved back to some memory location. For example, two values might be fetched, multiplied together, and the product stored back in memory.

If data needed to be moved to or from external devices, the CPU would control both via the I/O system. The CPU would tell the I/O system to either input data from a particular device into a specific location in memory, or move data from a specific location in memory to a specific device.

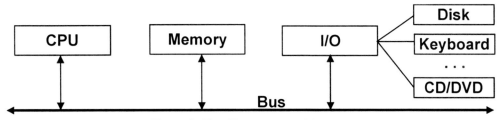

Figure 2. Von Neumann architecture

Interestingly, modern computers have several Von Neumann architectures in them in the form of special-purpose microprocessors, not just in the main CPU. Each of these microprocessors is, in itself, using a Von Neumann architecture because they have built-in "cache" memory, a processing unit, an internal bus, and an I/O function. Most circuit boards in the computer (and also the hard drive) have their own microprocessor, in fact. However, these microprocessors have specialized functions and run "read-only" programs rather than programs from the disk or main memory.

Hardware Evolution

This section explores the evolution of three significant aspects of computer performance: (1) memory construction and size; (2) disk size; and (3) CPU speed.

Discrete Memory (relays, tubes, transistors, core)

Virtually all computer memory is inherently binary in nature, having only the two states of "off" and "on," although combinations of binary devices have been combined in the past to create other structures like the decimal coding in IBM® 1620 and 1401 computers (1960). In the late 1800s, these binary devices were relays, like those used in Hollerith's tabulating machine, with access speeds measured in tenths and hundredths of seconds. Mechanical relays gave way to much faster vacuum tubes during World War II in computers like the ENIAC, which had 18,000 tubes.

The early 1950s saw the advent of core memory in the form of small rings of magnetic material called "toroids," which were programmed by changing the direction of a magnetic field. Core memory had access times in the 20 to 25 microsecond range, giving another significant increase in speed.

In 1949, William Shockley invented the discrete germanium transistor. Transistors had many advantages over vacuum tubes in both speed and heat dissipation and they soon began to replace tubes in the CPU. However, their cost compared to core memory made them impractical to use for the bulk of computer memory.

The Integrated Circuit

The greatest single breakthrough in computers, both in CPU design and memory design, was the integrated circuit. In addition to cost, discrete transistors on a circuit board have disadvantages in their size and heat dissipation, which are much less of an issue with integrated circuits. Furthermore, the speed limitation on discrete transistor-based CPUs was caused by the length of the wires connecting the transistors; that is, the speed of light became a limiting factor, and it remains so today (along with power dissipation).

In 1958, Jack Kirby, working at Texas Instruments Incorporated, developed the integrated circuit (IC). The IC had the advantage of greatly reducing the space required for transistors as well as reducing the length and number of the connecting wires. Kirby's first IC had one transistor, three resistors, and one capacitor, and was about the size of a small fingernail. Today's ICs contain transistors numbering in the hundreds of millions.

Integrated circuits continue to develop at an exponential pace (see Moore's Law below) with the design objectives always being more and faster transistors. Unfortunately, as you increase the speed of the chips and raise the transistor count, power consumption increases as well. One of the current limits on the technology is heat dissipation, which is why you see such large fan systems on many CPUs. Previously the domain of enthusiasts, water cooling in a PC might be a mainstream feature soon.

Moore's Law

One of the most obvious characteristics of the computer industry (or most industries for that matter) is the rapid rate of technological advancement. In fact, this growth in technology has been following an exponential path for many years now. In exponential growth, the number of something multiplies on itself and therefore expands at an ever-increasing rate. For example, bacteria grow exponentially in a Petri dish until reaching the saturation point.

This exponential growth applies in the computer world to several things:

- Computer memory sizes measured at the same cost
- Hard drive sizes for the same cost
- CPU and bus clock speeds

The phenomenon was noticed by several different scientists in the past but was made most famous by Gordon E. Moore, who, in 1965, noted that the number of transistors on a single IC chip had doubled every year since the year the IC was invented. He predicted the trend would continue for the next 10 years, a prediction that would come to be quite accurate. This, however, was partly due to the fact that semiconductor manufacturers used this trend in planning new products and scheduling research and development. Due to the prediction's success, the term "Moore's Law" was coined in 1970. In 1975, Gordon Moore revised his estimate to every two years, but industry experts now say the doubling is currently occurring about every 18 months.

As a related example, consider hard drive sizes. In 1983, typical hard drives for the IBM® PC were 5 megabytes, with the largest being about 20 megabytes. Now drives in the 5 terabyte range are available for which you would pay about the same as for a 20 megabyte drive in 1983 (in constant inflation-adjusted dollars). Using 28 years as the exponent in an exponential function, this growth corresponds to a doubling roughly every 18 months. Computer RAM has experienced similar growth; in 1983 most machines had 500 kilobytes of RAM, while current machines usually have 4 to 8 gigabytes.

Development of the Internet

Circuit Switching and Dedicated Circuits

Circuit switching was an early technology used by the telephone companies. With circuit switching, relays created a complete electrical circuit from one point to another within the same city or perhaps even across the country. For telephone service, these connections were temporary, created with the dialing process; other circuits, though, could be created as "dedicated circuits" that were maintained over time, frequently using leased lines. These dedicated circuits were used to connect computers and had a capacity of about 50k bits per second, which is about the speed of a fast dial-up modem (a bit being a single binary digit that can take two values: 0 or 1).

Since circuit switching uses a single path, a break in the path along the line would disconnect the computers using the circuit. Imagine that we wanted to create a network where any node (computer or server) could communicate with any other node without having to disconnect and reconnect. To create a network using circuit switching, you would need a different circuit between every pair of nodes (that is, computers or servers). With a direct connection between each of the other nodes, you would need 6 circuits; with 5 other nodes, you would need 10 circuits; and with 6 other nodes you would need 15 circuits (mathematically, this is the number of ways of choosing 2 items out of n items). Obviously, with hundreds of millions of nodes as we have today, it would be impossible to create such a network using circuit switching. Thus a new method for connecting computers was needed, and the solution came in the form of packet switching.

Packet Switching

The original driving force behind the development of the internet as we know it today was a desire by the Department of Defense (DOD) to have a network that was redundant and able to survive a nuclear attack. (This drive was particularly strong after the launch of Sputnik by the Soviet Union.) The DOD tasked the Defense Advanced Research Projects Agency (DARPA) to create such a network, and the network they created was ARPANET.

> **Packet Switching**
>
> In packet switching, a block of information is broken into smaller parts and each part is routed independently from source to destination. Packets may arrive out of order, so they are reordered using their packet sequence numbers. The advantages of packet switching over circuit switching include reliability, survivability, and automatic load balancing.

Before ARPANET could exist, however, a key technology had to be developed first: packet switching. During the cold war in 1962, DARPA created the Information Processing Techniques Office (IPTO) within DARPA and tasked it with the creation of a communications system that would be reliable and meet DOD requirements. Achieving survivability meant that the system should continue to operate even if one or more portions of the system became disabled. This implied multiple routes, with automatic rerouting in the event of failure.

To address this problem, studies by the Rand Corporation during the 1960s described the process of breaking information into small blocks. Working in parallel, developers in the United Kingdom described a similar technique which they called "packet switching," a term that ended up being accepted by the industry. The concept of packet switching was a significant enhancement from circuit switching because far fewer physical connections were required, enhancing reliability and scalability greatly.

DARPA's early packet network, ARPANET, went live at 10:30 p.m. on October 29, 1969. This network included 2 sites: UCLA and Stanford. By December 5, they had 2 more sites on the network (University of Utah and UC Santa Barbara). By 1981, there were 213 sites, which they termed *hosts*, and the underlying protocol for moving packets in the growing ARPANET was the Network Control Program, or NCP. In this architecture, the addition of nodes and control of the network was centralized.

Simultaneously, a variety of other networks were being developed in Europe (x.25) and in academia (Unix to Unix Copy, or UUCP). These networks used different rules (protocol) for routing information, so interconnectivity between these different networks was always an issue. As a result, DARPA commissioned the development of a new, unifying set of rules (again, protocol) for all networks. This new protocol was to reduce the network itself to a minimum, with the hosts (computers) themselves being responsible for the network, not a central agency.

The result of this design emerged in 1978, and after several enhancements, the design became known as TCP/IP (Transmission Control Protocol/Internet Protocol), as it is known today. It was also during this time that the term "Internet" came into common usage, which ARPANET was one piece of. (Later on, ARPANET would be gradually phased out, leading to its formal decommissioning in 1990.) On January 1, 1983, all computers in the world running NCP were shut down and restarted using TCP/IP. (Restarting everyone at once that day was not difficult because the number of computers numbered in the hundreds, instead of the hundreds of millions like we have today.)

Internet Protocol Basics – the Post Office Analogy

Now that you know the motivation for packet switching, let's examine TCP/IP in more detail. Consider, as an analogy, the US Postal Service. The post office initially receives mail via collection boxes (mailboxes). This mail is then routed to other distribution centers, and finally to the destination post office for final delivery. There is not a separate truck (or plane) flying from every post office in the country to every other post office, which would be analogous to the circuit switching system we discussed earlier.

So how does the post office know how to forward your mail to the right place, then? It uses the address on the envelope to determine the best routing. (In fact, this routing is simplified by the use of the zip code and zip plus 4.) All pieces of mail have a destination address; similarly, to be able to return a piece of undeliverable mail, you need a return address. Now, let's use this analogy to describe the Internet.

First, instead of having a dedicated circuit between each host/computer in the network, the Internet has a set of distribution centers (called carrier hotels) whose job is to move the mail (packets) from one geographic location to the next. In order to know how to route these data, TCP/IP requires each packet to have both a sender and receiver address. In TCP/IP these addresses are called the "source" and "destination" addresses, respectively. Instead of name, street, city, state, and zip like an address has, the IP address is a whole number. In IP version 4 (current), this is a 32-bit number (separated into 4 parts, called "octets") allowing for approximately 4 billion unique addresses. In IP version 6, this is a 128-bit number (separated into 16 parts) with, for all practical purposes, unlimited addressing (more on this later).

Say you want to access a web page on a server. At the server, the TCP part of TCP/IP takes that page and breaks it into a series of packets, and then hands those packets to IP for sending through the network. In IP, each packet might travel a different route from source to destination, and those packets might arrive at the destination in the wrong order, so TCP at the destination reassembles the packets in the correct order into the complete page. (Keeping the order implies that each packet will have a unique sequence number.)

For flow control and reliability, TCP uses end-to-end acknowledgement to guarantee delivery of packets. Flow control means that the source will not overload the destination with packets by just simply pumping out data (keeping in mind that various devices operate at different speeds). Instead, the sender and receiver cooperate in order to limit the number of packets en route at any one time.

Lost packets are detected by TCP by waiting for a specified time-out period for all packets to arrive (after the first one is received). If a packet has not arrived in that time and is declared lost, the destination node sends a message to the source node requesting retransmission of the packet. On the other hand, IP simply moves packets and does not detect lost packets.

As an example, consider Figure 3, which shows a network with eight different "postal workers" for packets. In IP, these postal workers are called "routers." A router is a special-purpose computer that understands how to route each received packet towards its destination. However, each router typically knows of multiple routes from itself to the destination (like any postal worker would). For example, router Q knows that it can forward the packet on towards its destination by sending it to router C, J, A, or T. The path chosen is based on the statistics on each path that are kept in tables within the router, and the router will make sure to choose a path that is functioning and either has the least load or is the "fastest" path. (How load or speed is determined is beyond the scope of this text.) Broken paths are detected by the router when communication is lost along a specific path.

> **Router**
>
> A router is a special-purpose computer that moves packets from one place to another using the "best" route possible. The router implements IP.

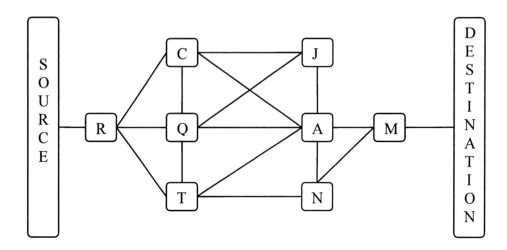

Figure 3. Sample network with eight routers

Our hypothetical web page might be broken into five separate packets during transmission (a packet can typically hold about 1,500 bytes): packet one might travel the route RQTNM; packet two might travel RCQAM; packet three might travel RQJATNM; and so on.

Note that packet three described above passes through more routers. This might be a result of the link between A and M being down when it was sent, which would show the survivability of the network and its ability to automatically recover from partial breaks.

Finding the IP Route

When a packet arrives at a router, the destination address may be unknown to the router. The router would then have to find a path from itself to the destination. This is done by sending "broadcast" messages over the router's known paths asking for information about routes to the destination. These messages would then be forwarded as many times as necessary until some router that knows of the destination is found. When a router is discovered that knows this path, it is forwarded back to every requester, so that every requester that had forwarded the inquiry on would now know the route and would save the route for future requests. With so many possible paths and nodes, you can imagine that routers have to maintain a lot of data as they work.

Keeping Track of Hosts/Computers (DNS)

In the early days of ARPANET, SRI was charged with assigning IP addresses to the various new hosts that wanted access to the network. These IP addresses and corresponding names of hosts were stored in a special file, called `hosts.txt`, which was located on every computer in the network. As nodes were added, SRI updated this file and distributed it to each computer.

> **Domain Name System (DNS)**
>
> DNS is a distributed database that maps IP addresses to hostnames (and vice versa). The database is distributed, in that there are many, many DNS servers, but none of them individually could realistically contain the complete database, due to its incredible size.

As you might imagine, this process became quite onerous when the number of nodes began to grow rapidly. What was needed was a way for the network to maintain that information for itself. As new nodes were added, the network would take care of routing the new node's information to the rest of the network. As a result of the design effort to tackle this problem, the Domain Name System (DNS) concept was introduced.

DNS is a distributed database that can map between hostnames and IP addresses. If the request to DNS supplies the hostname, DNS returns an IP address. Alternately, if the request supplies an IP address, DNS returns the hostname. The DNS database that does this mapping is distributed across many thousands of DNS servers throughout the world; furthermore, this database is so large (since there so many hosts) that it is unrealistic for any one server to contain the complete database (and there is no compelling reason for this database to be entirely contained in one place anyway). Instead, each DNS server only needs to know about nodes in its vicinity or nodes it has been requested to locate.

Automatic DNS Database Distribution

The database becomes distributed as follows. Say a new host is brought up in California, and a computer in New York tries to access a web page on that new host. The New York computer would access its closest DNS server and request a mapping from that hostname to the IP address. Assuming that the DNS server in New York does not currently have that mapping in its local store, it sends out a broadcast to the DNS servers that it knows about. These DNS servers continue forwarding the request through the network until a DNS server is found that knows the mapping. Then, the mapping is returned to each DNS server in the chain until it gets back to the New York DNS server, which then satisfies the original request.

Once a mapping is found, each DNS server in the route from New York to California would now know that mapping. (This is one reason why there is sometimes a significant delay in supplying the initial request for a web page, but subsequent requests are much faster.)

Examining the DNS Database (NSLOOKUP)

The Microsoft Windows® operating system includes a command-line utility, **NSLOOKUP**, which will send requests to the nearest DNS server and then display the mapping that was returned. To run this command, click **Start/Run**, type **CMD**, and press enter. This opens a command window as shown in Figure 4. (Note that this window was resized to reduce the size of the image.)

To find an IP address, type **NSLOOKUP** in the command window followed by the hostname, as shown in the first example in Figure 4. The first part of the reply from **NSLOOKUP** is the name ("frieda.nmu.edu") and IP address (198.110.199.20) of the nearest DNS server. The second part is the answer to the inquiry, which shows the name requested (**wdp.needlerat.com**) followed by the associated IP address (173.192.11.2).

To find a hostname from an IP address, type **NSLOOKUP** followed by the IP address, as in the second example in Figure 4. Again the identification of the server is given, followed by the name of the server. Note that the name returned is not exactly the same, though. This is because, in this case, **ns1.esperhosting.net** is the name of the site hosting **needlerat.com**.

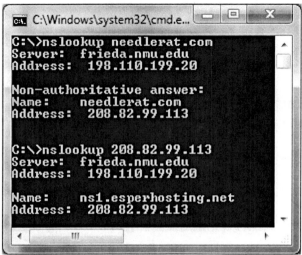

Figure 4. Examining DNS database with NSLOOKUP

IP (Version 4) Display Format

The current version of Internet Protocol (IP) is version 4, sometimes abbreviated as *IPv4*. This version of IP uses 32-bit (4-byte) addresses, and to make the numbers easier to write and to remember, the numbers are formatted using the "dot" notation as shown in Figure 4. For example, the IP address of **nmu.edu** is **198.110.200.4**. This notation can be understood by considering the 32-bit address as four bytes of 8 bits each. An 8-bit number can have a value between 0 and 255, and for this notation each byte of the address is converted to its decimal equivalent and separated by periods as shown. Compare **198.110.200.4** to the actual decimal value of the IP address: 3,329,148,932. The dot notation is easier for humans to remember and use.

IPv4 Address Exhaustion and IPv6

A 32-bit IP address allows for approximately 4 billion addresses (theoretically 4,294,967,296, but actually 3,706,650,624 in practice for various technical reasons). You might think that this would be a basically unlimited supply, but the Internet Assigned Number Authority (IANA) allocated the last of its blocks of IPv4 addresses on February 3, 2011.

IPv4 versus IPv6
IP version 4 (IPv4) uses 32-bit addresses, and the pool of addresses it can use has now been exhausted. IP version 6 (IPv6) uses 128-bit addresses that will provide a virtually unlimited set of addresses, plus a great deal of new capabilities.

Foreseeing this eventuality, the architects of the internet created a new IP version, IPv6, which uses a 128-bit address. This creates a virtually unlimited supply of addresses (one for every atom on the surface of the Earth, many times over) and adds many new capabilities. Due to the massive number of computers in the world, however, the industry does not have the privilege of shutting down every computer at the same time on IPv4 and restarting them with IPv6, as in the days of the conversion from NCP. Therefore, sites are bringing up both protocols in parallel currently, but this conversion will surely create significant headaches for system designers and will likely be a source of publicity in the future.

History of HTML[1]

Once various universities and corporations were connected via the internet, there arose a need to share information in a more meaningful way other than just sending files back and forth. During this same period, there were various text formatting schemes to create nice-looking printed documents. In the formatting programs that used these schemes, the format instructions were interspersed within the text of the document, and the format instructions were just normal printable symbols but used in a special way so that the program could distinguish between the text and the formatting. One such system was called ROFF (and there were other derivatives of it as well, like TROFF, GROFF, etc.); another system was SGML, which was IBM Corporation's version of GML.

In 1980, Tim Berners-Lee, a physicist with CERN, was using an in-house SGML text formatting system and decided to design an extension of it for the Internet. In 1991 he published an article called "HTML Tags," which described 20 elements for formatting text that became the original version of HTML (Hyper-Text Markup Language).

As HTML gained acceptance, many new features were desired. In November of 1995, version 2.0 was released, and in the following months, several other new features were added (file upload, tables, image maps, etc.). In January of 1997, version 3.2 was proposed by the World Wide Web Consortium (W3C), followed by proposed version 4.0 in December of 1997. Version 4.0 is the version most commonly being used today and is the version covered in this text.

---

[1] http://en.wikipedia.org/wiki/HTML

Review Questions

1. Describe the contribution to the evolution of computers made by the following people:
   a. Blaise Pascal
   b. Gottfried von Leibnitz
   c. Charles Babbage
   d. Herman Hollerith
   e. Alan Turing
   f. John von Neumann
2. What are the major components of von Neumann architecture? What is the function of each? Draw a diagram of von Neumann architecture.
3. What is Moore's Law?
4. What was the major breakthrough in the development of Integrated Circuits (ICs)?
5. What is the main difference between circuit switching and packet switching?
6. What were the main goals stated by the Department of Defense (DOD) in creating the packet network? In other words, what are the advantages of packet switching?
7. Research the early computer ENIAC. Find out how much memory it had, how it was constructed, how it was programmed, and how many instructions it could execute in one second.
8. What is the name of the network, created by the DARPA agency of the Department of Defense, that was the precursor to the Internet?
9. Describe the basic concept of packet switching, including addressing. Include the reasoning for why packets contain a sequence number.
10. What is the function of a router?
11. How does the Internet map between hostnames and IP addresses? What is the service that does this called?
12. What is the main difference between IP version 4 and IP version 6? Why was IPv6 necessary?

CHAPTER 2 – HTML BASICS

Evolution and Browser Support Issues

Many of the features included in today's HTML version 4 were originally designed and implemented as special features for particular companies' browsers. Microsoft would add features to its Internet Explorer® browser, and Netscape would add features to its browser, without any formal standardization beforehand. Most of these browser-specific capabilities were later added to the standard specification of HTML version 4.0, particularly those from Netscape. The problem was that adding new features sometimes meant that other features had to be removed or modified. In software, those features that are removed are said to be "deprecated," a term that means "no longer valid and should not be used (even though it might work)." Examples in HTML include such things as the `<align>` and `<center>` tags. However, when a change is made to the specification of HTML, this does not instantly cause all web pages that use the deprecated syntax to change. Therefore, browsers attempt to correctly render earlier versions of HTML so that older pages will still look the same.

> **Browser Variations**
>
> Browser companies tend to implement HTML specifications in slightly different ways. Therefore, some subtle and other not-so-subtle variations in the appearance of a page will exist depending upon the browser being used. **To be safe, you should test all of your pages with the most common browsers on the market,** which currently are Internet Explorer, Firefox, Safari, and Google Chrome.

Another major issue with browsers is that each company usually added features to their browser before the W3C standard that included those features was released. Therefore, they each implemented the HTML formatting in their own distinct ways. Although companies claim that their browsers follow the specification from the W3C, some subtle and other not-so-subtle variations in the appearance of a page may exist depending upon the browser being used and content of the page. The bottom line is that you should always test all your pages with all currently popular browsers.

Industry Standards – XHTML 1.0

Since there have been so many variations of HTML over the years – with different browsers each supporting different features – the W3C released a specification of HTML called XHTML in January of 2006. This document described functionality similar to HTML version 4.01, but also included a detailed a set of syntax rules and rules for tags. By following these rules, developers are able to create pages that are easier to maintain and require less special-case testing for browser variances. Therefore, if your pages follow the standards you can reliably expect them to function correctly (although they should still be tested on all popular browsers).

As a side effect of the standardization, some functions in previous versions of HTML were deprecated, to be replaced with the new "industry standard" methods. Pages contained in this text follow the XHTML standards, although brief mentions will be made about important deprecated features so you will recognize them in other pages you may encounter as you browse the Web.

There are tools on the internet that will allow you to verify that your pages meet the standards, one of which will be described later in this chapter. The details of the XHTML specification, however, will not be covered in this text.

Overview of HTML

HTML stands for Hyper-Text Markup Language. As noted above, it is designed for formatting pages using a technique of embedding formatting with the content. It should be noted that HTML is not a general-purpose programming language like C or C++, as it only provides formatting and not the more complex processing that is possible in those languages. The formatting information is included in what are called *tags* and these tags are included inside angle brackets. Our first example will make this clearer:

`<h1>Hello World</h1>`

Tags and Elements – Definitions

The example above uses the `<h1>` tag. This tag says that what follows it is to be formatted as the largest type of heading (see Table 1). The tag itself will not appear on the page that the user sees, however. Note that just having the `<h1>` tag is not sufficient, because there needs to be some way to mark the end of the area that is to be a heading. If there were only the `<h1>` tag, everything from then on to the end of the file would be in the large print of heading 1. As a result, most format elements are terminated with an ending tag that looks like the beginning tag, with the exception of an additional **/** as in the `</h1>` tag. Thus `<h1>` and `</h1>` bracket text to be displayed in the large heading format. Based on this description, here are some terms that will be used in this text to explain HTML:

HTML Terms and Definitions	
Term	**Definition**
Tag	A *tag* is a special set of characters that instruct the browser how to format text in a page. Tags start with a "less-than" symbol (`<`) and end with the "greater-than" symbol (`>`) and in between are characters that specify the type of formatting. In our example above, `<h1>` and `</h1>` are tags.
Beginning tag Ending tag	Most HTML elements are bracketed between matched tags. The first tag is called the *beginning tag* and the last tag the *ending tag*. The terms *opening tag* and *closing tag* are also frequently used.
Element	An HTML *element* consists of a beginning tag, data, and an ending tag (see heading example above). That is, an element is both the formatting instructions and the data to be so formatted. Note that there are some HTML elements that do not have an ending tag, and these are called *self-closing tags*. These elements are still closed, but in the opening element instead. The ` ` tag is an example of this, and is discussed later in this chapter.
Document	The collection of all formatting instructions and text, to be displayed as one complete unit by the browser, is known to you as the page creator as an HTML *document*.
Page	The page is what you see on the screen after the document is opened in a browser.
Attribute	Attributes provide additional information to the browser about various HTML elements (like where to go on a link). Attributes are covered in chapter 3.

Table 1. HTML terms and definitions

Structure of HTML Documents

All HTML documents have a certain minimum structure so that the browser knows how to interpret the content. This means that there are a certain minimum number of tags that must be included in every document. To start with, every document must start with the `<html>` tag and end with the `</html>` tag.

These two tags and the data between them constitute the `<html>` element and the full document itself. Next, every page needs a `<body>` tag and a `</body>` tag, which the text will abbreviate as the `<body>` element. The `<body>` element is always nested inside the `<html>` element. In Figure 5, the top half is the document which uses the heading of the previous example. The bottom half of the figure is how the page appears in the browser.

```
<html>
  <body>
    <h1>Hello World</h1>
  </body>
</html>
```

Hello World

Figure 5. Hello World

Here is a brief explanation of the HTML in the top portion of Figure 5. The first line is the beginning `<html>` tag. The `<html>` opening tag will almost always precede any other HTML elements. Except for document type, comments, and meta-data, it will be the first item in a document. The `<html>` tag identifies the contents of the file as HTML, so that the browser will know how to process the rest of the file. The last item in the file is always the ending `</html>` tag.

The first section of data contained within the `<html>` element is the `<body>` element. Every HTML file will have a `<body>` element as well. Furthermore, all displayable text will be located within the `<body>` element.

In the top portion of the figure, note how the text is displayed. The `<body>` tag is indented in from the `<html>` tag and the `<h1>` tag is indented in from the `<body>` tag. This is a good practice and should be followed in all HTML documents that you create. The reason for this indenting is so that you can clearly see identify each HTML element (and its contents) by aligning the left edges of its opening and closing tags. The choice of how much to indent is up to you, and this is usually a setting in the editor of your choice. With this information, you should now go and work through exercise 1 at the end of the chapter.

> **The `<body>` Element**
>
> Every HTML file will have a `<body>` tag, and all displayable text will be located in the `<body>` tag. When there is a `<head>` element (required in XHTML compatible pages), it will always precede the `<body>` element.

In our example above, the only data inside the `<body>` tag is another HTML element (`<h1>`). However, the body could also just contain unformatted text as shown in Figure 6. In the absence of the `<h1>` and `</h1>` tags, the data is not bolded or in a large font but is instead shown in the browser's default text style and font. (The function of headings is described in more detail later in this chapter.)

```
<html>
  <body>
    Four score and seven years ago our fathers brought forth on this
    continent, a new nation, conceived in Liberty, and dedicated to
    the proposition that all men are created equal.
  </body>
</html>
```

Four score and seven years ago our fathers brought forth on this continent, a new nation, conceived in Liberty, and dedicated to the proposition that all men are created equal.

Figure 6. Simple text in the body

Tags Use Lowercase

By the XHTML standard, all HTML tags must be in lowercase. This standard is fairly new so you may encounter pages with uppercase tags anyway. In order to follow the XHTML standard, however, use lowercase.

`<head>` and `<body>` Sections and the `<title>` Element

After seeing a `<body>` element, did you wonder if there is a `<head>` element too? If so, then you guessed correctly, as most HTML documents contain two major sections, consisting first of the `<head>` element, then the `<body>` element following. The `<head>` section does not contain any displayable text but instead contains special instructions to the browser. This might include special page formatting (CSS), the `<title>` element, and perhaps even some JavaScript. (CSS and JavaScript are covered in later chapters.) The `<head>`, `<title>`, and `<body>` elements are all required by the XHTML specification and so should be a part of all pages that you create.

> **The `<head>` Element**
>
> Every HTML file should have a `<head>` element that precedes the `<body>` section. The `<head>` element may contain special instructions to the browser, including formatting (CSS), a title, and JavaScript.

The `<title>` element is used by the browser to identify the page, and the text in the `<title>` element appears in the banner at the top of the browser window. Consider the revision to the Hello World HTML from Figure 5 as shown in Figure 7.

```
<html>
  <head>
    <title>My First Page</title>
  </head>
  <body>
    <h1>Hello World</h1>
  </body>
</html>
```

Figure 7. Hello World with title – HTML source

Notice how the text in the title element ("My First Page") in Figure 7 appears at the top of the screen in Figure 8. Not only does the title appear on the top of the page, it also appears when the page is added to favorites and when the page is scanned by search engines.

> **The `<title>` Element**
>
> Every HTML file should have a `<title>` element in the `<head>` section. The title appears at the top of the browser, is included in favorites, and is referenced by search engines.

Remember, XHTML standards require that you include the `<title>` element in all web pages.

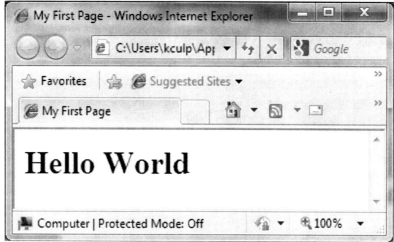

Figure 8. Hello World with title – browser

Whitespace (Tabs, Spaces, and Newlines)

The appearance of data between the opening and closing tags can, in general, be formatted in any way you want. It is the HTML tags that determine how the pages are formatted for the viewer. For example, you can include any amount of whitespace (tabs, blanks, and newlines) needed to improve the readability of the source document. The indenting that you do for nested HTML elements does not affect the way the page is displayed.

> **Whitespace**
>
> Whitespace (tabs, spaces, and newlines) is combined by the browser into one blank space. You can use whitespace to improve the readability of your document.

Special Symbols and Extra Space

Since multiple whitespace characters are combined, the question arises of how to add extra spaces when you really want them. However, there is a simple solution: use a special symbol for a blank that is not combined with other whitespace. This special symbol is ` `. There are other more advanced solutions to positioning text, which are described later; things like tables (chapter 3) and CSS columns (chapter 4).

This symbol is just one of a large number of other symbols defined in a similar fashion (that is, starting with the ampersand and ending with a semicolon). The letters in the special symbol mostly serve as a mnemonic. In this case, the ` ` symbol is a "non-breaking space."

Also, the less-than (<) and greater-than (>) characters frequently need to be written using special symbols, because the browser will think it is looking at HTML tags instead of regular characters. For this reason, when you want to write the characters themselves, the < character is replaced with `&lt;` and the > symbol with `&gt;`.

For example, say you are creating a web page that describes HTML elements, as shown in the bottom half of Figure 9. If you inserted "<head>" in your document as part of the text, the browser would think this was another `<head>` section and not data in the `<body>` element.

> **Warning**
>
> Never use the less-than or greater-than characters in your HTML source other than for creating HTML elements. Replace < with `&lt;` and > with `&gt;`.

In summary, use **<** for less-than and **>** for greater-than any time you use these symbols in the content of a document and not as HTML elements.

```
<html>
  <head>
    <title>HTML Elements</title>
  </head>
  <body>
    <h1>HTML Main Elements</h1>
    &lt;head&gt; - Heading section<br />&lt;body&gt; - Body section
  </body>
</html>
```

HTML Main Elements

<head> - Heading section
<body> - Body section

Figure 9. Less-than (**<**) and greater-than (**>**) special symbols

A partial list of these special symbols is given in Table 2. In this table, the symbol itself is shown along with its decimal equivalent symbol and its mnemonic symbol (when defined). You can use either the mnemonic or the decimal equivalent in your text. Also, note the symbols for single and double quotes.

Special Symbols in HTML			
Symbol	**Decimal**	**Mnemonic**	**Notes**
<	&#60;	&lt;	Use the decimal or mnemonic instead of the character in HTML data. Otherwise, the browser will interpret as an HTML tag.
>	&#62;	&gt;	
'	&#39;		Single quote. Use it to put quotes inside quotes.
"	&#34;	&quot;	Double quote. Use it to put quotes inside quotes.
%	&#037;		Percent sign.
°	&#176;	&deg;	Degrees.
•	&#8226;		Dot that can be used for math multiply symbol.
©	&#169;	&copy;	Copyright.
®	&#174;	&reg;	Registered.
¹	&#185;	&sup1;	Superscript 1.
²	&#178;	&sup2;	Superscript 2.
³	&#179;	&sup3;	Superscript 3.
±	&#177;	&plusmn;	Math: plus or minus.
≠	&#8800;		Math: not equal.
≤	&#8804;		Math: less than or equal.
≥	&#8805;		Math: greater than or equal.

Table 2. Special symbols

Headings

HTML simplifies creating nice headings for sections of your page. There are six separate headings defined in the standard (`<h1>` through `<h6>`). The logical difference in these is that `<h1>` is used for a major heading, `<h2>` for a sub-heading, etc. The display difference between them is the size of the font being used, with `<h1>` using the largest font and `<h6>` the smallest (see Figure 10). The font and size of each heading is a function of the browser defaults. You will see how to modify this with CSS later in chapter 4.

> **Headings**
>
> There are 6 headings (`<h1>` through `<h6>`). Each has a different font size, with `<h1>` being the largest and `<h6>` the smallest. By default, there is a blank line before and after a heading.

```
<html>
  <head>
    <title>Headings</title>
  </head>
  <body>
    <h1>Heading 1</h1>
    <h2>Heading 2</h2>
    <h3>Heading 3</h3>
    <h4>Heading 4</h4>
    <h5>Heading 5</h5>
    <h6>Heading 6</h6>
  </body>
</html>
```

Heading 1
Heading 2
Heading 3
Heading 4
Heading 5
Heading 6

Figure 10. Heading example

Note that headings (like paragraphs below) are displayed with a blank line before and a blank line after the heading. However, if you have multiple headings in a row, only one blank line is supplied between them.

At this point it is a good idea to recall what happens if you omit the ending tags. If you left off the ending tag for a heading and had a paragraph following that heading, everything in the paragraph would be in the font and size of the heading.

Paragraphs and Quotes

While browsing HTML pages, you have probably noticed that the text is not formatted into paragraphs as it is in books. In books, a paragraph starts on the next line down with an indent on the left. In web pages, a paragraph is marked by a blank line between blocks of text with no indent at the start of a paragraph. The HTML paragraph element is `<p>` and always appears with the beginning and ending tags. Paragraphs in HTML guarantee that there will be a blank line both before and after a paragraph (in the default setting). However, if you have two paragraph elements in a row, there will only be one blank line between them. Figure 11 shows how three paragraphs would appear in the editor and then in the browser. Note that the data between the beginning paragraph tag and the ending tag can appear in any format you like (even one word to a line if you wanted). The browser will assemble the data into one paragraph on the screen and will rearrange the paragraph as you shrink or enlarge the window.

As a matter of style, you should use paragraph elements for paragraphs and not some other construct (like `<br />` described below). This will simplify the updating of your pages in the future.

For convenience, HTML also includes a special paragraph element called `<blockquote>`. This element is similar to a paragraph in that it will always place a blank line before and after the element. However, it will also create margins on both sides of the element, as shown in the center paragraph of Figure 11.

```
<html>
  <head>
    <title>Gettysburg Address</title>
  </head>
  <body>
    <p>
      Four score and seven years ago our fathers brought forth on
      This continent, a new nation, conceived in Liberty, and
      dedicated to the proposition that all men are created equal.
    </p>
    <blockquote>
      Now we are engaged in a great civil war, testing whether that
      nation, or any nation so conceived and so dedicated, can long
      endure. We are met on a great battle-field of that war. . .
    </blockquote>
    <p>
      But, in a larger sense, we cannot dedicate -- we cannot
      consecrate -- we cannot hallow -- . . .
    </p>
  </body>
</html>
```

Four score and seven years ago our fathers brought forth on This continent, a new nation, conceived in Liberty, and dedicated to the proposition that all men are created equal.

> Now we are engaged in a great civil war, testing whether that nation, or any nation so conceived and so dedicated, can long endure. We are met on a great battle-field of that war...

But, in a larger sense, we cannot dedicate -- we cannot consecrate -- we cannot hallow -- . . .

Figure 11. Paragraph element

Divisions

In addition to the `<head>` and `<body>` sections of a page, you can create your own major divisions in the body section using the `<div>` element. The `<div>` element includes both the beginning and ending tags, like most other HTML elements. The XHTML 1.0 standard also requires that the `<body>` section include all information in either a `<div>` or a paragraph (`<p>`). Like paragraphs and headings, there will always be a blank line before and after the division. Also, paragraphs can be included within divisions but not the other way around. The logical order is for `<div>` elements to be located in the `<body>` and paragraphs inside the `<div>` elements.

Divisions are primarily used in conjunction with style attributes, which will be covered in chapter 4. In general, however, a set of style attributes can be applied to a division and this style would then affect all elements within that division.

Line Breaks

You may want to start text on a new line without leaving a blank line as would be done with the paragraph tag. This is done using the `<br />` element. For example, say you wanted to show your address and telephone number on separate lines, as shown in the bottom part of Figure 12. If you placed each line of the address and phone number in its own paragraph element, then there would be a blank line between each line of text. Instead, the source uses the `<br />` element, which locates the next line immediately below the previous.

The line break tag is a new type of element for our discussion, in that it has no ending tag. Instead, the standard is to close the element in the opening tag by adding a space and a slash before the ending greater-than sign. Thus, the source has a single-tag line break at the end of each line of data. To make the source look somewhat like the displayed page, each line of data is likewise started on a new line.

Another change from previous examples is that the `<head>` section is all on one line. Typing the `<head>` section this way shortens the length of the page in the source, thereby allowing you to see more of the rest of your file. However, writing the `<head>` section this way does not change the way it appears in the browser.

```
<html>
  <head><title>Line Breaks</title></head>
  <body>
    <h1>Address and Phone</h1>
    1234 E. 5th Street<br />
    Somewhere, TX 77777<br />
    (800) 555-1212
  </body>
</html>
```

Address and Phone

1234 E. 5th Street
Somewhere, TX 77777
(800) 555-1212

Figure 12. Line break example

Horizontal Rules

On occasion, you will want to separate portions of your web page with a horizontal line. This is done with the `<hr />` element, another element that has no closing tag. When this element appears in your source, a light gray solid line (horizontal rule) is drawn the full width of the screen.

```
<html>
  <head><title>Horizontal Rule</title></head>
  <body>
    <h3>Part 1</h3>
    <hr />
    <h3>Part 2</h3>
  </body>
</html>
```

Part 1

Part 2

Figure 13. Horizontal rule example

Making Text Stand Out

Sometimes you want certain text to stand out on your page. There are many ways to do this: bold, italics, underline, different colors, colored backgrounds, and the like. XHTML defines two elements for making text stand out: `<strong>` and `<em>`. (To remember `<em>`, think **em**phasized text.) In general, browsers interpret `<strong>` to mean bold text and `<em>` to mean italicized text. (Later on, in the discussion of CSS, you will see ways to change those defaults.)

Both `<strong>` and `<em>` are elements with a beginning and an ending tag. That is, text between the beginning and ending tag will have the characteristic specified. Consider the example in Figure 14. Note that there is always a blank line after headings, but a line break had to be added after the strong text so the emphasized text would be on the next line.

```
<html>
  <head>
    <title>Emphasized Text</title>
  </head>
  <body>
    <h1>This is a heading</h1>
    <strong>This is strong</strong><br />
    <em>This is emphasized</em>
  </body>
</html>
```

This is a heading

This is strong
This is emphasized

Figure 14. Strong and emphasized text

Previous versions of HTML prior to the XHTML standard had other ways to emphasize text. For strong text, there was a `<b>` or bold element. For italicized text, there was the `<i>` or italic element. Both of these are now deprecated and should not be used. The advantage of using `<strong>` and `<em>` is they relate to how we view and read the text. Also, you can change how these appear using CSS, as described in chapter 4.

> **Underlining**
>
> In the web world, underlined text is usually a link. For this reason, you should never underline text just to give it emphasis. Only underline links (which should happen automatically already). For emphasis, you should use `<strong>` or `<em>`.

Textbooks and other printed material frequently underline text that is to be emphasized. However, in the web world anything that is underlined is considered to be a link. For this reason, you should never underline anything but a link.

HTML Comments

As your web pages become more complex, it will become more difficult to locate and modify sections of the page in your editor. You will find that HTML comments will ease this problem a lot, however. An HTML comment is contained in a single tag that starts with `<!--` and ends with `-->`, and when the browser encounters this tag, it ignores it completely; nothing is displayed on the page. The comment is just for you, the designer, to use to highlight major sections of your page (or note anything else you like). Figure 15 has three comments which appear in italics. Note that the comments can be anywhere in the HTML file: before the starting `<html>` tag, in the `<head>` section, or in the `<body>` section.

You should make extensive use of comments in your files while writing them. In fact, for this class every HTML page you create should have at least one comment at the top which has your name and the section of the class you are attending. Think of HTML comments as "sticky notes" that are pasted in your HTML source. These notes might be useful for you in the future (you'd be surprised how quickly you forget things about the pages you make) or for someone else that might end up changing or reviewing your pages.

XHTML Validation

If you properly set up your page while making it, you can have the syntax validated against the XHTML 1.0 standard when you are finished. The validation website is http://validator.w3.org/ , but to use the site, you need to follow a basic template as shown in Figure 15. In the template, the lines in italics are comments and are there only to highlight the extra parts of your page that are needed for validation. You can use the template yourself by copying it to your page when you first create it and then filling in the needed content.

The first change is the addition of the **<!DOCTYPE>** line. This line defines the standard being followed by this page and should be a part of all HTML documents that you create. A **DOCTYPE** of *html* causes Internet Explorer to function close to the XHTML standard. The other part of the line is to request strict XHTML standards (xhtml1-strict.dtd).

The next change for validation is to the **<html>** element, where we have added an *xmlns* attribute (a term we'll cover a bit later; don't worry about it for now). Finally, inside the head section is a **<meta>** tag that defines the type of content. You do not need to remember any of these details to use the template; just copy it as-is.

```
<!-- Enforce strict XHTML editing rules -->
<!DOCTYPE html PUBLIC "-//W3C//DTD XHTML 1.0 Strict//EN"
       "http://www.w3.org/TR/xhtml1/DTD/xhtml1-strict.dtd">
<html xmlns="http://www.w3.org/1999/xhtml">
  <head>
    <title>Sample XHTML-compliant Page</title>

    <!-- Define character set and content type -->
    <meta http-equiv="Content-Type" content="text/html; charset=utf-8"/>
  </head>
  <body>
    <!-- Validator likes all your content to be inside a div or p -->
    <div>
      <h1>Sample XHTML-compliant Page</h1>
    </div>
  </body>
</html>
```

Figure 15. XHTML validator template

Using the Validator and Common Errors

Figure 16 below is the original Hello World page, but now with additions for validation. (The comments in the template were removed for brevity in this example.)

```
<!DOCTYPE html PUBLIC "-//W3C//DTD XHTML 1.0 Strict//EN"
          "http://www.w3.org/TR/xhtml1/DTD/xhtml1-strict.dtd">
<html xmlns="http://www.w3.org/1999/xhtml">
  <head>
    <title>Hello World</title>
    <meta http-equiv="Content-Type" content="text/html; charset=utf-8"/>
  </head>
  <body>
    <div>
      <h1>Hello World</h1>
    </div>
  </body>
</html>
```

Figure 16. XHTML version of Hello World

We will now validate the page using the W3C validator. Open http://validator.w3.org/ , select the tab labeled "Validate by Direct Input," and paste the text of the page into the window. Then click the Check button. The screen should look something like that shown in Figure 17. The result should appear as follows: "**Passed, 1 warning(s)**". The warning is because we pasted the input into the page and it had to assume the character type from the `<meta>` tag. If you save the file to your computer and use the Validate by File Upload method instead, this warning will not appear and you will get the following acknowledgment.

(**NOTE:** Any web page validator is subject to change constantly, so the results you get may be slightly different.)

This document was successfully checked as XHTML 1.0 Strict!

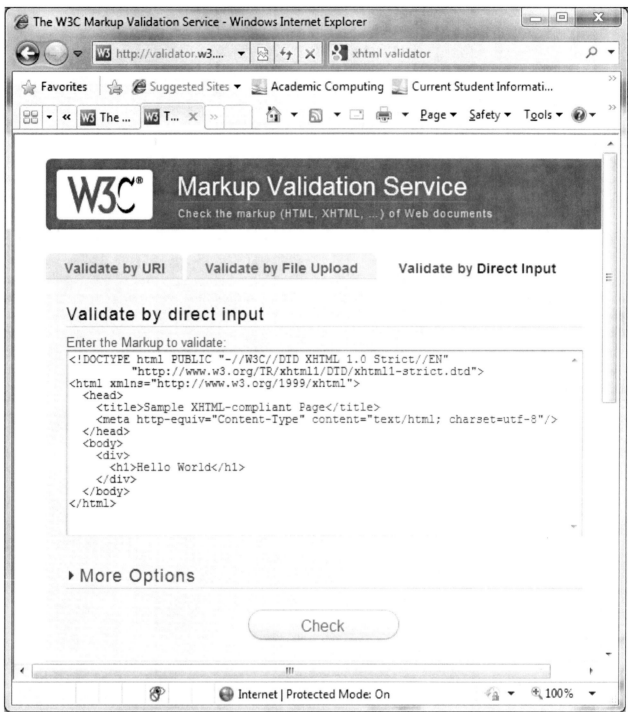

Figure 17. Validating Hello World

To show the usefulness of the validator, errors will now be intentionally added to the file and the validation repeated. First, change the ending `</h1>` tag to `<h1>` so the line now reads `<h1>Hello World<h1>`. This is a common mistake where the slash is omitted from the ending tag. This one error causes several errors to appear in the validation output (run the test to view the errors yourself). However, one line is quite clearly the problem:

> Line 10, Column 25: **document type does not allow element "h1" here; missing one of "object", "ins", "del", "map", "button" start-tag**

```
<h1>Hello World<h1>
```

The error highlights the ending tag and indicates that the second `<h1>` does not belong there. Now, remove the ending tag altogether so the heading line is `<h1>Hello World`. This time the error is very clear:

> *Line 11, Column 10*: **end tag for "h1" omitted, but OMITTAG NO was specified**

```
<h1>Hello World
```

Here the error is highlighted exactly. For the last test, leave off the closing greater sign for the ending tag on the heading line so that the line reads `<h1>Hello World</h1`. Now the error reads:

> *Line 11, Column 4*: **expected '>'**

Review Questions

1. What do the letters HTML stand for?
2. Why is it always good practice to test your pages in different browsers? Will the same page appear exactly the same in all browsers, and if not, why not?
3. What is XHTML and what is its purpose?
4. What constitutes a complete HTML element?
5. What are the minimum elements in a good HTML document?
6. What is the `<title>` element, where is it located, and what are its three uses?
7. What is whitespace and how is it handled by the browser?
8. How do you add extra whitespace to your page?
9. How many different types of headings are there and how do they differ?
10. What are the characteristics of the paragraph (`<p>`) element and how is it displayed?
11. How do you break a line to continue text on the line immediately below?
12. How do you draw a horizontal line across the page?
13. Describe the different ways to highlight text in a page.
14. Why should you never underline regular text?

Exercises

1. Open the HTML editor that you are using, type in the page shown in the top part of Figure 5, and then test it in your browser. Make sure the page says `Hello World` as in the example. Once that is working, change the page to say `Hello` followed by your name. Be sure to use the tab button or spaces to indent your HTML elements and content so it appears like the top part of Figure 5.
2. Add the validation lines to your Hello World application and then validate it (see Figure 16). Then create the errors described above at the end of this chapter, and try to create other errors as well. Study the resulting error report and come to class ready to discuss what you found.
3. Find the source to one of your favorite quotes or passages and make a web page out of it. Note: do not copy another page, simply copy the text. Use paragraph marks, line breaks, and emphasis as appropriate to format the text.
4. Write the HTML to create the web page shown below, making sure to put your name on the top line of the resume. You will need to use most of the HTML elements covered in this chapter to complete this exercise. Note that the word "GPA" is bold and the names of the educational institutions are italicized. At the end, add a paragraph about what your objectives are after getting your college degree and give it a heading of `Objectives`. Use the text highlighting techniques described above to improve the appearance of the paragraph. When you are completed, make sure to test your work.

Resume for <place your name here>

Address and Phone

1234 E. 5th Street
Somewhere, TX 77777
(800) 555-1212

Education

Thomas Jefferson High
GPA: 3.79

Northern Michigan University
Associates Degree in Welding

References

John R. Friendly
(555) 555-1212

Betty Watson
(555) 555-1234

CHAPTER 3 – HTML USING ATTRIBUTES

Attributes

Up to this point, your web development has been limited to simple HTML elements that have been used without any modifications. However, some HTML elements require additional information in order to be complete. Consider a basic web link. It usually appears in blue and is underlined, and if you click that link, you expect to see a different page. These links (described below) are HTML elements, but for these elements to work there has to be a way to specify the destinations of the links. This extra information is specified in the form of an *attribute*.

> **Attributes**
>
> Attributes are additional information included in the beginning tag of an HTML element. A single HTML element might have many attributes, or it might have none.
>
> Attributes are supplied in name-value pairs as shown below. Names should always be in lowercase.

An *attribute* is another piece of information that is added to the beginning tag of an HTML element in the form of a **name="value"** pair. This format must be followed precisely, with the attribute name followed by an equals sign and the value enclosed in either single or double quotes.

Below is the complete HTML used to create a link to www.needlerat.com. The destination page is specified with an attribute name of **href** which has as its value the URL to the page. Note that the page URL is inside quotes.

```
<a href="http://www.needlerat.com">Needle Rat Press, LLC</a>
```
Figure 18. Simple link example

All attributes like **href** are written in lowercase. This follows the XHTML standard, which says that tags should always be in lowercase. However, values inside the quotes can have any mix of upper- and lowercase letters.

<u>Core Attributes</u>

There are some attributes that will, on occasion, be found in almost all HTML elements. These are shown in Table 3. The **title** and **id** attributes will be described in this chapter, and **style** and **class** in the next. The **title** attribute is unusual because whatever is defined for the title will appear when the mouse is over the element. This frequently serves to give the page viewer extra information and is often used with forms, as will be discussed in chapter 8.

Core HTML Attributes		
Attribute	Value	Description
class	Class name	A valid CSS class name. Used to style the element using a style defined elsewhere in the stylesheet (see chapter 4).
id	ID	Specifies a unique ID for the element (see Defining Bookmarks below).
style	Style list	Styles element with inline style properties (see chapter 4).
title	Text	Extra information about an element that appears briefly when the mouse is moved over the element. For example, this can be extra instructions to the viewer of the page for input forms, as covered in chapter 5.

Table 3. Core HTML attributes

Links

The `<a>` (link) tag has two distinct purposes. First, it creates *links* to other pages (see example in the previous section). In other words, clicking the link will take you somewhere else outside the page. The other purpose is to define a place to go within a page, called a *bookmark*. It is from this second purpose that the term "anchor" is derived. First, though, we will look at the `<a>` tag as a link.

> **The Anchor (`<a>`) Element**
>
> The anchor (`<a>`) element has two purposes: (1) to create a jump to a different place (*link*); and (2) to define a place to go in the same page (*bookmark*).

Defining Links

Study Figure 18 carefully. Note that there is both a beginning and ending tag, with the *href* attribute given in the beginning tag. Between the beginning and ending tags are the words "click here." When the link appears in the text, only the words "click here" appear; the destination page does not appear anywhere.

Sometimes you want the underlined part to be a part of a sentence, perhaps within a paragraph. In this case you will simply add the link within the text wherever it is needed. Consider the example shown in Figure 19.

```
To follow the link,
<a href="http://www.needlerat.com">click here</a>.
```

To follow the link, click here.

Figure 19. Adding links within text

The words "click here" are underlined, but not the period at the end of the sentence, because the period is placed after the ending tag. There is a space between the comma and the link, though, because the first part of the sentence is on one line and the link on the next. This new line is interpreted as whitespace and converted to a single space. However, if the link is on the same line as other text before it, you will need to leave a space in the text before the opening tag of the link; otherwise the comma will be right next to the word "click." Remember, only the text placed between the beginning and ending tags is underlined on the page.

Defining Bookmarks

Bookmarks placed within a page allow for quick navigation to major sections within that page. You identify the major sections of the page with bookmarks and then use links to jump to those sections. A bookmark is defined using the `<a>` tag, like links, but with the change that the *href* attribute is replaced with an *id* attribute.

> **Defining Bookmarks**
>
> Bookmarks are defined using the anchor (`<a>`) element with the *id* attribute. When defining a bookmark, do not use the *href* attribute!

As a note, remember that *id* is part of the core attributes for all HTML elements, so any element can have an *id* attribute for a bookmark to link to. (The *id* attribute will be used much more in the material on JavaScript as well.)

Since a page could reasonably have many bookmarks, it is necessary to uniquely identify each of the bookmarks with its own *id*. For consistency, and to allow interaction with JavaScript, the *id* attribute value should follow certain naming rules (see the chapter on JavaScript for more details):

1. Start the *id* with a letter.
2. Follow this only with letters and numeric digits.
3. Use no symbols.
4. Use no whitespace (tabs or spaces) in the name.
5. Use a different value for each *id* attribute.

A bookmark requires an opening and a closing tag. If you place data between the opening and closing tags, it will be displayed on the screen as-is, complete with formatting. Many developers place no text between the opening and closing tags, though. They just place the bookmark in front of a major section heading, as shown in Figure 20. Figure 20 might be part of a single-page resume, with a set of links to the bookmarks and then four major divisions of the resume (personal, education, work history, and references).

```html
<!--Top of page with main heading-->
<a id="top"></a><h1>Resume for James Watson</h1>

<!--Table of Contents Links-->
<a href="#ed">Education</a><br />
<a href="#work">Employment History</a><br />
<a href="#refs">References</a><br />

<!--Personal information-->
    . . . . .
    . . . . .
<a href="#top">Top</a>

<!--Education-->
<a id="ed"></a><h2>Education</h2>
    . . . . .
    . . . . .
<a href="#top">Top</a>

<!--Employment History-->
<a id="work"></a><h2>Employment History</h2>
    . . . . .
    . . . . .
<a href="#top">Top</a>

<!--References-->
<a id="refs"></a><h2>References</h2>
    . . . . .
    . . . . .
<a href="#top">Top</a>
```

Figure 20. Example of bookmarks

Note the bookmark right after the beginning comment for top of page. The bookmark has no data, but is immediately followed by the `<h1>` element listing the name of the person this resume is for. The other three bookmarks precede the `<h2>` elements for the other sections of the page. The bookmark links do not show on the page, since they have no data; they only mark places to go in the page.

Referencing Bookmarks in the Same Page

Creating a link to a bookmark is similar to creating a link to a page. That is, the *href* attribute is used and text is placed between the beginning and ending tags. The difference between a page link and a bookmark link is the presence of the pound symbol (#), which tells the browser that what follows is a bookmark. When the pound symbol is used, it is followed by the value of the *id* attribute of the bookmark being jumped to.

> **Referencing Bookmarks**
>
> Bookmarks in the same page are jumped to using the anchor (<a>) element, with the *href* attribute set to a pound sign (#) plus the name of the bookmark. To link to a bookmark in a different page, set the *href* attribute to the page followed by # and the name of the bookmark. (See more info on this in the next section.)

Figure 20 shows several references to bookmarks within the page. Near the top of the page is a table of contents to the rest of the page, which consists of three links to other bookmarks in the same page. The first link (<a href="#ed">Education</a>) will appear in the browser as "Education," and when it is clicked, the screen will scroll until the education section is shown on the screen.

To return to the table of contents, each section links to the top of the page (<a href="#top">Top</a>). This link appears in the browser as "Top." Using a table of contents in addition to links back to the top of the page allows the person viewing it to easily navigate around the page.

Referencing Bookmarks in a Different Page

Creating a link to a bookmark in a different page involves a combination of a link to a separate page and a link to a bookmark. In other words, simply add the pound sign at the end of the website URL followed by the bookmark name. Figure 21 shows how you could have a link to the references section of your resume if this link were on another page.

```
To see my references,
<a href="http://www.example.com/resume.html#refs">click here</a>.
```

To see my references, click here.

Figure 21. Link to bookmark in a different page

Opening Links in a New Window

When you click a link, the new page referenced will usually replace the current page so that the back button, when clicked, would return to the original page. However, there is also an option to set the link to open in a new page or in a named frame. To change how the link works, set the *target* attribute. The most common values for *target* are shown below:

Value	Usage
_blank	Opens the new page in a new window or tab (browser setting)
_self	Opens the page over top of the current page (current window). This is the default.
Frame name	When using named frames, place the name of the frame here. Frames have been deprecated and are not generally used for new sites.

Table 4. Target values for links

Creating Email Links

To create a link to an email address, use the anchor tag with the keyword "mailto:" preceding the email address, as shown in Figure 22. The link would appear as shown. When the link is clicked, your default mail system will open the mail editor with the email address filled in. The key is to set the *href* attribute equal to the word "mailto", followed by a colon and then the email address.

```
To email me, <a href="mailto:kculp@nmu.edu">click here</a>.
```

To email me, click here.

Figure 22. Link to an email address

Advanced Email Links

You can also have the new email page brought up with the subject, carbon copy (CC), and blind carbon copy (BCC) fields filled in as shown in Figure 23. The link was broken down into several lines in this example to make it easier to read, but this is one case where whitespace is not ignored and should not be used in your pages. Therefore, in your pages you should have links be all on one line.

```
To email me, <a href="mailto:to@example.com?
  subject=Resume&
  cc=copy@example.com&
  bcc=blind@example.com">click here</a>.
```

Figure 23. Advanced email link

There are a lot of details to explain in this example. First, the email address is followed by a question mark (**?**). This denotes that a query string is being included with the link reference. In a query string, there are name and value pairs each connected with an equals sign, and each name-value pair is separated from the others with the **&** symbol. The most commonly used options for the parameters are shown below.

subject	Subject for the email
cc	Carbon copy address
bcc	Blind carbon copy address

You do not have to use all the above parameters in your links. In fact, subject is usually the only one specified. However, remember the syntax requires that the query string always starts with the "**?**" symbol.

If you are using Microsoft Outlook 2007 as your email client and you click this example link, your screen will look something like Figure 24 (except that the toolbars would also be shown).

Figure 24. Advanced email in Outlook

Images

Pictures and graphics are one of the things that make the Web so useful and pleasing to the eye, and there will be many times when you will want to enhance your pages with images using the `<img>` element.

The `<img>` element has two required attributes, *src* and *alt*, plus two frequently used attributes, *height* and *width*. Each of these attributes is discussed below. The `<img>` element is also closed in the opening tag, just like `<br />` and `<hr />`. This is because the opening element specifies everything the browser needs to display the image. Figure 25 is one example, containing the HTML to show a photograph of the US flag on the moon.

> **Warning**
>
> A common problem using the `<img>` element is that the picture is not in the same folder as your referencing page. When you make `<img>` links, open the folder containing your page and make sure you see the image files.

In the example below, a full URL is being used to specify the location of an image. It is relatively safe to use full URLs when the site you are referencing is your own site, but if you reference an image on someone else's site, they may move or remove the image. For best results (and to avoid using up other people's bandwidth), copy images to your own site's folder or subfolder.

```
<img src="http://wdp.needlerat.com/images/USflagOnMoon.jpg"
    alt="US Flag on Moon"
    title="US Flag on Moon" />
```

Figure 25. Image example – large

Image (`<img>`) Element Attributes	
Attribute	Description and Use
`src`	Required! This is the web address of the image. It can be a complete URL, as shown in the example, or if the image is located in the same folder as the page referencing it, the image can be referenced by just the image name (ex.: `src="USflagOnMoon.jpg"`). If the flag image is in a subfolder from the referencing page, then you can use relative addressing (ex.: `src="images/USflagOnMoon.jpg"`).
`alt`	Required! This is the text that will appear when the image cannot be displayed. In Internet Explorer, the alt text is also displayed when the mouse is moved over the image. However, to have the popup text show up in Firefox or Safari, also put this text in the `title` attribute.
`height`	Optional. This is the height the image is to occupy. The browser will compress or expand the image to fit the height and width specifications but still downloads the full image.
`width`	Optional. This is the width the image is to occupy. The browser will compress or expand the image to fit the height and width specifications but still downloads the full image.
`title`	Optional. The `title` attribute allows you to specify text that will appear when the mouse is placed over the image. This attribute can be applied to most HTML elements, in fact, but to guarantee functionality in all browsers, specify both the `title` and `alt` attributes using the same text (see Figure 25).

Table 5. Attributes for the `<image>` element

Sizing Images

Images can be very large on the Web, particularly with today's digital cameras; some can exceed 10 megabytes in size. If you reference a picture of this size, some browsers will wait until all 10 megabytes are downloaded before showing the image. Furthermore, these pictures might be huge, say, 3,000 pixels by 3,000 pixels. If you attempted to show one of these pictures in a browser on a screen of 1280 by 800 pixels, you would see the entire screen filled with the upper-left 15% or so of the picture. This would be of little value. Instead, you will usually want a picture to take up only a limited section of the screen.

> **Image Size**
>
> Always resize an image in an image editor to fit the area you need on a page. It is best to not use height and width attributes to make the image fit unless these are only small changes. The objective is to maximize performance of the browser (by reducing network traffic).

One approach to sizing the image would be to adjust the `height` and `width` attributes of the picture until it looks nice. To the browser user the screen would look right, but the full 10 megabytes of the picture would still be downloaded, wasting time and unnecessarily increasing the load on the network.

A better approach is to resize the image using a picture editor. To change the image in Microsoft Paint, open Paint, select the home tab, and then select the "Resize and Skew" icon. Type a percentage change until the picture has the size you like and save the image. To edit with Microsoft Office Picture Manager, open the image, click Edit Pictures and select Resize.

In general, the size of an image on a page is quite critical to the overall appearance of the page. For this reason, you probably should still include the `height` and `width` attributes of an image even when the image is resized in an image editor beforehand.

Images as Links

Practically any HTML element can be placed between the opening and closing tag of the anchor element, not just plain text. One of the most common elements to place in it is an image so that clicking on the image goes to a new site or bookmark. In the example in Figure 26, an image is used as a link.

```
<html>
  <head><title>Image Link</title></head>
  <body>
    <h1>Click the image to go to Needle Rat's home page</h1>
    <a href="http://www.needlerat.com"><img src="nrp.jpg" alt="NRP Home" /></a>
  </body>
</html>
```

Click the image to go to Needle Rat's home page

Figure 26. Image as a link

In addition to images, you can use any other HTML element as the link. For example, if you wanted a larger, bold link, you could use `<strong>` or `<em>` to highlight the underlined text. You can also nest the link inside a heading element (`<h2>`, `<h3>`, ...) to create the link of the desired size. Note that by XHTML standards, you should not nest a heading element inside the link (see Inline versus Block Elements in chapter 4).

Lists

When displaying data on web pages, you will frequently want to use lists. Two types of lists are available in HTML: ordered and unordered. Standard ordered lists have Arabic numbers marking each entry, and unordered list have symbols (squares, circles, and discs, to be precise). The ordered list uses the `<ol>` element and the unordered list uses `<ul>`.

Lists include varying numbers of items: some lists have many, others only a few. Thus the HTML syntax needs to provide a way of identifying individual elements in a list, which we'll see in a second.

Study the example in Figure 27 as you read the following explanation. The first list is ordered (`<ol>`), and the second, unordered (`<ul>`), as marked by the comments in the source. Both the `<ol>` and `<ul>` elements include three elements of type `<li>` between the opening and closing tags, which are the tags that identify individual lines. To add more items, add more elements of type `<li>`.

By default, ordered lists number items with Arabic numerals, and unordered lists use filled-in circles, which are called "discs." In the next section, you will see how to change the type of symbol used.

```
<html xmlns="http://www.w3.org/1999/xhtml" >
  <head>
    <title>Untitled Page</title>
  </head>
  <body>
    <!--Ordered List-->
    <ol>
      <li>Apple</li>
      <li>Orange</li>
      <li>Grape</li>
    </ol>
    <!--Unordered List-->
    <ul>
      <li>Apple</li>
      <li>Orange</li>
      <li>Grape</li>
    </ul>
  </body>
</html>
```

1. Apple
2. Orange
3. Grape

- Apple
- Orange
- Grape

Figure 27. Ordered and unordered lists

Changing List Symbol Type

The list element (`<ol>` or `<ul>`) includes an attribute (*type*) that allows you to specify the exact symbol to be used. In fact, if you specify a *type* attribute, the result will be the same regardless of whether the list element is `<ol>` or `<ul>`. Table 6 shows the various values that can be given for the *type* attribute. Figure 28 illustrates a couple of these options.

Note that using the *type* attribute is no longer recommended as part of XHTML 1.0 but it is still supported by all major browsers. The type attribute was covered for completeness here because it is still in extensive use. The better approach, though, is to specify a *style* attribute on the beginning tag for `<ol>` or `<ul>` and set the *list-style-type* style property to the type desired. Using styles with lists is covered in the next chapter.

Type Options for Lists	
Value for Type Attribute	Description and Use
1	Arabic numerals
A	Uppercase alphabet
a	Lowercase alphabet
I	Uppercase roman numerals
i	Lowercase roman numerals
disc	Solid circle (●)
circle	Open circle (○)
square	Solid square (■)

Table 6. List type options

```
<html xmlns="http://www.w3.org/1999/xhtml" >
  <head>
    <title>Untitled Page</title>
  </head>
  <body>
    <!--Ordered List-->
    <ol type="a">
      <li>Apple</li>
      <li>Orange</li>
      <li>Grape</li>
    </ol>
    <!--Unordered List-->
    <ul type="square">
      <li>Apple</li>
      <li>Orange</li>
      <li>Grape</li>
    </ul>
  </body>
</html>
```

a. Apple
b. Orange
c. Grape

- Apple
- Orange
- Grape

Figure 28. Different lists using the *type* attribute

Nested Unordered Lists

Lists can be nested inside lists. Figure 29 is an example of unordered lists being nested inside other unordered lists. Note in Figure 29 how the list for types of fruits is added after the word "Fruits" as a list item of the outside list (a list of edible plants, perhaps, though this is not specified). Also, inside the list item for apple is another list showing types of apples. Thus, to nest a list within a list, you place a complete list within the list element (`<ol>` or `<ul>`) and the associated list items (`<li>`) between the opening and closing tags of the list item of another list.

> **Nested Lists**
>
> To nest a list within a list, you place a complete list within the list element (`<ol>` or `<ul>`) and the associated list items (`<li>`) between the opening and closing tags of the list item of another list.

```
<html xmlns="http://www.w3.org/1999/xhtml" >
  <head>
    <title>Untitled Page</title>
  </head>
  <body>
    <ul>
      <li>Fruits
        <ul>
          <li>Apple
            <ul>
              <li>Braeburn</li>
              <li>Granny Smith</li>
            </ul>
          </li>
          <li>Orange</li>
          <li>Grape</li>
        </ul>
      </li>
      <li>Vegetables
        <ul>
          <li>Corn</li>
          <li>Peas</li>
          <li>Spinach</li>
        </ul>
      </li>
    </ul>
  </body>
</html>
```

- Fruits
    - Apple
        - Braeburn
        - Granny Smith
    - Orange
    - Grape
- Vegetables
    - Corn
    - Peas
    - Spinach

Figure 29. Nested unordered lists

The nice advantage of nesting unordered lists is that the browser will choose a different symbol for each internal list. The first symbol (by default) is the disc, followed by the circle, and finally followed by the square. If need be, though, you always have the option to override the symbols used with the *type* attribute (see Figure 28).

Creating an Outline List

When you nest ordered lists, the browser does not change the symbol used unless the *type* attribute is used. Instead, every list will use Arabic numerals. To create an outline list, you would need to specify a different *type* attribute on each list as shown in Figure 30.

```
<html xmlns="http://www.w3.org/1999/xhtml" >
  <head>
    <title>Untitled Page</title>
  </head>
  <body>
    <ol type="I">
      <li>Fruits
        <ol type="A">
          <li>Apple
            <ol type="1">
              <li>Braeburn</li>
              <li>Granny Smith</li>
            </ol>
          </li>
          <li>Orange</li>
          <li>Grape</li>
        </ol>
      </li>
      <li>Vegetables
        <ol type="A">
          <li>Corn</li>
          <li>Peas</li>
          <li>Spinach</li>
        </ol>
      </li>
    </ol>
  </body>
</html>
```

I. Fruits
    A. Apple
        1. Braeburn
        2. Granny Smith
    B. Orange
    C. Grape
II. Vegetables
    A. Corn
    B. Peas
    C. Spinach

Figure 30. Outline lists

Tables

Some data require more advanced presentation methods, like tables with multiple rows and columns. However, HTML does not have the concept of tab stops like a word processor does. As a result, HTML uses the `<table>` element to place data in columns. Note, however, that CSS columns can also be used to create columns in your documents as well, as discussed in chapter 4.

To understand HTML tables, consider a Microsoft Excel workbook. A workbook consists of *rows* and *columns*, and at the intersection of a row and column you have a *cell*. Furthermore, there is usually a bold *heading* at the top of each column of data, and some data have different formats, like numeric, right- or left-justified, or centered.

All of these characteristics of an Excel notebook can be created in HTML using tables. First, you define a table with the `<table>` element. Then within the `<table>` element you define rows. The concept of columns, however, does not exist in HTML in the same way as in Excel. Instead, within each and every row you define a group of cells, which you will have to manually make sure are in the proper "columns."

Cells in the same column in different rows may contain data that need different amounts of space to display them. To fit the data on the screen, the column widths are then adjusted to accommodate the widest cell. To illustrate all this, see Figure 31. Note that the left side of output portion of the figure corresponds to the source. (The right half will be discussed shortly.)

```html
<html xmlns="http://www.w3.org/1999/xhtml" >
  <head>
    <title>Table Example</title>
  </head>
  <body>
    <!--Table with three rows and two columns, column headings, and banner -->
    <table border="2">
      <tr><th colspan="2">Address Book</th>          </tr>
      <tr><th>Name          </th><th>Phone          </th></tr>
      <tr><td>Bill Smith    </td><td>888-555-1234</td></tr>
      <tr><td>John Stotdze  </td><td>888-555-1234</td></tr>
      <tr><td>Mary Thompson</td><td>888-555-1234</td></tr>
    </table>
  </body>
</html>
```

Address Book	
Name	Phone
Bill Smith	888-555-1234
John Stotdze	888-555-1234
Mary Thompson	888-555-1234

Address Book	
Name	Phone
Bill Smith	888-555-1234
John Stotdze	888-555-1234
Mary Thompson	888-555-1234

Figure 31. Simple table example

The `<table>` element has an optional attribute, *border,* for setting the width of the border of the table. If this attribute is omitted, there are no borders on the table and the data just appear in columns. Alternately, you can include the *border* attribute and set the value to zero for the same result. In either case (no border or border of zero), the table appears as shown in the right half of Figure 31.

The `<table>` element above has five `<tr>` elements nested between its beginning and ending tags. All of the rows except the first row have two cells defined (we will discuss the first row a little later). Row two has the column headings (Name and Phone), and the cells used for headings use the table heading (`<th>`) element. Cells created with `<th>` appear, by default, in the output as centered with bold font weight. Rows three through five have data and use the table data (`<td>`) element to create the cells. Cells created with `<td>` are, by default, left-justified and not bold (normal font weight).

> **Creating Table Cells**
>
> Table cells created with `<th>` appear, by default, centered and in bold font weight. Cells created with `<td>` appear, by default, as left-justified and normal font weight (not bold). Alignment and font weight can be changed using styling and CSS.

Missing or Empty Cells

If some rows have a different number of cells in them or if a cell contains no data, the table may not have the desired appearance. If there is nothing between the opening and closing tag of a cell element (`<th>` or `<td>`), then that cell is considered to be empty and the browser will show the cell as solid, but possibly without any borders. For example, say there was no phone number for Mary Thompson in the previous example. If the table has borders as in the left example, the resulting table would now appear in Internet Explorer and Mozilla's Firefox® browser as shown on the left in Figure 32. In Apple Inc.'s Safari® browser, the figure would look like the right-hand example.

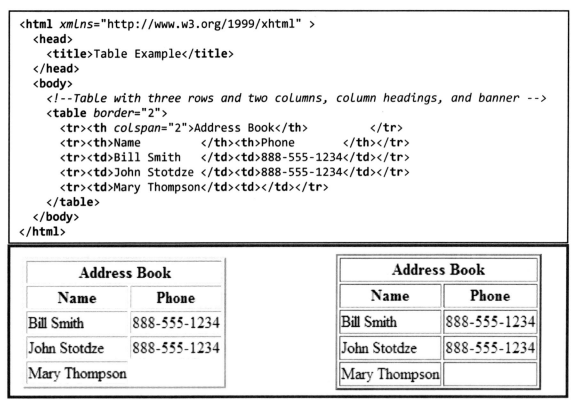

Figure 32. Table with empty cell and corrected version using

Now make a minor change to the HTML above by adding the non-breaking space (` `) between the opening and closing tags of the cell (`<td> </td>`). With that change, all browsers would look the same, showing an indented, bordered cell with no data. Note that the result of leaving out the last cell on the Mary Thompson row results in all browsers appearing as shown in the left example (Safari included). Since you will want your table to appear the same in all browsers, include the cell and use the non-breaking space.

> **Missing Data or Cells**
>
> If you do not have data for a particular cell, include the `<th>` or `<td>` element in the row and place a non-breaking space in the element. For example:
>
> `<td> </td>`
>
> Be sure all rows have the same number cells.

Spanning Rows and Columns

You can also define cells that will correspond to two or more columns. Consider the first table row in Figure 31 and Figure 32 (`<tr><th colspan="2">Address Book</th></tr>`). This row is the "Address Book" banner at the top of the table, and this cell has the attribute *colspan* set to 2, which means that this cell is to be counted as two cells *horizontally*. Thus this cell will span both the name and phone number columns defined in the next row. This makes all rows in this example actually have the same number of cells (two).

Consider Figure 33. In this example, there are two different phone numbers for John Stotdze. Thus the `<td>` element that includes his name has ***rowspan*** equal to 2. Since this `<td>` element is the first cell of that row, the cell will also become the first cell of the next row. The next row skips the name cell (as shown by all the spaces in the source) and only includes the cell for the phone number.

```
<html xmlns="http://www.w3.org/1999/xhtml" >
  <head>
    <title>Untitled Page</title>
  </head>
  <body>
    <!--Table with three rows and two columns, column headings, and banner -->
    <table border="2">
      <tr><th colspan="2">Address Book</th>                          </tr>
      <tr><th>Name                </th><th>Phone        </th></tr>
      <tr><td>Bill Smith          </td><td>888-555-1234</td></tr>
      <tr><td rowspan="2">John Stotdze </td><td>888-555-1234</td></tr>
      <tr>                                <td>888-555-4321</td></tr>
    </table>
  </body>
</html>
```

Figure 33. Example of rowspan

The `<colgroup>` and `<col>` Elements

Tables also can include the HTML elements `<colgroup>` and `<col>`. With these elements you can define the width of columns and, with some browsers, define the style of columns. However, browsers following Netscape's pattern (Firefox, Safari, and the Google Chrome™ browser) only allow the width of the columns to be defined with these elements. Since there are other ways to set column widths, these elements will not be covered here. They are only mentioned for completeness' sake.

Review Questions

1. What are HTML attributes and why are they needed?
2. Where are HTML attributes defined in the HTML syntax?
3. What is the purpose of the anchor tag and in what different ways can it be used?
4. What is a link and how does it work? Write down an example.
5. What is a bookmark and what is the value of a bookmark?
6. What is the syntax for defining a bookmark? Write down an example.
7. Describe how to create a link to an email address. What values can be passed to the email program when the email link is clicked?
8. What is the purpose of the *alt* and *title* attributes of an image element?
9. How should the *height* and *width* attributes be used with image elements? Should they be used to make a large image fit into a small space? Why or why not?
10. What are the two basic types of lists and how are they defined?
11. How do you change the type of a list using an HTML attribute?
12. What is the basic technique for nesting a list inside a list?
13. Describe the basic syntax for tables. What elements are nested inside what elements? Are columns specifically defined in tables? If not, how is the number of columns in a table determined?
14. How do you make empty cells appear correctly in a table in all browsers?

Exercises

1. Create two simple HTML documents. Place an `<h1>` element at the top of the first page that says "Page One" and an `<h1>` element on the top of the second page that says "Page Two". Then on page one, add a link that reads: "For page two, click here." Then on page two, create a similar link to page one.
2. On page one from exercise one above, create a link to your email address that reads "To email me, click here." Be sure to fill in the email subject and a carbon copy (CC) address.
3. On the Web (or elsewhere) find a fairly long document and copy the source into your own HTML document. Place a bookmark at the top of the page. Then define at least three section headings in the document and place a bookmark in front of each of these headings. Then place a table of contents at the front of the document with links to each of the bookmarked headings. Finally, at the end of each section define a link to the bookmark at the top of the page. This will create a page with complete navigation buttons. For help, study Figure 20.
4. Create an HTML document that has a link to the last section of the document created in the previous exercise. That is, this page will have a link to another page, and when that page is displayed, it will jump down to the specified bookmark. Make sure it opens that link in a new window or tab.
5. Create a link in any previous exercise HTML document using an image as the link.
6. Create an HTML document that has two images, and under each image put a heading describing that image. The images can be any pictures or images you want as long as the images are in good taste. First start with large images, and then resize them using an image editor so they better fill the page. Try to make both images about the same size.
7. Create an HTML document that is your to-do list numbered with Arabic numerals (1, 2, …). Then make the list use the solid square image for each item (▪).
8. Create an HTML document with a brief outline of any kind. Use three different levels in the outline, numbering the top level with uppercase roman numerals, the second level with uppercase alphabetic letters, and Arabic numerals for the third level. Use the *type* attribute to do so.
9. Create an HTML document with a table of ingredients for a recipe. At the top of the table, create a banner that spans all columns describing what the recipe is for (**Lemon Pie**, etc.). Then create two columns labeled **Ingredient** and **Amount**. Include at least three ingredients and amounts. Finally, at the end of the table add a row that spans all columns with preparation and cooking instructions.

CHAPTER 4 – STYLE, STYLESHEETS, AND COLORS

Overview

HTML is much more robust than what you have seen so far. The HTML described so far in the text has had no fine-tuning, with the result that every heading, table, or list looks exactly the same (except for the data included). This chapter will show how to not only change the display characteristics of HTML elements, but also how to add new ways to locate items, define borders, create columns, and much, much more.

The appeal and attractiveness of websites are greatly enhanced by styling them using *Cascading Style Sheets*, or *CSS*. With CSS, the web developer can create an overall look and feel to a website that makes it stand out with its own unique characteristics. Just browsing the Web for a little while reveals how different sites can have very different feels and appearances from page to page.

This chapter shows how to add style to a site. However, the choice of the best style for a page and an understanding of what styles work well is more art than it is science. How to achieve the proper visual effects by styling is a subject for Art, Design, and Communications Departments at various universities. We can, though, discuss the *mechanics* of adding styles to our sites.

Styling through CSS uses a syntax that is distinct from HTML, but the potential for confusion exists since their syntaxes can look similar. For this reason, the reader is encouraged to study CSS while comparing it to similar HTML in order to understand the proper syntax of each. In CSS, there are many different style settings – called *properties* – which can be changed. These properties can be set for any element inside the `<body>` element, and even on the `<body>` element itself. For example, you can change fonts, colors, text alignment (vertical and horizontal), borders, list types, etc. (If you search the Web, you can find several sites that have a complete list of CSS properties.)

Styles can be specified in three different ways, as shown in Table 7. Each of these methods is summarized here and then explained in detail later in this chapter. The first method, called inline, places the style attributes inside the quotes of the `style` attribute in the beginning tag of an HTML element. (The `style` attribute can be added to any HTML elements outside the `<head>` section.)

> **Inline Style**
>
> Inline styles are specified in the beginning tag of an HTML element using the *style* attribute. Style specified there applies to everything between the beginning and ending tags of the element. If there are other HTML elements nested in the styled element, the style would apply to them as well.

The second method is called an Internal Style Sheet, and in our example, is used to specify how `<h1>` elements are to look. As will be shown later, this global method would affect all `<h1>` elements in the page because it changes the default way that `<h1>` is being displayed. Styles defined using internal stylesheets are added to an HTML element by using the `class` attribute in the opening tag. (We will discuss the `class` attribute more a little later in "Defining Styles in the Stylesheet.")

The third method is almost the same as the second method, except that the style attributes are not defined in an internal stylesheet, but have instead been moved to an external page (`siteStyles.css`) in the same folder. There are many advantages to using an external page, which we will cover shortly. Like the second method, styles defined using external stylesheets are added to an HTML element by using the `class` attribute in the opening tag.

Defining Styles

Overview

There are hundreds of style attributes (properties) that can be specified for HTML elements. Some style attributes apply to many different elements; for example, alignment, font information, and colors would apply to almost all HTML elements. On the other hand, some HTML elements have special display attributes that you might wish to change. For example, lists need several specific attributes that you might want to specify, like *list-style-type* or *list-style-image*. Tables, too, have special attributes like *border-collapse* and *border-spacing* that would not apply to lists.

Given this level of complexity and the large number of possible attributes, this text will concentrate instead on basic techniques and leave you to research more advanced styling. Therefore, you should not only practice using each of the styles defined here, but also research other styles and try new things yourself. Find styles that you like as you browse the Web and then research the Web on how to achieve those styles. Make it a game to see how many different styles you can find and incorporate into your homework and projects.

Methods for Adding CSS to a Page	
Method	**Example**
Inline on a single element	```<html xmlns="http://www.w3.org/1999/xhtml" >
<head>
<title>Inline Style</title>
</head>
<body>
<h1 style="color:White; background-color:Black;">White on Black Heading</h1>
</body>
</html>```
Internal stylesheet	```<html xmlns="http://www.w3.org/1999/xhtml" >
<head>
<title>Inline Style</title>
<style type="text/css">h1 { color:White; background-color:Black; }</style>
</head>
<body>
<h1>White on Black Heading</h1>
</body>
</html>```
External stylesheet	```<!--HTML source with external stylesheet-->
<html xmlns="http://www.w3.org/1999/xhtml" >
<head>
<title>Inline Style</title>
<link rel="stylesheet" type="text/css" href="siteStyles.css" />
</head>
<body>
<h1>White on Black Heading</h1>
</body>
</html>```
	``/* External Stylesheet (siteStyles.css) */
h1
{
color:White;
background-color:Black;
}```
Result	**White on Black Heading**

Table 7. Methods for adding CSS

Style Name and Value Pairs

Browsers use internal tables to track the characteristics of each HTML element. When an element is styled using one of the above three methods, the browser makes changes to its internal tables, which track the current setting of many, many properties for each element. These include things like colors, borders, alignment, and fonts.

To change a particular property in CSS, the property is named and a new value for that property given. Consider the following example extracted from Table 7:

color:Black; *background-color*:White;

The first style property changed above is the foreground color (*color*) and the second is the background color (*background-color*). Each property is named and then assigned a new value, using the syntax of a name and value pair separated by a colon. Then each *name*:value pair is followed by a semicolon and a space. (Note that the semicolon is required for XHTML compatibility but the space is there only for increased readability.)

Also, if you like you can place the *name*:value pairs on separate lines to improve readability even more. This is the most common industry practice for methods 2 and 3 above.

> **Style name:value Pairs**
>
> To change a style's properties, specify the property **name** and the new **value** in pairs as shown:
>
> *color*:White; *background-color*:Black;
>
> The property name is followed by a colon and then by the new value. Next, add the required semicolon. The space between pairs is optional.

Since HTML also uses name and value pairs to specify attributes, it is good to compare these different ways of styling. Consider Table 8. On the left side is a series of HTML attributes that you have already seen; on the right, a set of CSS style properties. Note the use of the equal sign and a separating space for attributes, and the colon, a separating semicolon, and a space for properties. Be careful as you mix CSS and HTML so as not to confuse the syntax. Errors are common, so always check your work!

Comparison of HTML Attributes and CSS Style Properties	
HTML Attributes	**CSS Style Properties**
src="USflagOnMoon.jpg" *alt*="Flag on Moon" *href*="page2.html" *target*="_blank" *title*="User Security Code" *id*="code"	*color*:White; *background-color*:black; *text-align*:left; *font-weight*:bold; *font-size*:1.1em; *margin-left*:auto; *margin-right*:auto;

Table 8. Comparison of HTML attributes and CSS style properties

A quick study of Table 7 reveals how the style *name*:value pairs appear in all three methods for specifying style. The only way the methods differ is in how these pairs are included in the HTML. Each method is now described in more detail below.

Inline Styles (Changing One Element)

The inline style method makes changes to the display attribute for a single element, as shown in Table 7 and reproduced below:

`<h1 style="color:White; background-color:Black;">White on Black Heading</h1>`

For inline styles, the *style* attribute is included in the opening tag and style properties are placed within the quotes for that attribute. In fact, the *style* attribute can be included in any element within the `<body>` element, or also in the `<body>` element itself. (The reader should now work on exercise 1 at the end of this chapter to see this in action.)

> **Inline Styles**
>
> Inline styles are set with the *style* attribute of an element. The value of that style attribute is a series of *name*:value pairs separated by semicolons.

Many styles defined in an element will apply to all elements nested inside that element, too. If, for example, you change the font family to Arial in the `<body>` tag, everything in the body will use the Arial font (unless altered later by another style change). Similarly, if you change the foreground color to red in a table element, every cell in the table will be red unless changed at the row or cell level.

(Not all CSS properties are inherited by elements nested within them, though. For example, borders, margins, and padding elements are not changed for nested elements and will remain at the browser default settings unless specifically changed.)

Changes made using the inline style attribute of an element will affect only the element in which it is defined (and elements nested within it). Subsequent elements of the same type will return to the default settings for the browser. For example, `<h1>` elements after the white on black `<h1>` in figure 34 will appear normally and not be white on black.

There is no limit on how many style properties can be modified by an inline style. Furthermore, you can break up the line containing all these styles into multiple lines, rather than having one long line in the HTML source. In Figure 34, the style property list is so long it was broken across three lines.

```
<html>
  <head><title>Long Inline Style</title></head>
  <body>
    <h1 style="color:White; background-color:Black; width:450; height:40;
        font-family:Arial; border-style:solid; border-width:4px;
        border-color:pink; text-align:center;">
        White on Black Heading
    </h1>
  </body>
</html>
```

White on Black Heading

Figure 34. Complex inline style

Now consider what it would be like if your page had eight headings like the one shown here. You would have to include all the above styling for all eight of them. This would be a bit tedious, even with copy-and-paste. Methods two and three of Table 7 solve this problem by allowing for styles to be defined for multiple components at one time. These methods will be covered shortly.

Lastly, a note to those of you that may have wondered why the heading here is on the left side of the page and not centered, since the *text-align* style property is set to `center`. This is because only the text inside the heading is centered, since the style applies to only this element. To center the heading on the page itself, place the entire `<h1>` element inside a `<div>` that has centering set (more details below).

The Elements `<div>` and `<span>`

This section expands on the brief overview of the `<div>` element covered in chapter 3, and also covers a new element, `<span>`. The primary purpose of these two elements is to assign style attributes to content contained between the beginning and ending tags of these elements. The `<div>` element is used to define major divisions in an HTML document and, as such, it will usually contain multiple elements. Divisions, like paragraphs, will have a blank line both before and after them when rendered (although the size of this spacing can be modified using CSS). Style attributes applied to a `<div>` will apply to all elements nested within it as well. Typical style properties applied to a `<div>` and the elements contained therein include text alignment, CSS columns (see below), colors, and fonts.

> **The `<div>` Element**
>
> The `<div>` element is used to define styles for major divisions of a page, and the `<div>` usually has other nested HTML elements within it. The `<div>` element always has a blank line before and after it (by default).

The `<span>` element likewise is used to specify style, but instead of specifying style for multiple elements as with a `<div>`, `<span>` is usually used to change attributes on a set amount of text only. Therefore, you will frequently see just text within a `<span>` and not any HTML elements (since you could just style those elements by themselves).

Since the primary purpose of a `<span>` is to define style, it will always have some style associated with it. In the example below, the `<span>` element is used to make just one word – "red" – the color red.

```
Using the span element you can make just one word <span style="color:red">red</span>.
```

The advantage of `<span>` over `<div>` is that `<span>` does not add any blank lines around the text being changed. Instead, span makes changes to the text exactly where it is placed. Also note that there will usually be many style properties defined for a `<div>`, compared to only a few properties on a `<span>`.

> **The `<span>` Element**
>
> The `<span>` element is used to define styles for a single piece of text and will usually not include any nested HTML elements. Also, `<span>` has no blank lines or spaces surrounding it (by default).

The `<div>` element can be nested inside other `<div>` elements as needed, and you can nest `<span>` elements inside a `<div>` as well. However, a `<div>` cannot be nested inside a `<span>`, as this would not make sense, and a `<span>` should usually not be nested inside another `<span>`.

Inline versus Block Elements

At this point, we need to identify two major classifications of HTML elements and how these relate to the CSS process. The first type is the *block* element, and the second is an *inline* element. In a general sense, a block element tends to contain a substantial group of HTML statements or text, while an inline element usually only contains short pieces of text. These distinctions will become clearer as the material unfolds.

<u>Block-level Elements</u>

Block level elements are typically containers for nested elements and normally fill the full width of the page. Examples include headings (`<h1>` … `<h6>`), `<p>`, `<div>`, `<ul>`, `<ol>`, and `<form>` (see chapter 5). These elements are typically on their own line in the source or span across multiple lines. (Although headings usually do not contain other HTML elements, they are still considered block elements because they fill the full page width and because there is a blank line both before and after them in the page.) As they are containers for nesting, block elements can contain both block elements and inline elements (`<div>` inside a `<div>`, `<p>` inside a `<div>`, headings inside `<div>` or `<p>`, etc.).

Inline Elements

Inline elements will always be found inside another element, and typically include only a small amount of text between the beginning and ending tags. Examples include `<span>`, `<em>`, `<strong>`, `<cite>`, and `<a>`. As noted in the previous section, `<span>` is used to set the style of a small piece of text without adding any line breaks to the output (as `<div>` and `<p>` would). Inline elements will on occasion contain other inline elements, however. For example, say you wanted something bold and in italics:

> **Inline and Block Elements in XHTML**
>
> Block elements can include both inline and block elements, but inline elements should contain only other inline elements.

```
This is a <strong><em>big</em></strong> problem.
```

Here an inline element is nested inside another inline element. According to XHTML rules, though, inline elements must not contain block elements. For example, it would make no sense to nest a `<div>` inside a `<span>`. Instead, just specify the style attributes that you would use with `<span>` inside the `<div>` tag.

Using CSS with Inline and Block Elements

Inline elements are limited in what can be styled in them. Typically, you will be changing colors, fonts, and the like, and not be defining a size, location, or columns. On the other hand, block elements can be more extensively styled, including changes to location, size, padding, float (left or right), margins, borders, etc.

Stylesheets

Introduction

Inline styles only change the elements in which they are defined. Sometimes, however, you may wish to have a style applied to multiple elements of the same type. For this purpose, a stylesheet is created to define the style for single or multiple elements or to create named groups of styles. The style information is then located in a separate place either within the `<head>` section of the HTML (method two of Table 7) or in a separate file (method three of Table 7). This section only examines the format of the stylesheet, which is the same regardless of its location in methods two or three.

Example

Figure 35 is a stylesheet which defines attributes for the `<body>`, `<h1>`, and `<p>` elements. First, you can see that comments can be included in CSS by bookending the comment with a `/*` and an `*/`. Comments improve the readability of your stylesheets and are highly encouraged.

```
/*  StyleSheet1.css: Demonstrates simple CSS

/* Background for page is silver */
body
{
        background-color:Silver;
}
/* White centered headings on black */
h1
{
        color:White;
        background-color:Black;
        text-align:center;
}

/* Paragraphs that look like a book: indented with no blank lines */
p
{
        text-indent: 0.5in;
        margin-top: 0px;
        padding-top: 0px;
        margin-bottom: 0px;
        padding-bottom: 0px;
}
```

Figure 35. Sample stylesheet

Note how the style for all `<h1>` elements in the document is defined. The syntax includes the HTML opening tag (`<h1>`), followed by a left brace, followed by a set of *name:value* pairs (each ended with a semicolon), followed by the ending brace. The next two figures illustrate how the stylesheet actually works in practice.

Stylistically, the stylesheet in Figure 35 defines the background color for the page to be silver, and also defines headings to be white on a black background, centered on the screen. Finally, paragraphs are indented ½ inch, without a blank line before or after the paragraph. (This last change makes paragraphs look like they do in a book.)

```html
<html>
  <head>
    <title>Gettysburg Address</title>
    <link type="text/css" rel="Stylesheet" href="StyleSheet1.css" />
  </head>
  <body>
    <h1>Gettysburg Address</h1>
    <p>
    Four score and seven years ago our fathers brought forth on this continent,
    a new nation, conceived in Liberty, and dedicated to the proposition that
    all men are created equal. </p>
    <p>
    Now we are engaged in a great civil war, testing whether that nation,
    or any nation so conceived and so dedicated, can long endure. ... </p>
    <p>
    But, in a larger sense, we can not dedicate -- we can not consecrate --
    we can not hallow -- this ground. ...  </p>
  </body>
</html>
```

Figure 36. Document using stylesheet

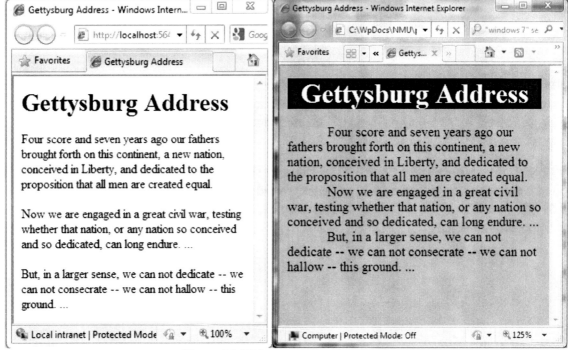

Figure 37. Web page using stylesheet

Figure 36 is the HTML source file for our CSS example. For simplicity, this page uses method three of Table 7, which means using the `<link>` element. The HTML itself contains nothing special other than one heading and three paragraphs. However, note how the presence of the stylesheet totally changes the appearance of the page (see Figure 37). On the left side is the page without any styling, and on the right is the page with the styling. (To see what the page would look like without styling in your browser, copy the HTML source in Figure 36 into your editor, delete the fourth line (the `<link>` element), and show the page.)

Defining Styles in the Stylesheet

There are several ways to define styles in a stylesheet. The example above applies changes to all elements. However, depending upon how styles are added to a stylesheet, the style element can apply to all elements (like above), some elements chosen in the HTML, or just one element chosen in the CSS. Furthermore, this choice has more to do with design objectives than the particular style being implemented. Each of these ways is described in the following paragraphs. Note that the techniques go from most general (covering the most elements) to the most specific (covering only one element).

Change All Elements of One Type

The stylesheet shown in Figure 35 makes style changes at the HTML element level. That is, it specifies changes to the `<body>`, `<h1>`, and `<p>` elements. Note that the source in Figure 36 has three paragraph elements, all of which are indented with no blank lines before or after them. Also, if additional `<h1>` elements were added to the source of Figure 36, all of them would be shown as white on black (see exercises at the end of this chapter).

> **Defining Style by Element(s)**
>
> If a style is defined in a stylesheet for an HTML element, the style changes will also apply to all elements of that type. In addition, the style changes will apply to all other HTML elements nested within that element.
> Multiple elements can be changed at one time by listing each element and separating them by commas.

Any HTML element can be styled with a stylesheet, and then the changes in that stylesheet would apply to all such elements in the page. As a reminder, a style applied to an element will also affect any element that is nested within it.

You can also update the style on multiple element types at once using only one group of properties. To do this, list every element type you want to apply changes to in the stylesheet, separate them by commas, and then add the braces and the style properties as shown in Figure 38. In that figure, the borders for a table and its cells are all changed as a group, causing the table to have a 2-pixel-wide green border around the outside and a 2-pixel green border between the cells. If you remove the *border-collapse* property (try it), there will be space between the cell borders as well as around the outside of the table.

```
td, th, table
{
 border-style:solid;
 border-color:Green;
 border-width:2px;
 border-collapse:collapse;
}
```

Figure 38. Defining CSS properties for multiple elements

Class Names (Styles for Selected Elements)

Sometimes you do not want to apply a style change to all elements of that type. For example, you might only want a few headings to be white on black, with the rest as normal. One solution would be to use an inline style on each of them; CSS, however, offers a better and more compact solution.

CSS allows you to define a group of *name:value* pairs in a stylesheet and assign a name to that grouping. Then that named group of styles is referenced in the HTML using the given name, as shown in Figure 39. Once the name is defined, you can apply that style to any HTML elements you want.

In this example, the stylesheet defines a class name using the period followed by a class name. Figure 39 uses the class name `rbHeading` but it can be any name that you like. However, the name should be meaningful so that it can be remembered and (at least partially) indicate the use for the class. The name should only contain letters and numbers and must not contain whitespace. This particular named class, `rbHeading`, has three *name:value* pairs defined to make the heading white on black but with fixed width.

To reference this named group of style properties, the HTML attribute *class* is given a value equal to the defined name (`<h3 class="rbHeading">`), and this class attribute can be applied to any HTML element outside of the `<head>` section. In other words, the named class is defined in the CSS and referenced in any HTML element. Other elements that do not have a *class* attribute pointing to this class will not use the style defined in it. Thus class names change only selected HTML elements (unlike using the element type of defining, which changes all elements of that type).

Sometimes you have multiple classes defined in the stylesheet and would like to reference more than one of those in a single element. Notice in Figure 39 how the second white on black heading is centered but the first white on black heading is not. This is because the second white on black heading also references the class name `center`. To reference multiple classes, set the *class* attribute to the list of class names and separate the names with a space. The order of the class names is important, as the changes are applied in the order specified (see Cascading Styles below).

> **Referencing Multiple CSS Classes**
>
> To reference multiple classes in an element, set the class attribute to the list of class names and separate the names with a space:
>
> `<h3 class="rbHeading center">`

```html
<html>
<head>
    <title>Using CSS Classes</title>
    <style type="text/css">
     .rbHeading       /* White on Black Heading */
     {
      color:White;
      background-color:Black;
      width:250px;
     }
     .center          /* Center Text */
     {
      text-align:center;
     }
    </style>
</head>
<body>
  <h3 class="rbHeading">This one is White on Black</h3>
  <h3 class="rbHeading center">White on Black centered</h3>
  <h3>This one is normal</h3>
</body>
</html>
```

This one is White on Black

White on Black centered

This one is normal

Figure 39. Using CSS class names

Class Names for Elements

When a class name is defined as described above, that class can be used by any HTML element. For example, the **center** class is generally useful for a wide variety of elements. Not every class is this general, though. (For example, say you are trying to style tables and want to define a style for table rows. This class would not be much use outside of tables.)

In this way, CSS allows you to restrict a class name to an individual element type. Consider the following example, which is a variation on the stylesheet in Figure 35.

```
p.bookFormat
{
        text-indent:     0.5in;
        margin-top:      0px;
        padding-top:     0px;
        margin-bottom:   0px;
        padding-bottom:  0px;
}
```

Instead of defining a style that could allow any kind of block-style text to be indented book-style, this change defines a named class that applies only to paragraphs. Then, when a paragraph needs to be in this special format, the paragraph would set the class attribute to **bookFormat**.

Adding Style to Only One Element

The last way to specify a style in a stylesheet is to apply the style to only one element. Since the style is being applied to only one element, the element must be identified using the *id* attribute in the HTML. Study Figure 40 for an example.

Note first how the initial **<h1>** element is defined and given an *id* of **mainHead**. Then, in the stylesheet the *id* is referenced by using the pound sign (**#**) followed by the *id* of the element. Keep in mind that this is a role reversal from class names; specifically, class names are defined in the CSS and referenced in the HTML, and here an *id* is defined in the HTML and then referenced in the CSS. Think about this distinction as you study and use CSS.

The *id* attribute, which can be added to any HTML element, is necessary so that the stylesheet can specify which element has that style. Note that since the *id* attribute must be unique inside one HTML page, only one HTML element is changed using the *id*.

The *id* Attribute

The *id* attribute can be defined on any HTML element. Within a single HTML page, all *id* attributes must be unique.

```
<!--Applying Style to HTML id Attribute -->
<html>
<head>
    <title>Applying Style to HTML id Attribute</title>
    <style type="text/css">
      #mainHead     /* Style for Main Heading */
      {
       color:White;
       background-color:Black;
      }
    </style>
</head>
<body>
  <h1 id="mainHead">This one is White on Black</h1>
  <h1>This one is normal</h1>
</body>
</html>
```

This one is White on Black

This one is normal

Figure 40. Referencing style using HTML *id*

Pseudo-Class Names for Links

The characteristics of external links can be changed in CSS. Specifically, you might want a link to grow larger and change color when a mouse moves over the link. Alternately, you might wish to specify how the link appears after it has been visited for the first time, or how it appears while the link is active (i.e. being clicked on or tabbed to). These characteristics use the concept of "pseudo-class names." For links, there are four pseudo-class names:

Link (<a>) Pseudo-Class Names	
Pseudo-Class Name	**Use**
a:link	Characteristics of an unvisited link.
a:visited	Characteristics of a previously visited link.
a:hover	Characteristics of link when the mouse is over it.
a:active	Characteristics of an active link.

Table 9. Link pseudo-class names

For the following discussion, see Figure 41. In that example all of the virtual classes are used to make minor changes to a link. (Note that an abbreviated style is used in the internal stylesheet to save space.) In the example below, the color of an unvisited link is changed from blue to fuchsia (not that anyone would ever want to do this), and when the mouse is over the link, the font size is enlarged from 120% to 140%. Finally, once the link has been visited the color becomes maroon, and while the link is actively being clicked the color becomes green (see exercise 3).

```
<!--Using Pseudo-Classes with Links -->
<html>
<head>
    <title>Using Pseudo-Classes with Links</title>
    <style type="text/css">
       a         { font-size:120%; font-family:Arial; }
       a:link    { color:Fuchsia; }
       a:hover   { font-size:140%; background-color:yellow; }
       a:visited { color:Maroon; }
       a:active  { color:Green; }
    </style>
</head>
<body>
  <a href="http://www.needlerat.com" target="_blank">Example Link</a>
</body>
</html>
```

<u>Example Link</u>

Figure 41. Link pseudo-class example

If you place any of these virtual class names in a stylesheet, then all links will take on the new characteristics. However, there will be times when you only want to modify the virtual class settings on certain links. To solve this problem, you can define named classes for links by appending a period to the end of the pseudo-class name and following that by the class name to be used. Consider the following variation on the last example, shown in Figure 42. Now the name **highlight** is added to each of the pseudo-classes, but only the first link includes the *class* attribute using this class name. (Note that another example of this is shown in Figure 54, an example that uses links as buttons.)

```
<!--Using Pseudo-Classes with Links -->
<html>
<head>
    <title>Using Pseudo-Classes with Links</title>
    <style type="text/css">
       a.highlight          { font-size:120%; font-family:Arial; }
       a:link.highlight     { color:Fuchsia; }
       a:hover.highlight    { font-size:140%; background-color:yellow; }
       a:visited.highlight  { color:Maroon; }
       a:active.highlight   { color:Green; }
    </style>
</head>
<body>
  <a href="http://www.needlerat.com" target="_blank"
     class="highlight">Special Link</a><br />
  <a href="http://www.needlerat.com" target="_blank">Normal Link</a>
</body>
```

<u>Special Link</u>
<u>Normal Link</u>

Figure 42. Named link pseudo-classes

Internal Stylesheets

CSS stylesheets can be defined internally or externally (methods two and three of Table 7). The previous example used the internal stylesheet method, so now we will describe them in more detail. Remember that the format of the stylesheet is the same, regardless of whether it is internal or external. The only difference is where the stylesheet is located. However, it is important to note that *internal stylesheets make changes only to the page in which they are defined!*

To create an internal stylesheet, use the `<style>` element and put the stylesheet between the beginning and ending tags of that element. The internal stylesheet portion of method two from Table 7 is reproduced here.

> **Internal Stylesheets**
>
> Internal stylesheets are defined between the opening and closing tags of the `<style>` element. The only attribute required on the opening tag is `type="text/css"`
>
> The `<style>` element is always located in the `<head>` section, and must contain only CSS, not HTML.

```
<style type="text/css">
  h1
  {
    color:Red;
    background-color:Blue;
  }
</style>
```

Figure 43. Sample internal stylesheet

The stylesheet is included as data for the `<style>` element. That is, between `<style type="text/css">` and `</style>` can only be CSS and *must not* contain HTML. The syntax for the `<style>` element is exact and must be followed precisely. Note also that the internal stylesheet is defined in the `<head>` section.

External Stylesheets

An external stylesheet is a separate file that contains only CSS, as described previously. The industry standard is for all external stylesheets to have a `.css` extension. Using a `.css` extension tells your editor what type of file it is so it can colorize the syntax for you. The number one reason for having external stylesheets is that *an external stylesheet can change the style of multiple pages.*

To create an external stylesheet, open a blank page in your editor and save it with a `.css` extension (to get proper colorization by the editor). Then add your style information as described above and save it again. Be sure to place the stylesheet in the same folder as the web page referencing it. Alternately, you could create a subfolder for all stylesheets (as described below) and use a folder reference.

> **External Stylesheets**
>
> External stylesheets exist outside any HTML page and are referenced in the head section using the `<link>` element. Only pure CSS is placed inside an external stylesheet (no HTML).
>
> Internal stylesheets can apply style changes to any page referencing it with the `<link>` element. Also, one page can reference multiple external stylesheets using multiple `<link>` elements. However, order is important (see the next section, Cascading Styles, for more information).

Once the stylesheet is defined, you need to tell the browser which page or pages will be using that particular stylesheet. This is done with the `<link>` element as shown here:

```
<link rel="Stylesheet" type="text/css" href="siteStyles.css" />
```

All but the *href* attribute is fixed and should appear exactly as shown in your page. The *href* attribute has a value equal to the filename of the stylesheet being used. If subfolders are being used, the attribute value would also include the folder name (see Folders and Folder References below).

The industry standard is to place all `<link>` elements in the `<head>` section of the HTML document. Also, if both an internal stylesheet and an external stylesheet are being used at the same time, you will normally place the `<link>` element *before* the `<style>` element for reasons explained under the next section, Cascading Styles.

Note that a single web page can reference multiple external stylesheets by simply including multiple `<link>` elements in the head section. Be sure to choose the best order for them, taking into account the cascading process described below.

Cascading Styles

Depending upon which method is used from Table 7 to change styles, the change might affect one element, or many elements. Students often ask the question, "What if a style property is set for an element multiple times?" For example, what if there is both an internal and external stylesheet for a page that defines the color of the `<h1>` element and these definitions end up being different? Say, for example, an external stylesheet changes the color, and then an inline style changes it. The question becomes: which one wins, and what is the color of the element?

> **Cascading Style Sheets (CSS)**
>
> Multiple styles may be applied to a single HTML element, through external and internal stylesheets and/or through HTML nesting. The styles of the element come from either the innermost HTML element (in the case of nesting) or from the order the styles are specified (with the last one specified determining the style).

The simple answer is that *the last one wins*. In our example, the inline style was the last one seen by the browser, as it is attached to the element itself. What would happen if there was no inline style, but only the internal and external stylesheets? Then the result depends on the order in which they are specified. To be safe, always place the `<link>` to the external sheet *before* the internal sheet. In that case, the color specified in the internal sheet would be the one used. Remember, a style change only changes a limited set of style properties. Any style property not changed in a stylesheet remains at its previous value, which could have been set in another stylesheet.

Another question about multiple specifications of styles arises from HTML nesting. For a ridiculous example that would never occur in the real world, consider this scenario: the font family is set to Arial on the `<body>` element, then a `<table>` is specified with a style that sets the font family to Lucida, then a table row (`<tr>`) is defined that changes the font family to Courier, and finally, a cell in the table (`<th>`) sets the family to Cambria. What would be the font of the cell? The answer is that the innermost element defines the style, so the font setting at the cell level would win and the cell's font would be Cambria.

Finally, note that multiple stylesheets will not always define styles for the same elements. It is only when they specify a new value for a style property that the latest change is applied. If one style property is only defined in the site-wide stylesheet, then that property applies regardless of other internal or inline style specifications.

Choosing a Styling Method

Table 7 defines three methods for adding style to a document: inline, internal, and external. The question is which one to use and where. As was mentioned in the introduction, much about style is an artistic decision. The designer first considers how the overall site should appear and what the look and feel of the site should be. Next the designer begins to plan individual pages, and for large-scale systems, a "storyboard" or mockup is drawn up before any real source is written. From these plans, an overall style policy is defined.

This site style policy would usually be implemented in one, or sometimes more, external stylesheet(s) and most, if not all, pages would be set to reference that stylesheet (or stylesheets). In this way, every page would have the same look and feel. This main external stylesheet would specify styles, using both element names and class names. Use of an *id* is not really appropriate in a site-wide page style, though, unless the same element with the same *id* occurs in almost every page of the site (and even then, a class name would be preferred). Finally, skeletons of the various pages would be created and tested for look and feel.

Internal stylesheets would then be added to those pages that require variations from the site-wide style. The `<style>` element for the internal stylesheet would be placed after the `<link>` element for the site-wide sheet, so that styles specified there would override styles in the site-wide stylesheet.

Finally, but rarely, a page will require some small tweaking with inline styles. However, most developers prefer to not use any inline styles to do this. Instead, they define classes in an internal (sometimes external) stylesheet and then use the *class* attribute to change the style. By never using inline styles and always placing the styles in a stylesheet, the HTML becomes cleaner and easier to create and edit.

Folders and Folder References

You may want to place all your images for your site in a separate folder under your main HTML document folder. This folder might be named **images**, for example. Similarly, you may want to place your stylesheets in a separate folder with a name like **styles**. In the examples below, these subfolders are assumed to be located in the same folder as the page itself:

```
<link href="Styles/StyleSheet1.css" rel="Stylesheet" type="text/css" />
<img  src="Images/mexico.gif" alt="Mexican Flag" title="Mexican Flag />
```

As seen in these examples, you simply preface the image or stylesheet name with the folder in which the image or stylesheet is located. A similar technique could be followed if you had a subfolder containing web pages. Assume that you had a set of instructional pages located in a directory called **HelpFiles**:

```
<a href="HelpFiles/orderform.html>Help with order form.</a>
```

Additional addressing techniques are available, but are beyond the scope of this book. (For example, using the "dot" notation, you can move between subfolders.) Check online for additional details.

Colors

One of the most common HTML style properties to change is color, and there are a lot of details on color selection that are covered online that may confuse the reader on the first pass. However, colors are relatively simple to use once you understand the basics.

Internally, the brightness of each primary color is represented by an 8-bit integer number that can have a value anywhere from 0 (no color, always black) to 255 (full color). The primary colors for computer monitors are red, green, and blue and thus form the letters RGB. When you combine the three 8-bit color numbers, you have a 24-bit number, giving rise to the term "24-bit color."

Note that the color white has a value of 255 for red, green, and blue. Also, black has a value of 0 for each of these colors. Between white and black are over 16 million different colors (2^{24} colors) with only a few of the most common ones having been named (red, blue, pink, orange, yellow, brown, white, black, etc.). For this reason, you will be better off always selecting a color by specifying the values for each of red, green, and blue, as described next.

RGB Color Specification

There are many graphical editing programs like Microsoft® Paint and Adobe® Photoshop® that have tools for selecting colors. These tools will then give you RGB values for each of the component colors. To illustrate, Microsoft Paint will be used to select a color and then that color will be applied as a background color to a heading using an inline style. If you are using an Apple computer, use one of the graphical editors on that platform (such as Adobe Photoshop).

Open Paint by clicking Start, All Programs, Accessories, and then Paint. The basic Paint screen is shown here.

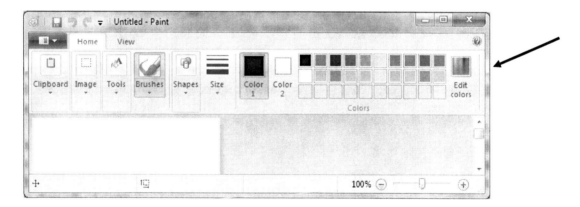

Click the Edit Colors button to display the color palate. Then, click the mouse somewhere in the middle of the color box to pick a color. To choose an exact color, though, it is necessary to type in three numbers for the RGB colors: in this example, red is 91, green is 184, and blue is 204. These values can now be used in CSS any place a color is needed.

For example, this color can be applied to the background color of a heading, also as shown in Figure 44. Note the syntax for using the RGB numbers: three values inside parentheses *with no whitespace between the values!* Using that notation, `rgb(255,0,0)` is the same as the name "red" because the value for red is at the maximum of 255 while green and blue are at 0. In other words, red is at its maximum and green and blue are off, leaving only red. Note, of course, that you would never use the RGB method of specifying red since the name "red" is already defined, shorter, and supported by all browsers.

```
<html>
  <head><title>Long Inline Style</title></head>
  <body>
    <h1 style="color:rgb(255,255,255); background-color:rgb(91,184,204); ">
        White on Black Heading
    </h1>
  </body>
</html>
```

Figure 44. Heading using custom color

Up to this point, absolute values have been used for each of the RGB colors. But you can also use a percentage value from 0 to 100 as well; for example, `rgb(100%,0%,0%)` would be red (100% red and nothing else). Also, you can create a whole range of gray colors by having the same percentage for each of the RGB values. For example, `rgb(90%,90%,90%)` would be a very light shade of gray (try it).

A final way to specify colors is to use the # character followed by the six hex color numbers. These colors can be found online but an explanation of the technique is beyond the scope of this text. For best results, use common color names or the RGB method.

Units for Defining Sizes

In CSS there are many places where you can specify the size of something. This might be the length or width of an element, the thickness of a border, settings and margins, padding, or many more things. This section looks at three of the various units that can be used to specify size: pixels, ems, and percentages (the others are not recommended in good web pages).

px (Pixels)

A pixel (`px`) is generally interpreted to be the size of the smallest dot on the screen. (A pixel may appear as more than one dot when the zoom feature is used in the browser, though.) Pixels are what you might consider absolute sizing, because the size will not change with changes in the window size or with changes in the current font. It is the easiest unit to use and can be quickly adjusted to make a particular page look good. However, if you want proportions and spacing to change as font sizes or window sizes change, try one of the next two units.

Em

The `em` unit is the size of the current font. For example, if you set the padding or margin around some text to 3 em and the font size was 14 point (`pt`), then the 3 em spacing would be equal to 42 point. The advantage of using em for padding and margins is that if the browser defaults have been configured for a different default font size (perhaps for the visually impaired), then the spacing would remain proportional to the size of the font. Note that a point is also a typeface size and represents 1/72 of an inch; however, points are not recommended for use in defining sizes since they do not play nicely with browser font resizing. (This is commonly done by many users, especially those with sight impairments.)

%

Percentage values are always relative to some other value, and that value depends upon the location of the element being modified by the CSS. For example, if you set the width of a `<div>` element that is immediately inside the body element to 30%, then the width of that element will be 30% of the width of the display page. However, if width is being specified on an element inside another element, it will be set to 30% of that containing element's width. Some experimentation and testing in various browsers may be necessary to achieve the best results.

Box Model (Margins, Borders, Padding, Height, and Width)

There are several ways to exactly locate HTML block elements in a specifically sized box, and furthermore, you can leave space in that box for the text and borders as well. The best way to understand this is to study the box model shown in Figure 45. After the size of the block-level element is specified (`height` and `width`), there are three other items that can be specified: margins, borders, and padding. Each of these three can be specified individually for each side, or all sides can be specified as a unit instead. The box model concept containing these three layers will be developed in the following paragraphs.

(Note in the figure that the dotted line around the text would not appear in the browser. It is included to highlight how the `height` and `width` style properties appear on the page. Also, you can see that as you increase any of the three properties (padding, margin, or border), you will also increase the area required for the completed block-style element.)

Space Required for Block Element

Any increase of any of the three block properties (padding, margin, or border) will also increase the area required for the completed block-style element!

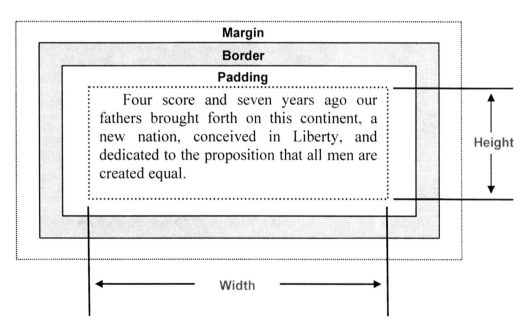

Figure 45. Box model

Margins

Margins specify how much blank space must be left outside the border (if any) between the element and any surrounding page content. Use margins to keep text from butting right up against an image. Alternately, you can reduce margins to keep the browser from leaving space above or below elements. Margins are also used to create CSS columns, to align tables in Firefox, and to add spacing to many other places.

Margins

Margins leave space between borders and any adjacent content.

For example, say you have an `<h1>` element at the top of your page. The browser will automatically leave (waste?) space above that heading, space that you might need elsewhere on the page. To free up that space, set the top margin on at least that particular `<h1>` element to zero.

Padding

Padding is the space to leave around an element before any border elements. As such, the padding area will take on the same background color as the element it surrounds. By increasing padding, you increase the space between the element and its border, if any. If no border is specified, padding will have a similar effect to margins.

> **Padding**
> Padding leaves space between an element and its border. It will have the same background color as the element itself.

Borders

Borders have more style options than padding or margins because a border, regardless of which side is specified, requires three pieces of information: color, style, and width (thickness). Furthermore, you can set the individual properties (size, style, and color) for all sides at once or one side at a time.

Due to the cascading characteristics of CSS, one strategy for borders is to first specify how you want all borders to appear, then redefining individual border characteristics to achieve a desired effect. For example, say you want a red border on the left, top, and right sides but a green border on the bottom. All borders are to be groove style (that is, they look like grooves in the page) and four pixels wide. The CSS would be as follows:

```
.specialBox
{
  border: 4px groove red;         /* Set size, style, and color for all sides */
  border-bottom-color: Green;     /* Override bottom border to make it green */
}
```

Browser Support for the Box Model

Earlier versions of Microsoft's Internet Explorer used a different (and faulty) set of rules for interpreting the settings in the box model. With later releases of IE (starting with version 6), they fixed the problem but had to continue to support the old method to not break existing pages. To solve this problem, IE checks for the presence of the **DOCTYPE** line. This line, if present, evokes full XHTML support, implying correct handling of the box model. The complete line is shown below:

```
<!DOCTYPE html PUBLIC "-//W3C//DTD XHTML 1.0 Transitional//EN"
    "http://www.w3.org/TR/xhtml1/DTD/xhtml1-transitional.dtd">
```

The only required part of the line is the first attribute *html*. However, for best results use the entire line, including the XHTML version of the `<html>` tag:

```
<html xmlns="http://www.w3.org/1999/xhtml" >
```

Positioning Elements

Elements can be positioned anywhere on the screen, or in the case of nested elements, anywhere within parent elements in which they are nested. Furthermore, there is an almost unlimited variety of ways in which elements can be positioned using CSS, where the method used becomes one of personal choice. These ways include positioning items relative to their order in the file (the default), positioning items absolutely on the screen, and positioning items relative to their normal positions. For this reason, this section will only give a brief outline of the positioning process.

Before you begin to position objects, you may find it useful for a period of time to draw borders around each element or give them different backgrounds. With this technique you will be able to see how the elements are being positioned exactly and how they are overlapping, if at all.

When a `width` and `height` are specified, most elements will be positioned by specifying their `top` and `left` properties; you can also use `right` and `bottom` if need be, however. This way, the item will remain locked as specified when the screen is resized.

Alternately, you can omit any size properties and just set the position of the element by using `left`, `right`, `top`, and `bottom`. In this case, the element will resize as the window is resized, with the box edges being tied to parent elements or the screen. Once the box is positioned, you specify what that position is relative to by setting the `position` property. The position property can be one of the values shown in Table 10, which also contains some specific comments on use of each value.

CSS *position* Property Values	
`position`	Description
`static`	Element appears just like it appears in the source HTML. This is the default setting.
`absolute`	Position element relative to a specifically positioned ancestor (not static). An ancestor is an element within which the element is nested. For example, once you position a `<div>`, you can position other elements exactly within that `<div>`.
`fixed`	Element is positioned relative to the browser window. Using this mode is unusual and will usually not appear right when the window is resized.
`relative`	The element is positioned relative to its normal position. If you set `top:40px;` and `position:relative;` then the object would be 40 pixels below where it would normally appear.
`inherit`	Positioning determined from the parent element.

Table 10. CSS *position* property values

The example below creates a simple page with a banner, a small navigation section, and a content section. These various sections are positioned using absolute positioning. First is the HTML.

```
<!DOCTYPE html PUBLIC "-//W3C//DTD XHTML 1.0 Transitional//EN"
  "http://www.w3.org/TR/xhtml1/DTD/xhtml1-transitional.dtd">
<html xmlns="http://www.w3.org/1999/xhtml" >
<head>
    <title>Absolute Positioning</title>
    <link rel="Stylesheet" type="text/css" href="position.css" />
  </head>
  <body>
    <h1 class="banner">Mama's Best Pasties</h1>
    <div class="navigation">
      <ul>
        <li><a href="#">About Us</a></li>
        <li><a href="#">Price List</a></li>
        <li><a href="#">Shipping Information</a></li>
      </ul>
    </div>
    <div class="content">
      <h2 class="center">About Us</h2>
      Using an old family recipe brought over from England, Mama Wilson used
      to sell pasties to the miners as they walked to the mine. We now use
      the latest in organic ingredients in her recipe to bring you the very
      best in pasties. Taste and see why all our customers rave about us.
    </div>
  </body>
</html>
```

Figure 46. Absolute positioning HTML

The HTML references the external stylesheet shown in Figure 47. After the centering class in that file, the body is set to a silver background and the margin and padding are set to zero. (These last two changes tighten everything up on the page.) From this point onward, the attributes of three classes are being defined: **banner**, **navigation**, and **content**. These classes correspond to the main sections of the page. Also, instead of defining all the CSS properties for each class and thereby duplicating some properties in each class, the common properties are defined first followed by more and more specific properties.

The first property sets absolute positioning on all elements by changing the **<body>** element. Next, the **banner** class is defined as covering the full width of the screen, centered, and with yellow on blue text. Then the **navigation** and **content** classes are set to start 50 pixels down to leave room for the heading, and the **navigation** class is given a different background color and a fixed width. After this the **content** class is positioned to start such that there is room for it after the **navigation** class.

Finally, the last set of properties in the CSS creates temporary green borders on the page. Since all class names are being changed in the definition, the borders will apply to all major sections of the page.

```css
/* Position.css */
.center { text-align:center; }
body   /* Silver background, no padding or margin */
{
  background-color:Silver;
  padding:0;
  margin:0;
}

.banner, .navigation, .content  /* Absolute positioning on all */
{
  position:absolute;
}

.banner { width:100%; background-color:Blue; color:Yellow; text-align:center; }

.navigation, .content   /* Navigation and content below banner */
{
  top: 50px;
}

.navigation   /* Navigation background and width */
{
  background-color:rgb(90%, 90%, 100%);
  width: 180px;
}

.content    /* Content to the right of navigation, 20px gutter from navigation */
{
  left:200px;
}
.banner, .navigation, .content /* Temporary borders for positioning */
{
  border: 1px solid green;
  padding: 2px;
  margin-bottom: 2px;
}
```

Figure 47. Absolute positioning CSS with temporary borders

The left side of the solution in Figure 48 shows the temporary borders, and the right side shows the results when the borders are removed by deleting this last set of CSS properties.

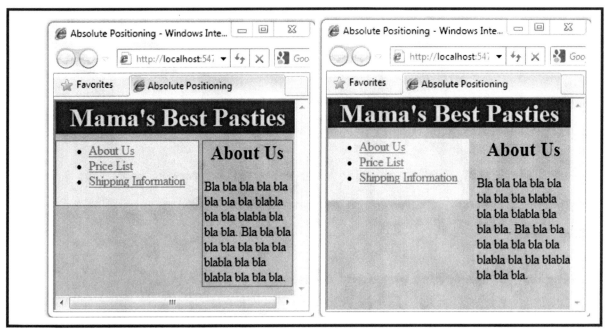

Figure 48. Absolute positioning results

An additional change you might try includes setting a height for the navigation class so it extends down to the end of the content section. Also, if you restrict the height of all three classes using percentages, the page will resize rather nicely. However, the font size of the text will not resize, so as you continue to shrink the window size a point is reached where the content will overflow the borders, making the result quite messy.

Styling Tables

Centering Tables with All Browsers

Different browsers operate differently when you are trying to place a table in the center of the screen. With most browsers, simply placing the table inside a `<div>` element that has *text-align* set to `center` would center the table. However, Firefox leaves the table at the left margin, so to center the table with all browsers, it is necessary to place the table in a centered `<div>` and to also set the table to be centered using a class designed for Firefox. This class sets the margins for Firefox to `auto` on the table so it will center, and the source for the solution is shown in Figure 49, with the results in the right half of the solution window. Note that the *class* attribute is set to `center` on the `<div>` and to `centerF` on the `<table>`.

> **Centering Tables**
>
> Firefox will left-justify a table even when it is in a centered `<div>`. Add a class to the `<table>` element that sets *margin-left* and *margin-right* to `auto`. This centers the table in all browsers.

```
<!--Centering Tables with All Browsers -->
<html>
<head>
    <title>Centering Tables with All Browsers</title>
    <style type="text/css">
     .center /* For IE, Safari */
     {
      text-align:center
     }
     .centerF /* For Firefox table element */
     {
      margin-left:auto;
      margin-right:auto;
     }
     td, th, table
     {
      border-style:solid;
      border-color:Green;
      border-width:2px;
      border-collapse:collapse;
     }
    </style>
</head>
<body>
  <div class="center">
    <h1>Centered Heading</h1>
    <table class="centerF" border="0">
      <tr><th colspan="2">Address Book</th>         </tr>
      <tr><th>Name           </th><th>Phone         </th></tr>
      <tr><td>Bill Smith     </td><td>909-231-1414</td></tr>
      <tr><td>John Stotdze   </td><td>725-4100</td></tr>
    </table>
  </div>
</body>
</html>
```

Figure 49. Centering tables in all browsers

Most elements inside a centered `<div>` are centered in all browsers. However, tables and other fixed-size elements in Firefox require the above documented setting for *margin-left* and *margin-right*. If the element is full width, there is no problem (like a heading without a width specified). However, if you limit the width of a heading as in the next example, the heading will remain at the left margin if the margin properties are not set on the heading. This is discussed below under Centering Headings with Borders.

Changing Table Borders

Figure 49 defines style attributes for `<table>`, `<th>`, and `<td>` as a single set. The result of these styles is a single two-pixel-wide green border as shown in the left half of Figure 49. The setting *border-collapse* eliminates space between the lines of the cells; if that is not set, the table is larger, with space between each cell as shown in the right half of the figure (try it). The rest of the style settings are self-explanatory.

Also note that the table setting for `<td>` is still at its normal setting of left justified even though the table is nested inside the centered `<div>`. That is because the `<div>` set the alignment of the table and not the elements inside the table. However, numeric and other data frequently need to be right aligned as shown next.

Aligning Numeric Data in Tables

To align data on the right in a table cell, you must set the *text-align* style property to `right` for that cell. This is generally done by creating a named class called `right` and referencing that *class* in every `<td>` (or `<th>`) element that must be right aligned. In the stylesheet add this line:

```
.right { text-align:right; }
```

Then change the two data lines in the source of Figure 49 as shown below. The result is that the phone numbers are right aligned; see picture on the right for the result.

```
<tr><td>Bill Smith    </td><td class="right">909-231-1414</td></tr>
<tr><td>John Stotdze  </td><td class="right">725-4100</td></tr>
```

Address Book	
Name	Phone
Bill Smith	909-231-1414
John Stotdze	725-4100

Centering Headings with Borders

As you may have noticed in some of the previous examples, a heading with a different background color creates a colored bar all the way across the screen. If centering is defined for just the heading (inline or by class name), the heading will be centered inside that full-width border.

There may be times, however, when you want a heading with a background color that has a fixed size as set by the *height* and *width* CSS properties. When you do this, centering has some interesting side effects, depending upon where it is defined. When you specify a width for a heading (see examples in Figure 51) there are two things being centered: the text inside the heading box, and the box containing the heading.

The following four figures illustrate the problem of centering. Figure 50 is the CSS used to create a boxed heading and to perform centering. Figure 51 is the HTML that shows four different combinations of centering on the element and also on a `<div>` containing the element. Figure 52 shows the four results in Firefox, and Figure 53 shows the results in Internet Explorer.

```
.center         /* Center Content inside Elements */
{
        text-align:center;
}

.centerF /* Center Firefox Elements */
{
  margin-left:auto;
  margin-right:auto;
}

.fancyHeads /* Fancy h3 Headings */
{
        border-color:rgb(255,140,140);
        border-style:groove;
        border-width:8px;
        background-color:Silver;
        color:Blue;
        width:350px;
        height:25px;
}
```

Figure 50. CSS for centered headings

The first heading in Figure 51 has a special format but uses no centering. The second heading uses the **center** class on the heading itself but does not use a **<div>**. The third heading still uses the **center** class on the heading, but adds the **center** class to the **<div>**, and the last heading also uses a **center** class for the **<div>** but uses the **centerF** class for the heading.

```html
<html >
  <head>
     <title>Centered Headings</title>
     <link rel="Stylesheet" type="text/css" href="CenteredHeadings.css" />
  </head>
  <body>
    <h4 class="fancyHeads">Left text and heading on all browsers</h4>
    <h4 class="fancyHeads center">Left heading centered text all browsers</h4>
    <div class="center">
      <h4 class="fancyHeads center">Centered heading and text except Firefox</h4>
    </div>
    <div class="center">
      <h4 class="fancyHeads centerF">Centered heading and text all browsers</h4>
    </div>
  </body>
</html>
```

Figure 51. HTML for centered headings

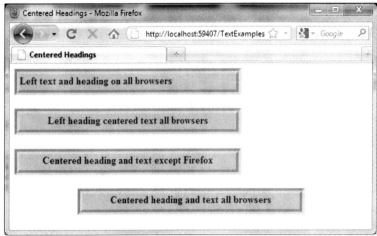

Figure 52. Centered headings – Firefox

Note the differences between Firefox and Internet Explorer on the third heading. IE centers while Firefox does not. The fourth heading, however, appears correctly in both browsers and is the technique that should be used. Specifically, set `text-align` to `center` on a `<div>` containing the heading, with `margin-left` and `margin-right` set to `auto` on the heading itself. Note that this pattern is the same as for tables (see above) as well as for other elements that need to be centered in Firefox.

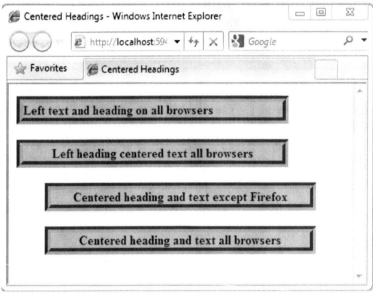

Figure 53. Centered headings – Internet Explorer

Links as Navigation Buttons

By using the pseudo-classes defined for links and adjusting other style settings, it is possible to make a link look like a navigation button. These navigation buttons might be used on a multi-page site (such as the resume project described at the end of the chapter). Navigation buttons will all share the same style, including having a fixed-size-width a box around them (borders), a larger font size, and a change in appearance when a mouse is moved over them. Using CSS, all these links (anchor elements) can be made to take on that button appearance. The difficulty is making all browsers treat them the same way.

Figure 54 shows one possible solution of a blue on pink link button. The first frame of the figure is the external stylesheet; the second is the HTML; and the third is the result in the browser (rendered here in black and white). You can change the colors and size to fit your needs, but some of the other CSS is needed to make the buttons appear the same in all browsers. These necessary features are described next.

The font name and size is set to your taste. The *text-decoration* property is set to **none** so the links are no longer underlined (the button box and contents imply a linking function already), and *display* is set to **block** so that Safari and Firefox will accept the exact box dimensions set by *width* and *height*. (Otherwise, these properties will not change the size of the box.) The *border-style* property needs to be set to some value other than **none** so there is a border around the box, and *height* and *width* are set so that the box clears the edges of the longest text in any of the buttons, leaving room for a little blank space on both sides.

Setting *text-align* to **center** causes the link text to be centered inside the box. Then, a *margin-top* of **0** reserves no space above the button; instead, a three-pixel space is being reserved at the bottom with *margin-bottom* set to **3px**. But these settings will be needed only if you place a set of these buttons stacked vertically. With a horizontal arrangement, use a *margin-left* of **0** and *margin-right* of **3px**.

```html
<!--LinkButton.html: Shows 2 links using LinkButton and one without. -->
<html>
  <head>
    <title>Link Buttons</title>
    <link rel="Stylesheet" type="text/css" href="LinkButton.css" />
  </head>
  <body>
    <!--Place buttons in a div slightly larger than the buttons so each button is-->
    <!--on its own line. Thus, the spacing between each button is set by-->
    <!--margin-bottom.-->
    <div style="width:270px;">
      <a href="http://wdp.needlerat.com" class="linkButton">Link to Text Site</a>
      <a href="http://www.needlerat.com" class="linkButton">Link to Publisher</a>
      <br />This is a link to <a href="http://www.needlerat.com">the publisher</a>.
    </div>
  </body>
</html>
```

```css
/* LinkButton.css: Creates fixed-size, boxed links with no underlining */
a.linkButton
{
  font-family:arial;          /* Use a blocky-style font */
  font-size:larger;           /*   with a larger face */
  text-decoration:none;       /* Turn off underlining */
  display:block;              /* So that Firefox/Safari accept size settings */
  border-style:groove;        /* Border: groove style */
  border-color:blue;          /*         blue color */
  border-width:4px;           /*         4px thickness */
  width:260px;                /* Set box width: adjust to fit largest set of text */
  height:25px;                /* Set box height to leave some space around text */
  text-align:center;          /* Align link text in center of box */
  margin-top:0;               /* No extra space above a link button */
  margin-bottom:3px;          /* Leave small space between buttons */
}
/* Make visited and unvisited buttons use same color scheme */
a:link.linkButton, a:visited.linkButton
{
  color:blue;
  background-color:rgb(250,170,220);
}
/* On mouse over, reverse the colors */
a:hover.linkButton
{
  color:rgb(250,170,220);
  background-color:blue;
}
```

Figure 54. Links formatted as buttons

Where you place the buttons depends upon how the CSS appears (see previous paragraph) as well as the HTML you use. Just as an example here, the link buttons are placed in a `<div>` with a fixed width that is only slightly larger than the buttons. This causes the buttons to be arranged vertically. If you place buttons vertically on a page with content to the right of them, use either frames or CSS columns instead. If you use frames, make the button frame slightly larger than the size specified on the buttons. If you use CSS columns, set the width for the button column to be slightly larger than the button `<div>`, and set the *margin-left* property for the right column to be a few pixels larger than the button column (see CSS Columns below).

CSS Columns

CSS allows you to create columns on a single page in such a way that the alignment of text in one column does not affect the alignment or position of content in the next. This is particularly useful when you want to place navigation buttons on the left side of a page and then have content change on the right side. This section includes only a brief description of columns and alignment; for more information, search the Web for "CSS columns."

Figure 55 shows a stylesheet that creates the columns and Figure 56 shows a sample of HTML that would use the columns. Figure 57 shows the result. The key to two CSS columns is to specify the *float* and *width* properties on the left column and the *padding-left* property on the right column. Setting *float* to `left` moves all content in that column to the left side and fits it inside the specified width, and setting *padding-left* on the right column makes it start to the right of the left column. Also note that *padding-right* should be somewhat larger than the width of the left column in order to create a gutter (blank space) between the columns.

If *padding-left* is replaced with *margin-left* on the right column, the text in the right column would be able to wrap under the bottom of the text in the left column when the text in the right column requires more vertical space than the left. *padding-left* constrains the right column for any length.

To make a footer (usually containing company contact information or the like), the CSS for the column defines

> **Creating Two CSS Columns**
>
> Two CSS columns are defined by setting the left column to float to the left and giving it a fixed width. Then the right column is set to have a left margin so as to leave room for the right column plus some extra space for a gutter (so texts in the columns don't run together).
>
> The footer is defined by clearing the columns defined previous to it.
>
> Note that you can specify other style properties in each of the columns and footer as needed.

an area that is below both columns by setting the *clear* property to `both`. This setting removes all column settings and returns the style to full screen width, with subsequent elements starting at the left.

The example HTML in Figure 56 initially loads two external stylesheets. The first is the `LinkButton` class from the previous section and the second is the CSS shown in Figure 55. The HTML for the example then defines three `<div>` elements, one for each of the two columns and one for the footer. In the left column, four link buttons are added. In the right column is a portion of the Gettysburg Address. And, in the footer, another portion of Lincoln's address is present.

```
/* CSSColumns.css: Creates two columns */
.colLeft                    /* Left Column */
{
  float:left;               /* Force to left side (required) */
  width:262px;              /* Width of column (required) */
}

.colRight                   /* Right Column */
{
  padding-left:272px;       /* Room for left column + 2px extra */
}                           /*   Note: 10 pixels larger then width of */
                            /*   left column to leave a border between */

.footer                     /* So we can center content under columns */
{
  clear:both;               /* Cancel columns from now on */
  text-align:left;          /* Set back to default alignment */
}
```

Figure 55. CSS for columns

```
<!--CSSColumns.html: Shows 2 links using LinkButton and one without. -->
<html>
  <head>
    <title>Link Buttons</title>
    <link rel="Stylesheet" type="text/css" href="LinkButton.css" />
    <link rel="Stylesheet" type="text/css" href="CSSColumns.css" />
  </head>
  <body>
    <!--Place buttons in a div that is slightly larger than the button so that each-->
    <!--button will be on a different line. In this way, the spacing between each-->
    <!--button (as set by margin-bottom) will be the only space between buttons.
-->
    <div class="colLeft">
      <a href="http://wdp.needlerat.com" class="linkButton">Link to Text Site</a>
      <a href="http://www.needlerat.com" class="linkButton">Link to Publisher</a>
    </div>
    <div class="colRight">
      <p>Four score and seven years ago our fathers brought forth on this continent,
        a new nation, conceived in Liberty, and dedicated to the proposition that
        all men are created equal.
      </p>
    </div>
    <div class="footer">
      But, in a larger sense, we can not dedicate -- we can not consecrate -- we can
      not hallow -- this ground.
    </div>
  </body>
</html>
```

Figure 56. HTML for columns

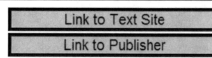

Four score and seven years ago our fathers brought forth on this continent, a new nation, conceived in Liberty, and dedicated to the proposition that all men are created equal.

But, in a larger sense, we can not dedicate -- we can not consecrate -- we can not hallow -- this ground.

Figure 57. HTML and results for CSS columns

Floating Images

CSS also allows you to float other objects. In the example here, text is located around a photo which is moved to the right side of the screen. The solution is shown (in Figure 58) along with the result (Figure 59).

```html
<html>
<head>
    <title>Floating Image</title>
    <style type="text/css">
      .photo
      {
        float:right;         /* Image to right and fill text on left */
        margin-left:10px;    /* Keep text away from left side of photo */
      }
    </style>
</head>
<body>
  <div>
    <img src="Lincoln.jpg" alt="Lincoln Photo" class="photo" />
    <p>Four score and seven years ago our fathers brought forth on this continent,
       a new nation, conceived in Liberty, and dedicated to the proposition that
       all men are created equal.</p>
    <p>Now we are engaged in a great civil war, testing whether that nation, or any
       nation so conceived and so dedicated, can long endure. We are met on a great
       battle-field of that war. </p>
    <p>But, in a larger sense, we can not dedicate -- we can not consecrate -- we can
       not hallow -- this ground. </p>
  </div>
</body>
</html>
```

Figure 58. Wrapping text around an image (HTML)

Figure 59. Wrapping text around an image (result)

Styling and Centering Lists

The correct way to change the type of a list is to use CSS. Although the *type* attribute for the `<ol>` and `<ul>` elements was described above, this attribute has been deprecated and should not be used. Instead, you should use the *list-style-type* CSS property for the list. Although there are a variety of values for *list-style-type*, all browsers support the following: `none`, `circle`, `disc`, `square`, `decimal`, `lower-alpha`, `lower-roman`, `upper-alpha`, `upper-roman`, and `inherit`. Figure 60 creates a list numbered with uppercase roman numerals.

```html
<html>
  <head>
    <title>CSS Styled Lists</title>
    <style type="text/css">
      .uRoman   { list-style-type:upper-roman; }
      .center   { text-align: center; }
      .centerFF { margin-left:auto; margin-right:auto; }
    </style>
  </head>
  <body>
    <div class="center">
      <table class="centerFF"><tr><td>
        <ol class="uRoman">
          <li>Apple</li>
          <li>Orange</li>
        </ol>
      </td></tr></table>
    </div>
  </body>
</html>
```

Figure 60. List styled with CSS

If you place a list inside a centered `<div>` element, the numbers or symbols marking each item will not be aligned. Instead, the items in the list are centered, so longer items start to the left of shorter items (try it). Furthermore, different browsers tend to handle these lists differently. The solution to this problem requires steps similar to centering tables (described earlier in this chapter).

If you view the page from Figure 60, you can see that the list is centered in the middle of the screen but the list items themselves are left justified. This was accomplished by placing the list inside a single table cell created with `<td>`. The `<td>` element uses left justification, which left-aligns the list, but the table is centered on the screen using techniques described above for centering tables (centered `<div>` for IE and automatic margins for Firefox). Since browsers automatically adjust the width of tables to their widest elements, the longest element of the list will be centered and the other elements will be left justified under this longest element. Also, no `border` attribute was specified for the table, in order to avoid having a box around the list.

> **Centering Left-Blocked Lists**
>
> List items inside a centered `<div>` are centered instead of left justified. To left-justify the items, place the list inside a table with a single cell created using the `<td>` element. Also, set the border on the table to zero or omit the *border* attribute entirely.

Review Questions

1. A complete online practice exam on chapters 2, 3, and 4 is available at http://wdp.needlerat.com. Your answers will be stored between browser sessions but the exam is not self-grading. For best results, take the exam with your HTML editor open. Try the exercises with no notes open and check if your solution works. If you make mistakes, wait a few hours or a day and try it again until your HTML/CSS is exactly correct.

   > **HTML/CSS Practice Exam**
   >
   > Take the practice exam several times with no notes until your answers are perfect. You can consult your notes as needed when you get stumped but you should eventually be able to take the exam without error.

2. What do the letters CSS stand for?
3. What is the purpose of style and stylesheets?
4. Which HTML attribute is used to add an inline style to an element?
5. What HTML syntax is used to add an internal stylesheet to a page? How is an external stylesheet applied to a page?
6. Inline styles can change how many elements at one time?
7. What are the purposes of the `<div>` and `<span>` elements? How do these differ?
8. What is the purpose of a stylesheet?
9. Using a stylesheet, how do you change the appearance of all elements of one type in an HTML page?
10. How do you create collections of style properties that can be assigned to one or more elements as a group?
11. How, in a stylesheet, can you define a group of style properties that will apply to only one instance of an element on an HTML page?
12. Write a single line of HTML that references an external stylesheet called `mystyle.css`.
13. Write the complete `<head>` section of an HTML page using an internal stylesheet that makes all paragraphs use the Arial font. Include both the HTML and the CSS.
14. What are pseudo-classes and how are those used with links (i.e. anchor tags)?
15. What is meant by the "cascading" in Cascading Style Sheets?
16. Under what circumstances should each style method be used (inline, internal, and external)?
17. What are CSS columns, and how are they created?

Exercises

1. Create each new HTML document page described in the exercises from scratch (without copying any other document), and use an inline style to change the colors (foreground and/or background) as well as the alignment for various elements.
2. Add an additional `<h1>` element to the source shown in Figure 36, using a different set of styles, and show the result. Then add a third `<h1>` element with no inline style. How does this third heading appear? Is it different from the other two? If so, why?
3. Type the source from Figure 41 into your editor and see how changes that you make to the stylesheet affect the link.
4. Create the table at the right with the following features: (1) a single solid blue border, (2) a yellow background on the top table line heading, (3) the item descriptions as left justified, (4) the item and price column headings as centered, and (5) the price items as right justified.

Price List	
Item	Price
End Table	64.50
Steel Case Desk	439.95
Bedroom Suite	11,205.00

5. Create an HTML document with a brief outline of any kind. Use three different levels in the outline, numbering the top level with uppercase roman numerals, the second level with uppercase alphabetic letters, and using Arabic numerals for the third level. Use an inline style to define the type of the list.
6. In exercise 4 above, center the outline in the middle of the page but have the numerals of each type aligned at the left (the list being centered but with the items blocked on the left).
7. Create an HTML document with a heading that has a green background, a black grove border, and yellow text. Do this first using an inline style, followed by an internal stylesheet and then an external stylesheet. When using an internal or external stylesheet, use a class name.
8. Expand the document created in exercise 5 by making the border reduced and fixed width but with the heading centered on the line. Also, change the border color to use a custom color that you obtained from a drawing program like Paint.
9. Format some paragraphs in a page using book format: no blank lines between paragraphs, but with an indent for each paragraph.
10. Create a link that looks like a button. Draw a border around the link, turn off underlining, and have the link change color when the mouse is over the link. Be sure to center the link text inside the border. Test the results on various web browsers to insure it looks the same in each browser.
11. Use CSS columns to create two sections of a web page. Place a series of links in the left column and data in the right. (The links do not need to go anywhere.) Note that this could be part of the major resume project shown below, in that you can structure your resume with navigation buttons on the left.
12. Wrap text around an image on the page. Place the image on the right, test your results, and then place the image on the left and try again.

Multi-Page Resume Project

For this project you will create a multi-page resume, with navigation buttons on each page and a consistent style throughout. Design it as if this would be a real site that you would be willing for future employers to view. Note that each page should have the same heading and set of navigation buttons.

It is recommended that you research the web first and see first how different sites style their pages. Then, select a general look and sketch it to get a feel for your site on paper before creating any pages.

Required Pages

1. Personal Information (name, address, phone, email, website, etc.). Include a photo or photos. Use a filename like `personal.html`.
2. Employment History (list of each place worked and responsibilities). Format these in a table so each place worked is formatted in the same manner and is easily searched visually. Use a filename like `employment.html`.
3. Education (starting with high school and continuing to where you are now). Use a filename like `education.html`.
4. References (which can be fictitious if you want). Use a filename like `references.html`. Include at least two references (one for personal and one for work).
5. External stylesheet that contains at least 12 separate style definitions and is several screens long. Place all the style information here that applies to any two or more pages in the site. Add a substantial amount of style settings in your external CSS file to demonstrate that you have a good feel for the many capabilities of CSS. Finally, be sure to use a file extension of `.css`.

Optional Pages

6. Portfolio. If you have done anything special that either shows your successes (like art or design work) or highlights some special skills, put it here. For example, if you have volunteered as a fireman and were learning EMT skills, put that in this section. If your portfolio is significantly long, consider creating a top-level page for the portfolio with links to other pages. Use a style like the resume itself. Use photos where appropriate!
7. Add other pages you think appropriate (check with your instructor if you like).

Navigation and Appearance

Each page should have a consistent look and feel and the exact same set of navigation buttons. One solution is frames, with a banner frame and a navigation frame, so that when a link button is clicked only one frame changes to the new information. Since frames have been deprecated, however, the best solution is to use CSS columns as described earlier in this chapter.

CHAPTER 5 – JAVASCRIPT

Introduction

HTML is a structured "markup" language that allows web page content, including text and graphics, to be specified along with the formatting of that content. However, HTML does not allow any general programmatic functions, resulting in a static, non-interactive page. Things like `if`-statements, loops, user-input validation, etc. are not available in HTML. For this reason, HTML gains access to general programming constructs by adding scripting languages, one of which is called JavaScript. JavaScript is roughly styled after Sun Microsystems' Java language but is a very different language in use. However, if you have any familiarity with Java or other C-based languages like C++ or C#, JavaScript will be easier to learn.

JavaScript Characteristics

JavaScript is a programming language because it adds programming capabilities to HTML pages. However, it was once called a "lightweight" language because JavaScript had far less third-party library support than other programming languages, like Java, C++, and C#. Now, with the addition of JavaScript frameworks like jQuery, the capabilities of JavaScript are approaching that of many other programming languages, except that JavaScript is interpreted rather than compiled and is not strongly typed.

JavaScript is normally embedded directly into web pages as human-readable sequences of words and punctuation. As such, JavaScript is a *scripted* language and an *interpreted* language. "Interpreted" means that the browser reads one line of the script at a time directly from the HTML file. This differs from most computer languages, which convert the source into an executable program through what is called a *compilation* process. This executable program consists of machine instructions for direct execution by the target processor. In contrast, the browser has to read and interpret the original JavaScript source on the fly and then decide what to do with it. As you might imagine, processing is often slower with a scripting language as compared to a compiled language.

> **Scripted Language**
>
> A scripted language is interpreted one line at a time rather than being compiled into an executable program like other languages. Scripting languages often run more slowly than compiled languages.

Since JavaScript is interpreted by the browser, all you need to use JavaScript is a text editor. The major expense for professional web developers is for what is frequently called an Interactive Development Environment (IDE). An IDE is a tool that does much of the programming work for you, allowing you to lay out the page visually and then automatically have it create some pieces of JavaScript for you. These editors include a design mode with a what-you-see-is-what-you-get (WYSIWYG, pronounced "whizzy-wig") edit mode. Examples of IDEs include Adobe's Dreamweaver® and Microsoft's Visual Studio®. Microsoft offers a free version of Visual Studio for download, plus many universities have licenses for the professional versions of Dreamweaver and Visual Studio.

Although the name JavaScript contains the name "Java" and is styled after the Java language, the syntax and capabilities differ in significant ways from Java. If you have no experience with Java, these similarities and differences will not be of importance to you; however, if you have previously programmed in Java, you will need to observe the syntax more carefully. The major differences include the fact that JavaScript does not define simple data types and that JavaScript is interpreted (Java is instead converted to an intermediate form called bytecode that is somewhere in between compiled and interpreted code).

Why JavaScript?

The primary objective of JavaScript is to add interactivity to a web page. This interactivity frequently takes the form of validations. For example, if you leave out a required credit card number on a commercial site and try to go to on, you will receive an instant notification of the missing information. "Instant" in this case means that there was no round-trip network traffic to the remote server. Instead, the browser handled the validation locally.

> **JavaScript Objective**
>
> JavaScript is designed to add interactivity to web pages. It allows such things as validating user input as well as fancy formatting of the page.

Although most functionality achieved through local JavaScript could be done on a server, doing the work locally offers several benefits:

1. There is less traffic on the Web, thereby improving performance for everyone.
2. The server has to do less work. In the example above, instead of the server having to notify the user that they forgot a credit card number, the browser does it locally.
3. The user receives a much faster notification of the error, improving the overall user experience.

Your First JavaScript Program

You will be directly typing JavaScript as well as HTML into a simpler editor, rather than an IDE. So, open up your editor of choice and type the following web page exactly as shown below. Note: be sure to type the page and do not cut and paste from the online source. The typing process aids learning!

```
<html>
  <head>
      <title>My First JavaScript</title>
  </head>
  <body>
    <script type="text/javascript">
      alert("Congratulations!");
    </script>
  </body>
</html>
```

Figure 61. First JavaScript program

Save the page with the name `FirstScript.html` (or similar name) in a folder created for this class and then view the page in your browser. This example shows nothing on the page, but it does pop up a message of congratulations. The way this message appears differs between browsers; Figure 62 shows how it appeared with

> **The alert() Function**
>
> The `alert()` function displays a message included as a parameter in a small box on the screen (see examples in Figure 62).

three currently popular browsers at the time of publication. (The exact appearance is continually changing as new versions of the browsers are released.)

Examine Figure 61 and study the organization of the page. In this, your first JavaScript program, we have put a "script" block in the body section (more details below). Between `<script>` and `</script>` is one line of JavaScript (`alert("Congratulations!");`). This line of JavaScript uses a pre-defined tool (a.k.a. function) called `alert()` which displays one of these windows depending upon your current browser:

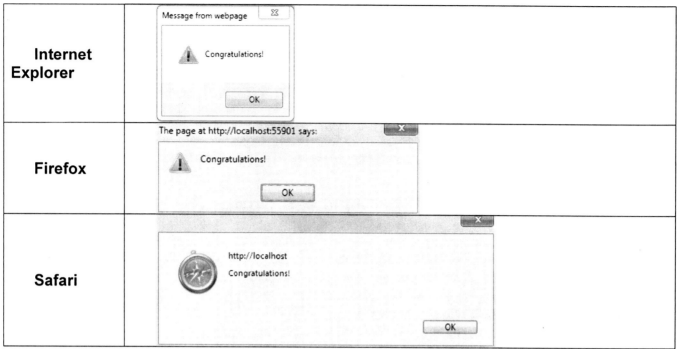

Figure 62. Alert box in three popular browsers

Adding JavaScript to HTML

Multiple JavaScript blocks can be added in two places within a single HTML document: the `<head>` section or the `<body>` section. Alternately, JavaScript can also be located in an external file. Although this will be covered in more detail later, the type of JavaScript code varies with the section in which it is located. The `<head>` section normally contains functions (also called methods) such as event handlers (see Web Forms in chapter 8). These functions, for things like button clicks and validations, would then be used as tools for JavaScript that will later be placed in the `<body>` section.

> **JavaScript Location**
>
> JavaScript can be placed in either the `<head>` or `<body>` section of a web page. When placed in the `<head>` section, it usually takes the form of a function that is referenced by other functions in the `<head>` section, or by button events in the `<body>` section. JavaScript in the `<body>` section is processed when it is encountered.

The browser always processes the HTML page from top to bottom, so it will process JavaScript in the `<body>` section as it is encountered (along with the HTML). Thus, any JavaScript encountered in the `<body>` section may interrupt display of the HTML on the page. Keeping this in mind, JavaScript in the `<body>` section should be code that makes changes to the HTML on the fly, like making special changes to the format of the page, displaying messages, changing display characteristics, and the like. It should also do things like specify actions on mouse clicks, mouse hover, and other events that result from user interaction with the screen. Later on, we will look at placing some JavaScript in the `<head>` section that will be used to support JavaScript that is defined in the `<body>` section. Specifically, functions that are added to the `<head>` section are called by events in the `<body>` section. (This will be covered in chapter 7.)

Internal JavaScript is added to pages between the `<script>` and `</script>` tags (the ending tag is absolutely essential!) The complete syntax is shown below on the left side. On the right side is the HTML for adding CSS to your page; notice the similar syntax, which might help you remember both.

```
<script type="text/javascript">          <style type="text/css">
    Your script goes here...                 Your CSS goes here...
</script>                                 </style>
```

JavaScript can be located in a separate file and referenced with the *src* attribute of the `<script>` command, as in the examples below. The advantage of external JavaScript is that the script can be used by multiple pages without having to reproduce it (like external CSS). When the external JavaScript file is in the same directory as the page (as in the first example below), it is referenced just by name. Alternately, you can also specify the location with a full URL, as in the second example.

```
<script type="text/javascript" src="myScript.js"></script>
<script type="text/javascript" src="http://www.mySite/myScript.js"></script>
```

Fetching User Input with `prompt()`

JavaScript, like many other topics, suffers from the problem that one needs to learn multiple things first so that the other items can be understood. To ease you into the material, the `prompt()` function will be introduced now, since it will be needed for the next few examples. If you struggle some with this content, start with just trying to get the big picture, and later, as you work through other examples in the chapter, this material will become clearer. You will find it useful to review this material after you complete this chapter.

> **The `prompt()` Function**
>
> The `prompt()` function displays a small input box, with a prompt at the top and a place for input underneath. The function needs two pieces of information: (1) the prompt in the box and (2) the default value for the input field.

The `prompt()` function is used to obtain a single piece of information from the person using your web page. Knowing this, consider how you might modify the page shown in Figure 61 so it says "Congratulations John" instead of just "Congratulations". Specifically, we need the page to first ask for a first name and afterwards show the popup box with the name included in the message. Type the solution shown in Figure 63 in your editor and then show the page. It will display a box asking for the first name, and when the OK button is clicked, the page shows the congratulations message as desired.

```
<html>
    <head>
     <title>Using the Prompt Function</title>
    </head>
    <body>
        <script type="text/javascript">
            var firstName = prompt("Enter first name", "");
            alert("Congratulations " + firstName);
        </script>
    </body>
</html>
```

Figure 63. Obtaining user input with `prompt()`

The JavaScript works as follows. The first change that was made was to add a new line above the `alert()` function that requests the user's first name, using the `prompt()` function. The result obtained from the user is placed in a local variable called `firstName` (variables are described in detail below) and then the `firstName` variable is used as part of the message displayed with the `alert()` function. (This function displays a small box, which has instructions as to the type of input desired as well as a place to enter that information.)

> **Variables**
>
> A variable is a named memory location in which to store data. It is like the memory function on a calculator: you can place numbers or text there and, later, you then get back what you put there earlier. Variables are used to store intermediate and final results of calculations as well as text data like names.

The `prompt()` function needs two pieces of information called *parameters* before it can display the box (functions and parameters are covered in chapter 7). First, it needs to know how to label the box; that is, it needs the instructions to give the user. Secondly, it needs the default value for the input field. This default value is there when the box is displayed so that if the user likes that value, nothing else needs to be typed. Also, this default value can be blank so the user must enter some information (more on this shortly).

In the example above, the instructions are "**Enter first name**". The second value specified is the default content that is displayed in the box, which in this case is the empty string. By using the empty string (`""`), the user must supply some information to the prompt or click the Cancel button.

Figure 64 shows how the box appeared in three popular browsers at the time of publication. (Browsers are continually modifying how these prompt boxes appear.) Locate where the phrase "Enter first name" appears in each one. Although each browser's prompt appears differently, they all have the same two buttons (OK and Cancel) as well as a place to supply the requested information.

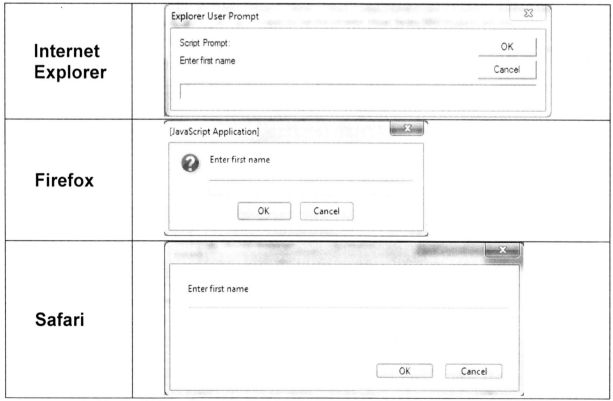

Figure 64. Prompt box in popular browsers

To review, the phrase "Enter first name" is placed inside the parentheses of the prompt() function as the first of two entries separated by a comma. The second entry (also called "value") is the default value. In the previous example, this consisted of two double quote marks (""), but it can also contain data. For example, say the first line of the JavaScript is changed as follows:

```
var firstName = prompt("Enter first name", "Billy Bob");
```

Then the prompt box would now appear as shown in Figure 65. Note that the input box now has been filled in with the name "Billy Bob." Also, this value is preselected, as indicated by the highlighting. If the user wants to use the highlighted value instead of typing something new, they can simply click the OK button (hence its name, "default value"). Alternately, they can begin to type new information easily also; since the default value is highlighted, any value typed erases what was there and the new data replace it.

Figure 65. Prompt with initial value

For example, say most users of an input box on a page are from Michigan, and the box prompted for a state abbreviation. You could then set the second parameter to "MI," so that any user from Michigan would be saved the time of typing the state abbreviation.

Once the OK button is clicked with input data present, the variable firstName is initialized with the value typed by the user. Now the contents of this variable need to be combined with the word "Congratulations" to create the complete message for the alert() function. This combination uses a technique called string concatenation and is implemented with the + sign. What is inside the alert() function is shown below:

```
"Congratulations " + firstName
```

This creates a new message, called a string, that consists of the word "Congratulations " (including the space added after the word) followed by the contents of the variable firstName. For example, if you typed "Joe" the full string would be "Congratulations Joe".

Writing Text to the Screen

In addition to writing text to a popup box with alert(), you can also write and format data to the screen using document.write(). The write() function takes as input any text data (i.e., a string), including HTML information. Figure 66 has a script block embedded between two <h1> elements. The alert() function in the first line of the JavaScript, used just to pause the screen so you can see the results up to that point, is followed by the document.write() function call, which writes the next heading out to the screen. Notice the text inside the function call: it is just an <h2> HTML element, complete with beginning and ending tags. Type the document in Figure 66 and observe the results when you view the page in your browser.

```
<html>
  <head>
    <title>Writing HTML with document.write()</title>
  </head>
  <body>
    <h1>Demonstration of document.write()</h1>
    <script type="text/javascript">
      alert("The screen is paused while the alert box is displayed");
      document.write("<h2>This heading is from JavaScript</h2>");
    </script>
    <h1>Appears after closing the prompt box</h1>
  </body>
</html>
```

Figure 66. Writing HTML to the screen (with `document.write()`)

When the page is viewed, the alert box appears and the result on the screen is as shown in Figure 67. Initially the first `<h1>` is displayed and the alert box appears. However, neither the heading to be written by JavaScript nor the last `<h1>` is displayed.

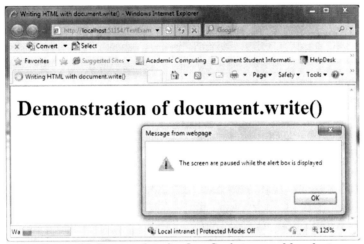

Figure 67. Page update by JavaScript paused by alert

Once you dismiss the alert box (click OK), the screen appears as shown in Figure 68. Notice that the `<h2>` element written by JavaScript appears after the initial `<h1>` element and before the final `<h1>` element. Here is the key: page updates produced by `document.write()` appear in the order where the JavaScript is encountered in the HTML of the page. As always, the browser processes the HTML in the body in a top-to-bottom fashion.

> **JavaScript `document.write()`**
>
> Page updates produced by `document.write()` appear in the order the JavaScript is encountered in the page HTML, in top-to-bottom order.

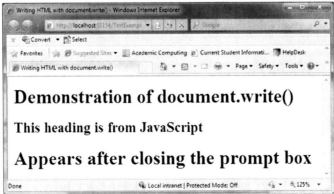

Figure 68. HTML mixed with `document.write()` data

In summary, the `document.write()` function is a tool that you can use to display JavaScript results in HTML on the screen. Any amount of HTML can be displayed using `document.write()`. For example, Figure 71 creates an entire table in a string and then displays that table on the page.

JavaScript Syntax

Overview

JavaScript consists of a series of statements that use a very special vocabulary and follow a rigid set of grammatical rules. Before trying to explain the vocabulary and grammar of JavaScript, though, consider the English language. Each word is separated by a space, or sometimes some other punctuation marks (periods, commas, etc.) and a space.

> **JavaScript Syntax**
>
> JavaScript has syntax, just like the English language. The specific rules for the words used, the order of the words, and the punctuation must all be followed for your script to function correctly.

Words in English are of two different major types. The first type is words that have meaning in the syntax of the language: *ball*, *jump*, *and*, *of*, etc. These meaning of these words can be found in any dictionary. The other type of words is what we call "proper nouns," names that refer to a specific person, place, etc. Proper names are chosen by individuals (like parents) and are not found in a dictionary (except, perhaps, for famous people or places).

In a similar fashion, JavaScript has two kinds of words, called *tokens*. The first type of token is the vocabulary of the language. These "vocabulary" tokens were chosen by a committee and follow a worldwide, published standard. These tokens that are part of the syntax are called *reserved words*, meaning that you cannot use the tokens when you create your own names/tokens.

> **Reserved Words**
>
> Words that are defined as part of the JavaScript syntax are called *reserved words*. You should not use any of these reserved words for any name of an *id*, variable, or function.

JavaScript Style

Each browser more-or-less follows the JavaScript standard and does the same thing when it encounters tokens within the syntax. Most reserved words that are part of the JavaScript syntax start with a lowercase letter but may include uppercase letters after that. These words include built-in functions like `prompt()` and `alert()` as well as instructional words (`var`, `function`, `if`, `while`, etc.) and the names of the various attributes of HTML elements (like `document`). Special things, like the Math and Array classes, start with a capital letter, and constants, like the value for PI, are given as all capital letters. When a token consists of multiple words run together, the first letter of each additional word is then capitalized (a convention called "camel case"). An example of this is the `getElementById()` function (described in chapter 8). See how this capitalization style makes each word stand out? The words are run together for a technical reason, because separating them with spaces would create multiple tokens that would each be interpreted separately. If our example above were written `get element by id`, JavaScript would attempt to ascribe a meaning to `get`, to `element`, etc.

JavaScript Comments

Comments in JavaScript allow you to describe, at a high level, what the code is doing and how the code works. Comments, therefore, will significantly improve the readability of your code and help you understand your code when you come back to it at a later date.

There are two types of comments in JavaScript. One is single-line comments that start with a double slash (`//`). In this comment type, everything from the `//` to the end of the line is a comment. Single-line comments can occur on a line by themselves, or after other JavaScript on the line, as shown in the first two lines of Figure 69.

```
<script type="text/javascript">
  // This is a single line comment on a line by itself

  var f = (9.0 / 5.0) * c + 32; // This comment follows other JavaScript

  /*
    This is a multiline comment. Multiline comments can span multiple
    lines and are bracketed between the start and end markers, as
    shown here.
  */
</script>
```

Figure 69. JavaScript comments example

The second type of comment is multi-line comments. You can add multi-line comments to your JavaScript by bracketing them between `/*` and `*/`. These comments can span multiple lines, as shown above, or can be on one line, like the single line comment. Multi-line comments are handy when you need to add substantial amounts of documentation to your JavaScript.

There is, however, an inherent risk to using multi-line comments. The problem arises when you forget to add the ending `*/` after the comment, which makes the rest of your program become a comment and therefore will not run correctly. For this reason, check your multi-line comments carefully to make sure that they are correctly formed.

JavaScript Names and Tokens

The second type of word (token) in JavaScript is a user-defined name. These are names that you, as the JavaScript programmer, choose. Although you are choosing the token, there are still several rules and style issues that apply as noted in the next section.

With JavaScript and HTML you will be naming three things: (1) Any HTML elements using the `id=""` attribute (this includes the form, input controls, and any other element); (2) variable names; and (3) function names. The `id` attribute of HTML elements allows those elements to be referenced within the HTML (like bookmarks) as well as accessed within JavaScript code (see chapter 8). Variables are named storage locations where intermediate and final results can be stored. And function names are referenced in either HTML elements or by other pieces of JavaScript (see chapter 7).

> **Variables**
>
> A variable is a named storage location in which you can place information such as user input, results of computations, etc.

Valid HTML `id`s, as well as JavaScript function and variable names, are subject to several constraints and a couple of style recommendations. These are listed below:

Constraints (i.e. requirements)
1. Reserved words cannot be used (you can't name a variable **var**).
2. Variable names must begin with a letter.
3. The first letter can then be followed by any combination of letters and number digits (0 – 9).
4. No special characters can be used except the underline character.
5. No whitespace (tabs, spaces, newlines, etc.) can be used, because a blank would indicate a different token or name.

Style Recommendations (these are used throughout the industry)
1. Names should start with a lowercase letter.
2. Capitalize the first letter of each new word (**getElementById**).

Remember that JavaScript must be able to distinguish between the names for every distinct thing (HTML elements, functions, and variables); therefore, all names should be unique. Also, functions will always appear with parentheses, and between these parentheses may or may not appear some parameters.

HTML *id* examples:	`form1, txtName, chkCredit, top`
Variable name examples:	`salesTotal, age, milesPerHour`
Function name examples:	`compute(), pageLoad(), sayHello(), getArea(2.5, 4)`

JavaScript Punctuation Overview

This section is just an overview of JavaScript punctuation. Additional details are given later in the discussion of each JavaScript statement type.

Most JavaScript statements end with a semicolon. Exceptions include loops (**while**, **do**, **for**) and conditional (**if**) statements. The browser will frequently allow you to get away without a semicolon but they are required for strict compatibility with the XHTML standard. The requirement for a semicolon depends upon the type of statement, so as you study the examples in the remainder of this document, look at where semicolons are used and where they are not.

JavaScript uses a matching pair of parentheses **()** in two ways: (1) in mathematical expressions and (2) in function declarations and references. Both of these uses are described later. For now, just remember that parentheses will always occur in matching pairs (as in English). JavaScript mathematical expressions may also have parentheses within parentheses due to the fact that brackets and braces have a different meaning in JavaScript (see below).

Brackets ([]) are used in JavaScript for arrays, which are covered in chapter 9 (Advanced JavaScript), while braces ({}) are used to combine multiple statements into a single statement, which is called a *block* statement. (This is needed where a particular syntax specifies only one statement but multiple are requested – see Block Statements below.) Just like parentheses, brackets and braces are also always used in matching pairs. Finally, also like parentheses, braces may be found inside another pair of braces (block statements within block statements).

JavaScript uses both single quotes and double quotes to denote character data (much like English does), and finally, JavaScript uses commas to separate parameters in a function definition and the semicolon to separate parts of a **for**-loop.

JavaScript Variables

A JavaScript variable is a named location in memory in which to store data, such as results of calculations, names, etc. A named memory location is analogous to numbered memory locations on larger calculators. For example, if you have used the M+ button on a calculator, you have been using memory. JavaScript allows you to specify as many "memories" as you need and to name those locations instead of having to use numbers. Our first variable, `firstName`, was shown in Figure 63.

Variable Declaration and Initialization

All JavaScript variables are declared by using the `var` keyword followed by the variable name. This syntax applies regardless of the type of the data being used, as noted below. For those readers who are familiar with other programming languages with typed data, the keyword `var` encompasses many data types: `int`, `long`, `double`, etc. Instead of specific data types, JavaScript uses a universal data type that can contain various types of data.

Even though there is a universal data type, JavaScript still understands the difference between integers and floating point numbers, strings, booleans, etc. In JavaScript, the type is often determined by what lies on the right side of the replacement statement (to the right of an equals sign). If the right side of the replacement is a string, that piece of data is stored as a string. If the right side is a number, that piece of data is stored as a number. If it is a boolean constant like `true`, then a boolean value is stored.

JavaScript variables must have a valid name to be declared (see JavaScript Names and Tokens above). This can, optionally, be followed by a replacement statement to initialize the value of the variable. Alternately, variables can be defined on one line and then initialized later in the program (therefore being on separate lines). Here are some examples:

```
var pi = 3.14159273;
var stateName = "Michigan";
var milesPerHour;
milesPerHour = 60;
```

Note that the first example defines the variable and initializes it by setting it equal to a value. Note also that initializing a variable in one place of your JavaScript does not prevent it being changed in another place by simply setting the name equal to a new value, as in the example below:

```
milesPerHour = 37;
```

JavaScript Variable Types

A JavaScript variable can store data in a wide variety of formats, including user-defined formats. For the purposes of this text, we will look at the following types:

>Integer (whole) numbers (-20, 30, 104, etc.)
>Fractional numbers (3.14149, 2.71828, 1.5, etc.)
>Strings (collections of characters, such as "Joe", "Hello World", "3.14159", etc.)
>boolean (`true` or `false`)
>Objects (pointers to complex things, like an input text box)

This variety of types sometimes complicates the implementation of programs, and it is sometimes necessary for JavaScript to convert between these types. This is especially true when dealing with numbers and strings.

Numbers and Computations

Number Internal Structure

You don't really have to know any of the following material to use JavaScript; it is included for completeness and to help you understand some of the stranger numerical results that can occur in the language.

All numbers inside JavaScript are stored using a standard format (IEEE 754) for storing fractional numbers. The numbers are stored in what can be described as sort of a scientific notation, in that there is a base number plus an exponent. The actual range of the numbers is about $\pm 1.7 \times 10^{308}$. With this format, fractional computations are accurate to about 15 or 16 decimal digits, and integers can be represented in the range of $\pm 2^{53}$.

One thing that tends to surprise new users is that you cannot always represent precisely a fractional number using this structure. In fact, truncation errors can occur. For example, an algebraic computation might yield a value of 2.0 whereas JavaScript computes 1.9999999999199997. This value is close enough to 2 for most people, so you might choose to round the number off using `Math.round()` (see below) or round the result for display using the `toFixed()` function (also covered below).

Math Operators and Mathematical Expressions

You can create complex mathematical expressions using one or more of the five JavaScript math operators, combining them by using multiple sets of parentheses as needed. There are five main math operators: +, –, *, /, and %. Three of these are obvious (+, –, and /) and mean the same thing as in algebra. The asterisk means "multiply," since the letter x could not be used (as it would represent a variable) nor could the dot "·" (as it is not on a standard computer keyboard). Lastly, the % operator gives the remainder of an integer division. For example, 11 % 3 equals 2, which is the remainder after dividing 11 by 3.

+	-	*	/	%	( )
Addition	Subtraction	Multiplication	Division Quotient	Division Remainder	Parentheses

Table 11. Math operators

Although JavaScript enforces the standard mathematical order of operations (parentheses, exponents, multiply, divide, add, subtract), you should use parentheses liberally when it makes it easier to see what the expression is supposed to do. (There are several examples of these kinds of expressions in the remainder of the text.)

Temperature Conversion Example

To illustrate a math computation and an expression, consider the problem of converting a Celsius temperature to Fahrenheit. The algebraic representation of the conversion formula is:

$$f = (9/5) \cdot c + 32$$

A simple JavaScript solution to compute this formula is given in Figure 70. In the example, a fixed value for Celsius (zero) is used in the computation and the corresponding Fahrenheit value shown. Type the solution below into your browser and run it to see the answer.

Now study how the expression is written. The fraction 9/5 could have been simply written as 1.8, as that is the value of 9/5. However, it is clearer to see the fraction inside the parentheses as that fraction is part of the original formula. This fraction is then multiplied (*) by the Celsius temperature and then the constant 32 is added. Due to the precedence (order) of the operators, no parentheses are needed, so the multiply and add steps occur in the correct order. The answer correctly appears as "32" when displayed by the `alert()` function.

As an exercise, change the initial value of C to 100 to see that the computed Fahrenheit temperature is 212. Be sure to work out exercise 8 at the end of the chapter as well.

```
<html>
  <head>
    <title>Convert C to F</title>
  </head>
  <body>
    <h1>Convert C to F</h1>
    <script type="text/javascript">
      var c = 0;
      var f = (9.0 / 5.0) * c + 32;
      alert(f);
    </script>
  </body>
</html>
```

Figure 70. Simple Celsius to Fahrenheit conversion

Strings

Modern computers represent all data, including characters, internally as patterns of ones and zeros. In the early days, characters were represented in a simple 8-bit format called ASCII (though we now use a compatible but better standard called UTF-8), but as the computer world expanded and began to include countries with other languages (like Japanese, Chinese, and Arabic) there were not enough combinations possible in 8 bits, so a different, more complex format called Unicode is now used.

Just like there is a special structure in computers for storing characters as multiple bits, when you combine multiple characters together in JavaScript you create a special structure called a *string*. In other words, JavaScript strings are simply the high-level way that text data are stored by the computer. When the congratulations example was expanded (as shown in Figure 63) the variable `firstName` was stored as a string because `prompt()` obtains and returns text data.

JavaScript strings can contain any kind of text data, and they can vary immensely in size. A string could contain thousands of characters or it might contain zero characters (see The Empty String below). Internally, the computer stores the text data along with a count of the number of characters in the string for efficiency and for bookkeeping purposes. Strings also have special functions associated with them for changing or testing the content of the strings (see String Functions below).

The String + Operator

JavaScript defines an operator for strings so that more complex strings can be created from simpler strings, and this operator is the + operator. This operator places pieces joined with + end to end to make a longer string. This is called an *append* or *concatenate* operation. For example, consider the two lines below:

```
var message = "Hello" + " " + "World";
alert(message);
```

The above will display an alert box with the phrase "Hello World". This phrase was constructed by "adding" a space to "Hello" and then adding the word "World" after it. You can also add variables to strings, as was done in Figure 63 and reproduced below:

```
alert("Congratulations " + firstName);
```

Here, the contents of variable `firstName` (which were supplied by the user) are appended to the string "Congratulations ". Note that a blank was left after the word "Congratulations" so there would be a space between the words in the final string, making the full message "Congratulations Joe".

Appending Numbers to Strings

Frequently, you will want to show the results of a computation with `alert()`. However, you normally don't just want to show the number, but also add some descriptive information to it. In Figure 70, only the resulting temperature is shown. Would it not be nicer if the result said "100C = 212F"? That is, the result would show both corresponding temperatures. The change to Figure 63 to do this is shown below:

```
alert(c + "C = " + f + "F");
```

The concatenated string starts with the original value for `c`, then appends the letter C, a space, and "=". To this is appended the contents of the variable `f` (the computed Fahrenheit temperature) and this is followed by the letter F.

As a side note, when JavaScript encounters numeric data concatenated with string data, it will convert the numeric data to a string in its shortest possible form before concatenating. Specifically, no zeros are added to the right of a decimal point unless specifically requested by `toFixed()` as described below. Thus, any time JavaScript finds the need for a string concatenation using a variable that contains a number, JavaScript will convert the number to a string before appending.

String Constants

String constants in JavaScript are written with matching quotes at the beginning and end of the list of characters. The beginning and ending quote character can be either a single quote or a double quote, as in the following examples (but remember that the beginning and ending quote must be the same type). Note, however, where possible you should use the double quote format.

```
var lastName = "Jones";     // Preferred method
var lastName = 'Jones';
```

The Empty String

A string of zero characters is allowed in a JavaScript string and is called the empty string. For example, the following would declare a variable named `empty` and set it equal to a string constant with no characters between the quotes:

```
var empty = "";
```

Thus **empty** is a real, defined variable with a value, as opposed to an undefined variable. It is a string with zero characters. If you appended an empty string to another string, you would end up with the same value, because no additional characters would be added to that string. If you append something to an empty string, you would end up with what was appended to that string. It is the later technique, as it turns out, that is useful in converting from a number to a string. That is, to convert a number to a string, simply append the numeric value to an empty string, as shown in the example below. In this example, the numeric variable **area** is converted to a string and the result placed in the variable **areaAsString**.

```
var area = Math.PI * radius * radius;      // Area of a circle
var areaAsString = "" + area;
```

Building Complex Strings

Up to this point, strings have been relatively short and defined on just one line. However, there will be occasions where you may want to create complex and long strings from within JavaScript. For example, say you wanted to create the table of information shown at the right inside the box (excluding the box). The table is to be created as a string and displayed on the page using **document.write()**. The string for this table would contain several lines of HTML, as shown in Figure 71.

```
<html>
  <head>
    <title>Writing HTML with document.write()</title>
  </head>
  <body>
    <script type="text/javascript">
      var tableString =           "<h2>Sales Representatives</h2>";
      tableString = tableString + "<table>";
      tableString = tableString + "<tr><th>Name</th><th>Phone</th></tr>";
      tableString = tableString + "<tr><td>Jacob Smith</td><td>993-555-8181</td></tr>";
      tableString = tableString + "<tr><td>Mary Wilson</td><td>993-555-1221</td></tr>";
      tableString = tableString + "</table>";
      document.write(tableString);
    </script>
  </body>
</html>
```

Figure 71. Complex strings

The long string, **tableString**, is being constructed on several lines of JavaScript using the string append operator (+). Note that the variable name **tableString** appears on both sides of the equal sign in several of the lines. This is the standard replacement statement, where what is created or calculated on the right side of the equal sign is then placed in the variable on the left side. What happens is that JavaScript opens the variable **tableString** and obtains its current value, and to this value the next part of the string is appended, after which the result is then placed back in the variable **tableString**.

Strings within Strings

The table created in Figure 71 had an **<h2>** heading and no border. Suppose you wanted a border on the table and wanted the heading to be a row that spans the two columns, as shown at the right. In this case the table line would need to look like this:

```
<table border="2">
```

Specifically, the table command would need to have the **border** attribute given the value of `"2"`, specified inside quotes. (Up to this point, all values of attributes have been shown in double quotes, in fact.) So if the border attribute is added to the string using double quotes, the result would look like this:

```
tableString = tableString + "<table border="2">";
```

The problem is that the initial double quote in front of the value 2 would mark the end of the string being created. JavaScript would think the string being appended stops after the equal sign, as shown here:

```
tableString = tableString + "<table border="
```

JavaScript offers a simple solution to the problem by defining certain special characters using a two-character sequence. Within a JavaScript string (which starts and ends with a double quote), a double quote can be represented by the two characters `\"`. These are sometimes called *escape characters*. With escape characters, the `<table>` line would appear as shown below:

```
tableString = tableString + "<table border=\"2\">";
```

The line is a little easier to read now but still a little obscure until you get used to it. But this is the recommended solution if you just want to have a double quote appear within your string. (In fact, this is the approach taken by many other programming languages, like Java and C#.)

If you are dealing with the values of attributes, though, there is still yet another solution, which takes advantage of an HTML feature where either single quotes or double quotes can be used to define the values of attributes. Using this solution, the line then appears as follows:

```
tableString = tableString + "<table border='2'>";
```

Now the line is easy to read and also correctly interpreted by the browser. The complete solution to creating the table as pictured is shown in Figure 72. This solution adds the title row and the table line to the string using single quotes.

The solution also initially defines **tableString** as the empty string. That way, all the HTML lines are added in the same way, which makes the lines of HTML line up at their left edges. This is not necessary, but merely a cosmetic technique that you may wish to use.

```
<html>
  <head>
    <title>Strings within Strings</title>
  </head>
  <body>
    <script type="text/javascript">
      var tableString = "";
      tableString = tableString + "<table border='2'>";
      tableString = tableString + "<tr><th colspan='2'>Sales Representatives</th></tr>";
      tableString = tableString + "<tr><th>Name</th><th>Phone</th></tr>";
      tableString = tableString + "<tr><td>Jacob Smith</td><td>993-555-8181</td></tr>";
      tableString = tableString + "<tr><td>Mary Wilson</td><td>993-555-1221</td></tr>";
      tableString = tableString + "</table>";
      document.write(tableString);
    </script>
  </body>
</html>
```

Figure 72. Strings within strings

String Functions

There is a special set of tools (methods and properties) supported by strings that allow you to change the case of strings, to search strings, and to change specific parts of strings. Each of these tools is accessed by appending a period to the variable containing the string (called "dot" notation) and then appending the name of the tool. For example, the following would create two variables, the first with the string "Jones" and the second with the string "JONES".

```
var name = "Jones";
var nameUpper = name.toUpperCase();
```

Since the first variable, **name**, is a string, you can use the **toUpperCase()** method to create a new string that has all the alphabetic characters changed to uppercase. The table below lists many of the string functions that are available and can be used as a reference.

String Class Functions	
String Function	**Description/Use**
`toLowerCase()`	Method that creates a new string with all the alphabetical characters set to lowercase.
`toUpperCase()`	Method that creates a new string with all the alphabetical characters set to uppercase.
`length`	A property which returns the number of characters in the string.

`substring(first, last)`
`substring(first)`
• `first`: Index of first character
• `last`: First position after the last character
	A method that creates a new string starting at the first index and ending at the last index. Note that string positions (indexes) start at 0, so that the first character is numbered 0 and the last character is the length of the string minus 1. For example:
	
	`//         01234567890`
	`var name = "Jimmy Jones";`
	`var subS = name.substring(3, 7);    // subS = "my J"`
	
	The string **name** has a total of eleven characters, numbered from 0 to 10 (see comment above string). The variable **subS** has 4 characters, starting with the "m" at location 3 and ending with the "J" at position 6. This is because the **last** parameter is the first character past the end of the desired substring.
	
	If the **last** parameter is not given, then **substring** returns the string from the **first** index all the way to the end of the string.

`indexOf(str)` • `str`: The substring to search for.	Searches the string for the first occurrence of the specified single character or substring in **str**. If that character or substring is found, the index (in the range 0 to length minus 1) is returned. If the substring is not found, then -1 is returned. When the substring is found, the index returned is the leftmost character of the substring.
`lastIndexOf(str)`	Same as **indexOf()**, except it returns the last occurrence of the specified single character or substring.
`charAt(index)`	Returns a single character at the location specified in **index**, where **index** is a value from 0 to length minus 1.

`split(char)`	Creates an array of strings by splitting the string everywhere it finds the character in **char**. For example, the following would split the name on the space, thus placing the first name in the first entry and the last name in the last entry:
	
	`var name = "Jimmy Jones";`
	`var names = new Array();`
	`names = name.split(' ');`
	`alert("First: " + names[0] + " Last: " + names[1]);`

`replace(old, new)`	If the string value contained in **old** is found, it is replaced with the string in **new**.
	
	`var a = "Hello World";`
	`var r = a.replace("orl", "qrst");`
	`alert(r);`
	
	The result is that **r** has the string `"Hello Wqrstd"`. That is, the "orl" of "World" was replaced with "qrst".

Table 12. String class functions

Numbers and String Type Conversions

String Concatenation Examples

The following table shows a variety of string concatenation examples, and also highlights how the **toFixed()** function can be used to specify a fixed number of digits to the right of a decimal. (The **toFixed()** function rounds up to the specified number of digits.)

String Concatenation and Conversion Examples	
Code Segment	**Resulting String in Variable r**
`var a = "ab";` `var r = a + "c";`	`"abc"`
`var a = "ab";` `var r = a + a;`	`"abab"`
`var a = "ab";` `var r = a.toUpperCase() + a;`	`"ABab"` (Note that the contents of **a** are not modified by the first **toUpperCase()**.)

`var a = "ab";`
`var b = "cd";`
`var r = a + b;`
	`"abcd"`

`var c = 0;`
`var f = (9.0 / 5.0) * c + 32;`
`var r = c + "C = " + f + "F";`
	`"0C = 32F"`

`var a = 5.0 / 9.0;   // 0.555...` `var r = "5/9 = " + a;`	`"5/9 = 0.5555555555555556"`
`var a = 5.0 / 9.0;   // 0.555...` `var r = "5/9 = " + a.toFixed(3);`	`"5/9 = 0.556"`
`var a = 5.0 / 9.0;   // 0.555...` `var r = "5/9 = " + a.toFixed(0);`	`"5/9 = 1"`
`var a = "Hello World";` `var r = a.toUpperCase();`	`"HELLO WORLD"`
`var a = "Hello World";` `var r = a.toLowerCase();`	`"hello world"`

Table 13. String concatenation and conversion examples

Strings Cannot Be Changed

Strings are immutable in JavaScript, meaning that strings cannot be changed. The tools for changing case, making substitutions, or modifying the string do not actually make any changes to the original string. Instead, a new string is created with the desired changes while the original string remains unchanged. In the last two examples in Table 13, the original string (in **a**) still says "Hello World" afterward. If you want the string changed, then you would have to set the string equal to itself, as shown below. (Specifically, what happens is that a new string is created that is all uppercase and the contents of the original string are replaced with the uppercase value.)

```
a = a.toUpperCase();
```

Converting Strings to Numbers

Numbers are stored in a computer in a compact form that is ideal for the processor to use in arithmetic computations. In contrast, strings are sequences of characters. If the user typed 127 into a **prompt()** function, the value would be stored as "127," but in ASCII, this would be stored internally as 00110001 00110010 00110111. Unfortunately, the computer cannot perform arithmetic on text data, so to compute with "127" the computer would first convert the string "127" to its internal binary value, which can be expressed in only 8 bits as 01111111.

The problem with this comes in when JavaScript fetches input from the user. If the user typed in the number 127 as a Fahrenheit temperature to be converted to Celsius, it would be stored as a string. For the computer to perform a computation on this value, then, the value must first be converted to the shorter, computational form.

In some cases, JavaScript can tell that you are using a text input value as a number and will attempt to convert it for you. If you try to multiply an input string by a number, JavaScript knows that there is no multiply operator defined for strings and will try to convert the string to a number. Here is an example for an HTML document (Figure 73) that computes the area of a circle given an input radius. First a request is made for the radius of a circle, which will be stored in the variable **radius**. Using **radius**, the area of a circle is computed using the formula $a = \pi r^2$. Since the radius is being used in a multiplication, JavaScript will automatically try to convert the typed-in string to its internal numeric format before calculating. (Note that the JavaScript multiplies **radius** times itself as an easy way to square it.)

```html
<html>
  <head>
    <title>Area of a Circle</title>
  </head>
  <body>
    <h1>Compute Circle Area</h1>
    <script type="text/javascript">
      var radius = prompt("Enter radius of circle", "");
      var area = Math.PI * radius * radius;
      alert(area);
    </script>
  </body>
</html>
```

Figure 73. Area of a circle from user input

Unfortunately, JavaScript cannot always know when to convert a value for you. If you try to add something to a variable that is a string representation of a number, JavaScript will assume that you want a string "+" operation and will concatenate the two values instead. For example, study the JavaScript in Figure 74.

```html
<html>
  <head>
    <title>String Conversion Problems</title>
  </head>
  <body>
    <h1>String Conversion Problems</h1>
    <script type="text/javascript">
      // Grab a user value
      var aValue = prompt("Value to which 100 will be added", "");

      // Show results without any specific conversions
      var sum = aValue + 100;
      alert("Sum without specific conversion is " + sum);

      // Convert input value first and show results
      aValue = parseFloat(aValue);
      sum = aValue + 100;
      alert("Sum with specific conversion is " + sum);
    </script>
  </body>
</html>
```

Figure 74. String conversion error with addition

This page requests a single value from the user and then does the computation in two different ways, showing the results of each method after. First, no specific conversion is made. When you open this document (try it) and type a value of 32, the first **alert()** function returns "32100", not "132". The reason is that the variable **aValue** has the string "32" in it and not a numeric value. When JavaScript sees the plus sign followed by 100, it first converts the 100 to the string "100" and then concatenates the two strings, yielding "32100".

The fix to this problem is to specifically convert the user input from its internal string format into the internal computational format, as shown in the last part of the JavaScript. Here the variable **aValue** is set equal to the **parseFloat()** function with **aValue** passed as a parameter. This changes **aValue** from "32" to 32. Then when the 100 is added, the result is the correct value of "132".

The **parseFloat()** function of Figure 74 takes the string input and converts it to the type of number that can have a fractional part (like 3.14). Another function is also available called **parseInt()**, which converts to a whole number (integer) and discards anything to the right of the decimal point. These functions are summarized in Table 14.

Numeric Conversion Functions	
Conversion Function	**Description/Use**
parseFloat(value)	Converts a valid input string value to a number that can have a fractional part like 3.14. No change is made to the input value. Instead, the function returns the converted value.
parseInt(value)	Converts a valid input string value to a whole number. No change is made to the input value (other than truncating the decimal part, if one exists). Instead, the function returns the converted value.

Table 14. Numeric conversion functions

Each function takes, as input, a single parameter (that can be the name of a variable) that contains a string. This string value will usually have been obtained previously from the user using **prompt()** or from an input text box on a form (see Chapter 8).

Don't worry about the fact that in Figure 74 the variable **aValue** appears on both sides of the replacement statement. What happens internally is that the contents of **aValue** are fetched (a string), converted into a fractional number, and then stored back in `aValue`. The net result is just a change in the internal format of the information stored in `aValue`.

The following page is another illustration of trying to add two numbers (from two prompts) without a specific conversion:

```html
<html>
  <head>
    <title>F to C Form</title>
  </head>
  <body>
    <script type="text/javascript">
      var a = prompt("Enter first value", "");
      var b = prompt("Enter second value", "");
      var c = a + b;
      alert("" + a + " + " + b + " = " + c);
    </script>
  </body>
</html>
```

Figure 75. Simple adder with errors

However, the page does not function as you would expect. In this program, two values are asked for from the user and stored in variables (**a** and **b**). A third variable, **c**, is then set to the sum of those variables, and that result is shown in an alert box. If you run this program and type in the values "3.5" and "5.2", though, your answer will be "3.55.2" and not 8.7, as you might expect. This is because the variables **a** and **b** are both stored as strings and the "+" operation happens to be defined for strings. The result is then the concatenation of the two strings.

Although JavaScript will try to handle these type conversions for you, it will not always do so correctly, as you can see from the above. To be safe, you should specifically convert all user input with `parseInt()` or `parseFloat()` before performing any numerical computations on that input. Change the compute steps as follows:

```javascript
var a = prompt("Enter first value", "");
var b = prompt("Enter second value", "");
a = parseFloat(a);       // This line is new
b = parseFloat(b);       // This line is new
var c = a + b;
alert("" + a + " + " + b + " = " + c);
```

The result now is correct, because the values for **a** and **b** were first converted to numbers, and the "+" operation now means an arithmetic addition.

Note that you will find that you get the correct answer for a * b, a − b, and a / b without the `parseFloat()` function calls, because the multiply, subtract, and divide functions are not defined for strings. The browser, in its effort to read your mind, assumes that you wanted to do numeric computations, so it automatically converts the string values to numbers before the computation. However, you should not take advantage of this (since you may forget about the exception for +), but should instead always convert input numbers before using them in numeric calculations.

> **Converting User Input**
>
> You should always use either the `parseFloat()` or `parseInt()` function to convert user input before using input values in numeric computations.

Conversion Problems and `NaN`

The built-in functions `parseFloat()` and `parseInt()` do their best to convert user input, but if that input has invalid characters, the results can vary. First, there may be no valid characters in the input (say someone types `"cat"` as the value of the height of a triangle). In this case, a special value called `NaN` is returned. This stands for **Not a Number**, meaning invalid input. `NaN` is not a number and will not compare as equal to anything, not even another `NaN`. Furthermore, any computations with `NaN` always yield another `NaN`.

> **`parseFloat()` and `parseInt()`**
>
> `parseFloat()` converts user input from a string to a fractional number. The conversion stops as soon as an invalid character is encountered (alphabetic, symbolic, or a second decimal point).
>
> `parseInt()` converts user input from a string to a whole number. The conversion stops as soon as an invalid character is encountered (alphabetic, symbolic, or a decimal point).
>
> If no valid numeric values are found for either function, the value is set to `NaN`.

On the other hand, the string input might start with valid numbers and then have an invalid symbol, including alphabetic letters or symbols, as in, for example, `"36.1A"`. When invalid data are obtained after some valid data, `parseFloat()` and `parseInt()` both stop processing when the first invalid symbol or letter is found and keep the value obtained so far. For example, if the input is `"36.1A"`, `parseFloat()` would return 36.1. With the same input, `parseInt()` will stop processing when it encounters the first decimal point and would return 36. (Note also that `parseFloat()` will stop processing when it encounters a second decimal point.)

The value `NaN` can occur any time you try to convert user input. As a result, your JavaScript program should always check for invalid user input and request for him or her to correct the input if invalid. Testing for the `NaN` value is described in chapter 6.

Numbers to Strings

In addition to converting strings to numbers, JavaScript also converts numbers to strings. Usually, though, these conversions are handled automatically for you. For example, if you call the `alert()` function with just a number, JavaScript automatically converts the number for printing. Consider the following example:

```
var a = prompt("Enter value for a", "");
a = parseFloat(a);
alert(a);
```

Due to the `parseFloat()` call, the variable **a** is in numeric format (assuming **a** had a valid number in it). Say the user typed 23.1 as input for **a**. The alert would simply show 23.1, because `alert()` requires a string and JavaScript knows how to do that conversion for you.

If you really need to convert a numeric value into a string, simply append it to an existing string or an empty string (as demonstrated earlier in this chapter). Consider the following:

```
var a = 23.1;
var b = "" + a;
```

The variable **a** has a value equal to the number 23.1, but the variable **b** has a value equal to the string `"23.1"`. This is because JavaScript sees the + sign after the empty string and interprets the + as a string concatenation. It then converts the number into a string and appends it to the empty string. Since the value being prepended to **a** is an empty string, a four-character string results (`"23.1"`).

Another place where you need to specifically tell JavaScript how to convert a number into a string is when you want to show a numeric answer to only a specific number of places. Consider the following code segment (try it):

```
var area = Math.PI * 2 * 2;              // Computes area of circle with radius 2
alert("Area: " + area);                  // Shows 12.566370614359172
alert("Area: " + area.toFixed(2));       // Shows 12.57 (above rounded to 2 places)
```

The first line computes the area of a circle with radius 2, the second line shows a 17-digit-precision result of that computation, and the third line shows the same result with the area *rounded* to exactly two decimal places. The **toFixed()** function can be appended to any numeric value with the dot, taking as input the number of decimal digits required to the right of the decimal.

.toFixed()

By referencing the function **.toFixed()** of a numeric value, you can control the number of significant digits shown in a result. The function takes a whole number as input, which is the number of digits to be used to the right of the decimal point. The result is rounded to the specified number of places.

Review Questions

1. What is the purpose or objective of using JavaScript in web pages? What advantages does it offer the web developer?
2. In what parts of the HTML page can JavaScript be placed? When should the script be placed in one place rather than another?
3. What is the difference between an interpreted language and a compiled language?
4. What are reserved words?
5. What is a function parameter?
6. How are parentheses used in JavaScript punctuation?
7. What is the purpose of the `alert()` function and what parameter(s) does it take?
8. What is the purpose of the `prompt()` function, how many parameters does it take, and what are the parameters used for?
9. What is the purpose of `document.write()`?
10. Can HTML be included in the string passed to `document.write()` in order to format the data?
11. Write one line of JavaScript that asks the user for their telephone number.
12. Try to reproduce, from memory, the code that asks for a name and says congratulations to that name (see Figure 63).
13. What are the naming rules for JavaScript IDs, variables, and functions? That is, should they be uppercase or not? Can symbols or whitespace be used? Etc.
14. What is a variable?
15. Define a variable called `phone` and set it to "555-1212".
16. How large of a positive number can be represented in JavaScript (use scientific notation for your answer)?
17. List all the Math operators.
18. What is a string? What is meant by appending or concatenating strings?
19. Can modifications be made directly to existing strings?
20. What functions are used to create an all uppercase or all lowercase string? Do these functions change the value of the original string?
21. Describe the problems that occur because of the + sign being both the math addition operator and the string concatenation operator.
22. What function converts a string fractional value into a number? How about a whole number?
23. In chapter 2 you learned that values for attributes need to be in quotes. How would you include values with quotes in them in a JavaScript string? List the three possible ways.

Exercises

1. Study the example shown in Figure 61 in detail. Then open a blank page in your editor and try to recreate it without looking at the text or your notes. See how much you can remember. When you get stuck, look back as needed. At a later time, try again. The more you practice, the easier JavaScript will be. To remember how to type the `<script>` block, note its similarity to a `<style>` block.
2. Create a new script similar to the one shown in Figure 63 that asks the user for their age and then displays a message that reads something like "Your age is 23" (assuming they typed 23). You will need a variable to hold the age, as in the example, but instead of `firstName`, use the variable name `age`.
3. (More difficult) Modify the program in Figure 63 to ask for two pieces of information: a first name and a last name. Then have the congratulations say something like "Congratulations Joe Smith". You will need two variables, one for `firstName` and one for `lastName`, which can be filled by using the `prompt()` function twice, after which you can use both names in a single `alert()` function call. If your first attempt does not have a space between the names, add the space using the + sign and a single blank (" ").
4. Write the JavaScript to compute the area of a rectangle, placing the script in the `<body>` section. Define a variable called `length` and set it equal to 8, define a variable called `width` and set it equal to 3, and define a variable called `area` and set it equal to the product of the previous two variables. Show the results with `document.write()`.
5. Write the JavaScript to compute the volume of a sphere using the formula $a = (4/3) \cdot \pi r^3$. Place the script in the `<body>` section. Define a variable called `radius` and fetch it from the user with `prompt()`, and define a variable called `volume` and show the results with `document.write()` so that your answer appears as shown below (assuming a value of 3 was typed in response to the request for radius):

   ```
   A sphere of radius 3 has a volume of 113.1.
   ```

6. Rewrite exercise 4 to prompt the user for the length and width of the rectangle. Convert both input values to fractional numbers and then compute and display the area.
7. Rewrite the code in Figure 75 so that it properly shows the sum of the numbers instead of the string concatenation.
8. Do the reverse computation of that shown in Figure 70. That is, compute a Celsius temperature from a Fahrenheit temperature using the formula $c = (5/9) \cdot (f - 32)$. Show the results with the `alert()` function.
9. Create the list shown below using `document.write()`. Then create the list in a string (see Figure 71) and display it.
   - Apple
   - Orange
   - Pear
10. Create the list shown below using `document.write()`. Then create the list in a string (see Figure 72) and display it. Use an inline style on the `<ol>` element (`style="list-style-type:upper-roman"`) to force roman numerals.
    I. Apple
    II. Orange
    III. Pear

CHAPTER 6 – CONDITIONAL EXECUTION AND LOOPS

Up to this point, all JavaScript code we have seen proceeded sequentially from the first line of the script to the last line. However, the primary purpose of JavaScript is to add interactivity to the web page, to validate user input, and to add the ability to loop (i.e. repeat commands). The objective is to offload work from the server and the network by doing as much as possible locally in the browser, guaranteeing that the data sent to the server is accurate. Also, response time is always faster when the server is not involved, providing a better user experience.

In order to validate data, JavaScript needs to be able to ask questions or perform tasks a varying number of times depending upon the contents of various data items (variables and/or input fields). This chapter looks at different constructs for asking questions and for looping in JavaScript, but prior to covering these topics, you will need to understand block statements and how to compare things.

Comparison Operations

Conditional processing is frequently based on the result of a test such that, when the test passes, a set of statements are processed, but if the test fails, the statements are not processed. In most cases, these tests consist of comparisons between variables and constants, or between variables. JavaScript has eight comparison operators, which are listed in Table 15.

<	<=	>	>=	==	!=	===	!==
Less than	Less or equal	Greater than	Greater or equal	Equal after possible conversion	Not equal after possible conversion	Equal format and equal value	Unequal format or unequal value

Table 15. Comparison operators

Note that "==" and "!=" should generally *not* be used (unless you know exactly what you are doing). You should use "===" and "!==" instead, since they don't try to convert the types of variables like "==" and "!=" do.

if-Statements Comparing to Whole Numbers

One type of conditional execution is achieved by using **if**-statements in conjunction with a comparison operator. An **if**-statement tests a logical condition, created by comparing two values using one of the comparison operators shown in Table 15. The following four examples illustrate comparing a variable (containing a whole number) to a constant number:

```
1.
if (age >= 21)
   message = "Adult";

2.
if (age >= 21)
{
   message = "Adult";
   alert(message);
}
```

```
3.
if (age >= 21)
{
   message = "Adult";
   alert(message);
}
else
{
   message = "Minor";
   alert(message);
}
```

```
4.
if (age < 21)
   message = "Minor";
else if (age < 60)
   message = "Adult";
else
   message = "Antique";
```

117

The first example tests the age variable and, if the age is greater or equal to 21, sets the message to "Adult". The second example uses a block statement to not only set the message but to show it as well. The third example uses the `else` keyword to also set a message when the condition is false. The final example shows nested `if`-statements to separate three different possibilities.

(As an additional note, the statement following the `if`-statement and the statement following the `else`-statement can be replaced with block statements in the examples above.)

if-Statements Comparing to Strings

Since strings contain a variable number of characters, testing strings is a bit more complex than the testing for whole numbers we showed above. For example, what does the "greater than" operator mean with strings? What does it mean when we say strings are "equal"?

First, strings are ordered alphabetically: as 2 > 1 for numbers, `"B"` > `"A"` and `"ABCE"` > `"ABCD"` in strings (in JavaScript, anyway). In the second example, both strings have four characters and differ in only the last character. The first of the two is larger because E comes later in the alphabet than D, which is logical.

However, what happens when we compare `"ABCD"` and `"ABC"`? Now the first is longer but has the same first three letters. By definition in JavaScript, the longer string will be considered "larger" because "D" is larger than "nothing".

Next, consider `"ABCD"` and `"abcd"`, which both have the same letters. But, one is all uppercase and the other is lowercase. If you just compare the two as shown above, you will find that the lowercase version is "larger." This result arises from the fact that the internal storage format for letters is such that the lowercase letters occur after the uppercase letters. If you would like more details, search Google for "Unicode plane".

Sometimes you need to compare two strings and do not care whether lowercase or uppercase letters are used. To handle this comparison correctly, you can use either the `toLowerCase()` or `toUpperCase()` string method.

> **.toUpperCase() and .toLowerCase**
>
> Functions `.toUpperCase()` and `.toLowerCase()` of a string variable create a new string that consists of all uppercase or all lowercase letters, depending upon the function used.

Consider the following examples:

```
var x = "aBcD";                 var x = "aBcD";                          var x = "aBcD";
if (x === "abcd")               if (x.toUpperCase() === "ABCD")          if (x.toLowerCase() === "abcd")
    alert("Found match");           alert("Found match");                    alert("Found match");
```

In the first example, the strings are being compared exactly as they are, so they would not be equal and the alert would not be displayed. In the second case, a new string is first created from the variable `x` that is all uppercase letters and then is compared to `"ABCD"`. Since the new string is uppercase, the alert message would be displayed. In the last example, a new string is created with all lowercase letters and then compared to `"abcd"`. This would likewise result in the alert message being displayed.

Block Statements

All loops and `if`-statements take a single JavaScript statement in the standard syntax. However, in most cases you really want to have multiple statements. A block statement allows the single statement to be replaced by a set of statements set off by a pair of braces, as shown below in the example:

```
{
    statement;
    statement;
    statement;
    . . .
}
```

The block statement allows any statement to be replaced with a series of statements of any kind. In fact, some of the statements within a block statement can be other block statements, nested to any level.

The `confirm()` Function

Included with the JavaScript library of functions is a function that can prompt the user for a yes/no answer to a question. This function, the `confirm()` function, is similar to `prompt()` in that you pass it a message that is displayed on a box; however, the user's response is not text, but just a mouse click on either an OK button or a Cancel button. Figure 76 shows the HTML and JavaScript to display the Confirm dialog box, and Figure 77 shows how the dialog box appears in Internet Explorer currently (it is similar in other browsers).

The Confirm dialog box is most often used to make sure the user wants to perform a particular task. In the example, there is a button that would perform an irreversible step of deleting the user's profile. In case the button was clicked by accident, the user is asked to confirm his or her intent. Run the program and see the difference between clicking the two buttons. If the OK button is clicked, the message displayed is "Profile deleted". If the Cancel button is clicked, the message displayed is "Ok. No changes made". Since the `confirm()` function returns `true` if the OK button is clicked in the dialog and `false` if Cancel is clicked, the `confirm()` function is most often used inside an `if`-statement.

```
<html>
  <head>
    <title>Using the Confirm Function</title>
    <script type="text/javascript">
      var curUserName;      // Name of current user
      function delUser()
      {
        if (confirm("Are you sure you want to delete the profile for this user?"))
          alert("Profile deleted");
        else
          alert("Ok. No changes made");
      }
    </script>
  </head>
  <body>
    <form id="form1">
      <input type="button" value="Delete User Profile" onclick="delUser();" />
    </form>
  </body>
</html>
```

Figure 76. Using the `confirm()` function

Figure 77. Example of `confirm()` dialog box

Complex Conditions

Sometimes, a simple comparison is not enough to handle more complex situations. In addition to the comparison operators shown in Table 15, there are three *logical operators* as shown in Table 16. These operators are combined with the comparison operators to create more complex conditions. (The material in this section is needed to understand some of the examples under `while`-loops below.)

\multicolumn{4}{c}{**Logical Operators**}
Operator	**Description**	**Example Condition**	**Resulting Condition**
!	Logical NOT. Inverts the logical value and reverses the sense of the test (as shown here in the last three examples).	`!x`	If `x` is `true`, `!x` is `false`. If `x` is `false`, `!x` is `true`.
		`!isNaN(s)`	If `s` is a valid number, the condition `!isNaN(s)` is `true`. If `s` is invalid, the condition `!isNaN(s)` is `false`.
		`!(x < y)`	Same as `(x >= y)`.
		`!(x >= y)`	Same as `(x < y)`.
		`!(x === y)`	Same as `(x !== y)`.
&&	Logical AND. *All* conditions connected with AND must all be `true` for the result to be `true`. If `false` appears anywhere in a list of conditions connected by AND, the result is `false`.	`x && y`	If both `x` and `y` are `true`, the result is `true`. Otherwise the result is `false`.
||	Logical OR. If *any* of the conditions connected with OR are true, the result is `true`. All conditions must be `false` for the result to be `false`.	`x || y`	If either `x` or `y` is `true` or both are `true`, the result is `true`. If both are `false`, the result is `false`.

Table 16. Logical operators

For a not-so-real-world example, say that you want to test whether someone is able to retire based on two conditions: money in the bank, represented by the variable **savings**, and age, represented by the variable **age**. Say that someone could retire if their age is greater than or equal to 62 by drawing Social Security, or alternately, one could retire if his or her savings were $1 million. Assuming that one could retire if either condition existed, the first example code segment in Figure 78 shows how such a test could be constructed. (Notice that the two logical comparisons are connected with the OR operator.)

```
<html>
  <head>
    <title>Logical Operator Examples</title>
  </head>
  <body>
    <script type="text/javascript">
      // No error checking done on input values
      var age = parseInt(prompt("Enter your age", ""));
      var savings = parseFloat(prompt("Enter your savings", ""));

      // Example 1: Simple OR logical operator
      // Either $1M in bank or over 62
      if (age >= 62 || savings >= 1000000)
        alert("1: Ok to retire");
      else
        alert("1: Keep working for a while");

      // Example 2: Simple AND logical operator
      // Both $1M in bank and over 62
      if (age >= 62 && savings >= 1000000)
        alert("2: Ok to retire");
      else
        alert("2: Keep working for a while");

      // Example 3: Mixed logical operator
      // Either $2M in bank, or both $1M and over 62
      if ((savings > 2000000) || (age >= 62 && savings >= 1000000))
        alert("3: Ok to retire");
      else
        alert("3: Keep working for a while");
    </script>
  </body>
</html>
```

Figure 78. Logical operator examples

A more realistic approach (given that one probably cannot retire on just Social Security) is to add the requirement that both a savings of $1 million (or more) and an age greater than or equal to 62 are required. This solution is shown in example 2 in Figure 78. There, the two logical conditions are connected by the AND operator.

Finally, another scenario is to assume it is OK to retire if you have $2 million in savings, regardless of age, or that you can retire with $1 million as long as you are also over age 62. The logical expression from example 2 (both $1 million AND age 62) is placed in parentheses to make it a single logical value, and this condition is connected with OR to a test for savings of over $2 million. Study and play with the example until you can understand how it works. Try different combinations of age and savings and see which test allows for retirement.

Loops

Frequently in JavaScript, you will need to perform a set of steps several times. One frequent need for loops is in processing arrays, for example. Although arrays are an advanced topic reserved for chapter 9, you can think of arrays as a series of boxes that are accessed using a box number. A loop might then open each box using its box number and add up the numbers.

Another use is math computations. For example, you might want to add up the sum of all odd numbers from 73 to 1,341 (admittedly an unusual task); another example might be the computation of trigonometric functions using what is called the Taylor series polynomial expansion (Figure 83). Loops give JavaScript a way of repeating a group of statements a set number of times to compute mathematical results like these.

Basic Loop Operations and Types of Loops

JavaScript supports three different kinds of loops: `for`-loops, `while`-loops and `do-while`-loops. All these loops share three basic operations, detailed in Table 17.

Basic Steps of All Loops	
Step	**Description**
Initializations	One or more variables are initialized before the loop. For example, if you are adding up a set of numbers, you would define a variable to hold the sum (in the future) and set that value to zero. Other initializations might be for variables that will be used to control the number of times the loop executes (which will be tested in the next step).
Testing Loop Continuation	A test is made to see if the loop should continue or stop. If the condition tested is `true`, the loop continues (or starts, if this is the first time). If the condition tested is `false`, the loop stops and the instruction following the loop is the next instruction to run.
Updating Loop Control Conditions	Some variable or condition is changed such that the continuation test will, at this time or at a future time, cause the looping to stop (see Infinite Loops below).

Table 17. Basic parts of all loops

With `for`-loops, all three basic steps can often be done within the loop syntax itself (although some additional initializations may occur before a `for`-loop). In a `while`-loop, the continue test occurs at the top of the loop and the loop control update occurs inside the loop, and in a `do-while`-loop, the loop control update also occurs inside the loop but the continue test is done at the end of the loop. In either type of `while` loop, the loop control update step is most often the last step of the loop (but occurs before the test, in the case of the `do-while` loop).

A final characteristic of virtually all loops is that the loop control update should change a variable or condition that is being tested within the continuation test; otherwise, the loops will never end (see Infinite Loops below). As you study the three types of loops, look for these three basic steps and their locations in the loop.

for-Loops

The `for`-loop is the easiest loop to learn and most compact of the loops. It is normally used when the number of loops (times through the set of statements) is known in advance, either as a constant number or a value contained in a variable.

> **`for`-Loop Usage**
>
> `for`-loops are generally used when the number of loops is known in advance, either as constants or values stored in variables. The continuation test and updating loop control steps of the `for`-loop normally use a loop variable.

The `for`-loop runs the series of statements in the loop *for* a set number of times using a step variable. Setting up this variable – frequently called the *loop variable* – is part of the initialization step. The continuation test is usually a logical expression involving the loop variable, and finally, the incrementing step changes the value of the loop variable. The compact syntax of this loop allows for all of the basic parts to be specified within the syntax, as shown here:

```
<Possible Initializations>;
for(<Initializations>; <Continuation Test>; <Update of Loop Variable>)
     <statement>;
```

<Possible Initializations> Frequently there will be initializations (not associated with loop control) that are included just before the `for`-loop. For example: defining a variable called `sum` and setting it to zero.

<Initializations> Normally, this defines a loop variable and gives it an initial value, as shown in the example below.

<Continuation Test> This is a logical expression, normally in the form of comparing the loop variable to some limiting value. If the condition tests `true`, the loop continues. When the test fails (is `false`), the loop stops. This test is made at the beginning of the loop. Therefore, *if the condition fails on the first pass, the loop never executes*.

<Update of Loop Variable> This statement changes the loop variable. This usually means adding something to the loop variable (forward loops) but it can also mean subtracting something. Be sure to specify the same loop variable in the increment step as the one in the continuation test; otherwise the loop is infinite and never ends.

Example:
```
// Add all integers from 1 to 10
var sum = 0;
for (var i = 1; i <= 10; i = i + 1)
   sum = sum + i;
```

If more than one statement needs to be executed in the loop, create a block of statements by including multiple statements between braces. Also note that it is possible to create an "infinite loop" if the loop variable is never changed during the loop in a way that makes the continuation condition `false`.

while-Loops

The `while`-loop syntax (see below) is used to run a series of statements as long as a specified condition is met. It differs from the `for`-loop, where the number of loops is usually known in advance, in that the loop tests a single condition and continues to run as long as that condition is true. This makes it better for loops where the number of times you will need to process something is not known beforehand. Loop termination is caused by changing something inside the loop that is tested in the condition.

> **while-Loop Usage**
>
> `while`-loops are generally used when the end of the loop relies on something occurring inside the loop. For example: when the user enters a specific or valid value.

The **while**-loop is handy for obtaining valid user input by looping until valid data are entered. In this case the continuation test will keep checking the last value entered by the user (see Looping for Valid Input with *while*-Loops next).

The syntax for the **while**-loop is below. Note that the braces that create the block statement are not actually required, but are found in most loops of this type since a single-statement **while**-loop is rare.

```
<Initializations>
while(<Continuation Test>)
{
        <statement(s)>;
        <Update Loop Test Data>
}
```

<Initializations>   Loop test conditions are set up before the **while** statement. In addition, other initializations might be done here. For example, if you are summing a set of values, then the sum variable would be declared and set to zero before the loop.

<Continuation Test>   This is a logical expression, normally in the form of comparing the loop variable to some limiting value or testing user input. If the condition tests **true**, the loop continues.

When the test fails (is **false**), the loop stops. This test is made at the beginning of the loop. Therefore, *if the condition fails on the first pass, the loop never executes.*

<Update Loop Test Data> This statement changes the data used by the loop test. This might take the form of requesting additional information from the user, or performing a computation on a loop variable.

Looping for Valid Input with *while*-Loops

A good example of using a while-loop is forcing the user to enter a numeric value from the **prompt()** function. In the first example in Figure 79, the user is simply asked for a numeric value. If a numeric value is entered, it is used for a computation, but if an invalid number is entered (as determined by the **isNaN()** function), the user is again prompted for a numeric value instead. This requesting continues until a valid numeric value is given, after which the user is thanked. Run the code for yourself and see how the loop works.

The loop continues as long as the tested condition is **true**. Since the function **isNaN()** returns **true** when the value tested is not a number, the net result is that the loop continues as long as the input value is not a number and stops as soon as a valid number is entered. Note that if the user enters a valid number on the first prompt, the loop never runs (which is OK in this case).

```
<html>
  <head>
    <title>While-Loop Input Examples</title>
  </head>
  <body>
    <script type="text/javascript">
      // Example 1: Just force a numeric input
      // Note: The parseFloat() function disallows a blank input
      var inputValue = prompt("Enter any valid number", "");
      inputValue = parseFloat(inputValue);  // Try to make it a number
      while (isNaN(inputValue))
      {
        inputValue = prompt("Invalid number. Enter any valid number", "");
        inputValue = parseFloat(inputValue);  // Try to make it a number
      }
      alert("Thanks. You entered " + inputValue);

      // Example 2: Force a numeric value from 1 to 10
      // Note: Three conditions make the loop continue with a new prompt:
      //          - Any invalid number
      //          - A valid number less than 1
      //          - A valid number larger than 10
      //        These conditions are connected with the OR logical operator
      var inputValue = prompt("Enter a whole number from 1 to 10", "");
      inputValue = parseInt(inputValue);  // Try to make it a number
      while (isNaN(inputValue) || inputValue < 1 || inputValue > 10)
      {
        inputValue = prompt("Invalid number. Enter a whole number from 1 to 10", "");
        inputValue = parseInt(inputValue);  // Try to make it a number
      }
      alert("Thanks. You entered " + inputValue);
    </script>
  </body>
</html>
```

Figure 79. while loops for input validation

The second example in Figure 79 not only forces a numeric input value, but also forces the user to enter a value between 1 and 10. To do this, the loop must both test the validity of the input value and compare it to an upper and lower limit. For these numeric comparisons, values must be in numeric format and not strings. This is another reason that the input value is first parsed to a number before the loop (and also inside the loop).

To force a valid numeric input value in the range of 1 to 10, the loop needs to continue asking for a new number any time any one of these 3 conditions exist: (1) the input is not a number, (2) the input is a number but less than 1, or (3) the input is a number but is greater than 10. Thus the logical OR operator is used to connect all 3 conditions.

Note that in both of the examples in Figure 79 there are two sets of two almost identical statements: one set outside the loop and one set inside the loop. The first line of the pair prompts for a value, and the second of the pair attempts to make it a number; at a higher level, the first pair of lines constitutes the initialization step for the loops (see Table 17), and the second set updates the value being tested in the loop. For better readability, the first prompt just asks for the number, while the second alerts the user to the fact that their previous try was in error before asking for a new number.

do-while-Loops

The **do-while**-loop syntax (see below) is very similar to the **while**-loop in that it also runs a series of statements until a specific condition is achieved. But the **do-while**-loop differs from the **while**-loop in that the **do-while**-loop tests for continuation at the end of the loop, where the **while**-loop tests at the beginning. The syntax of the **do-while** loop is shown below. *Note that the continuation test is at the end of the loop and is followed by a semicolon!* (This semicolon is often forgotten.)

> **do-while-Loop Usage**
>
> **do-while**-loops are generally used when the loop needs to run at least once. Since the continuation test occurs at the end of the loop, the loop will always run at least once.

```
<Initializations>
do
{
        <statement(s)>;
        <Update Loop Condition Data>
}
while(<Continuation Test>);
```

(NOTE: The semicolon pointed to by the arrow should be present!)

<Initializations> — Loop test conditions need not be set up before the **do-while** loop. Instead, the loop conditions can be done within the loop since the conditions are tested at the end of the loop. However, there are frequently initializations before the loop anyway for clarity's sake, like clearing a **sum** variable.

<Continuation Test> — This is a logical expression which is normally in the form of testing a function or comparing a loop variable to some limiting value. If the condition tests **true**, the loop continues. For example, it might test whether some input value from the user is valid or not (and continue looping when it is invalid).

When the test fails (is **false**), the loop stops. This test is made at the end of the loop. As a reminder, remember that **do-while** loops *always* run at least once.

<Update Loop Test Data> — This statement changes data used by the loop test. This might take the form of requesting additional information from the user, or performing a computation on a loop variable.

Looping for Valid Input with *do-while*-Loops

The **do-while**-loop, like the **while**-loop, is also useful for forcing the user to enter a numeric value from the **prompt()** function. However, the code actually becomes a little bit simpler as compared to the **while**-loop, in that there is only one prompt and one conversion to a numeric value. The code in Figure 79 has been converted to use **do-while** loops here and is shown in Figure 80.

```
<html>
  <head>
    <title>Do-While-Loop Input Examples</title>
  </head>
  <body>
    <script type="text/javascript">
      // Example 1: Just force a numeric input
      // Note: Only need to define the variable before the loop
      var inputValue;
      do
      {
        inputValue = prompt("Enter any valid number", "");
        inputValue = parseFloat(inputValue);  // Try to make it a number
      } while (isNaN(inputValue));
      alert("Thanks. You entered " + inputValue);

      // Example 2: Force a numeric value from 1 to 10
      var inputValue;
      do
      {
        inputValue = prompt("Enter a whole number from 1 to 10", "");
        inputValue = parseInt(inputValue);  // Try to make it a number
      } while (isNaN(inputValue) || inputValue < 1 || inputValue > 10);
      alert("Thanks. You entered " + inputValue);
    </script>
  </body>
</html>
```

Figure 80. do-while loops for input validation

The **do-while** loop is shorter than the **while**-loop because the **do-while** loop always runs at least once, so the prompt and conversion to a number is done inside the loop before the continue test is made. In the **while**-loop, you have to prepare everything before the test at the top of the loop. Then, inside the loop you have to do the same thing again before it loops to the next test at the beginning.

In comparing Figure 79 and Figure 80, you may have noticed that the prompt to the user inside the loop had to change in the first figure. In the first example, before the **while**-loop the user was just prompted for a numeric value, but inside the **while**-loop the person was told that what they entered was invalid and that the data must be reentered. In a **do-while**-loop, there is only one message, so there is no invalid data warning, just a request for a valid number.

Making *while*-Loops Execute At Least Once

You can force a **while**-loop to always run once, just like a **do-while** loop, by initializing the loop conditions in such a way that the **while**-loop executes on the first pass. The simpler code of Figure 80 is revised for a **while**-loop and shown in Figure 81. The revised code works as follows:

The value of the loop variable, **inputValue**, is set to the character **"a"**, which will cause the **isNaN()** test to return **true** and the loop to execute the first time. Then the data are prompted for only once inside the loop. This technique basically converts the **while**-loop into a **do-while** loop, since it always causes the loop to execute at least once. With techniques such as this, you really only need the **while**-loop to do whatever you need, and for this reason **do-while** loops are seldom used.

```
<html>
  <head>
    <title>Simpler While-Loop Input Examples</title>
  </head>
  <body>
    <script type="text/javascript">
      // Example 1: Just force a numeric input
      var inputValue = "a";  // "a" will cause isNaN() to return true
      while (isNaN(inputValue))
      {
        inputValue = prompt("Enter any valid number", "");
        inputValue = parseFloat(inputValue);  // Try to make it a number
      }
      alert("Thanks. You entered " + inputValue);

      // Example 2: Force a numeric value from 1 to 10
      var inputValue = "a";  // "a" will cause isNaN() to return true
      while (isNaN(inputValue) || inputValue < 1 || inputValue > 10)
      {
        inputValue = prompt("Enter a whole number from 1 to 10", "");
        inputValue = parseInt(inputValue);  // Try to make it a number
      }
      alert("Thanks. You entered " + inputValue);
    </script>
  </body>
</html>
```

Figure 81. Revised while-loop for input validation

Studying Loops

As a review, the three loop types will now be compared and contrasted. Loops vary in where they are best used, where the loop test is done, and in how initializations are done. Also, different loops might never run, run at least once, or run an infinite number of times. Look for these characteristics as you read the following paragraphs.

Loop Test Location

The first characteristic to note is that **while**-loops and **for**-loops may never run, because the continuation test is executed *before* the loop is run. On the other hand, the **do-while**-loop always runs at least once since the continuation test is done at the end of the loop.

Best Uses for Loops

Although it is possible to use any loop type to solve any problem, some loop types are better suited to certain types of problems than others. For example, the **for**-loop is the best to use when the number of loops is either a constant number or an integer value that is stored in a variable. The **for**-loop is thus most often seen in computations and in the processing of arrays (see chapter 9).

Note, however, that many developers will use the **while**-loop for numeric computations even when the number of loops is known. This may be because of comfort with using the **while**-loop, or just a simple personal preference. Examples of using **while**-loops with numeric computations are given below so the loop types can be easily contrasted.

On the other hand, `while`-loops and `do-while`-loops are most often used when the end of the loop is determined inside the loop. In the previous examples, the loop was terminated once a valid number was entered that was in the specified range, making a good case for using a `while`-loop.

Infinite Loops

An infinite loop is a loop that never ends; it is like the Energizer® Bunny that keeps going and going and going. In earlier versions of web browsers, the browser would lock up during infinite loops, forcing the user to kill the application. Modern browsers detect this condition, though, and issue a warning in which you are given the opportunity to stop the loop.

Infinite loops all result from a disconnection between the loop's continuation test and the update to the loop test data. Thus, when a change is never made inside the loop to make the continuation test fail, the loop will never stop. Typical causes include not updating the loop variable, updating the wrong loop variable, or changing the loop variable in the wrong direction. Figure 82 shows three examples of infinite loops. Since these loops can lock up your browser, you should not try them yourself.

```
<html>
  <head>
    <title>Examples of Infinite Loops</title>
  </head>
  <body>
    <script type="text/javascript">
      // 1. Infinite while-loop: test variable a, change b
      var a, b;
      while (isNaN(a)) {
        b = prompt("Enter any valid number", "");
      }
      // 2. Infinite for-loop: test variable i, change j
      var i, j;
      var sum = 0;
      for (i = 1; i <= 10; j = j + 1)
        sum = sum + i;
      // 3. Infinite for-loop: test variable i, change i in wrong direction
      var i, j;
      var sum = 0;
      for (i = 1; i <= 10; i = i - 1)
        sum = sum + i;
    </script>
  </body>
</html>
```

Figure 82. Sample infinite loops

The first example in Figure 82 shows a `while`-loop to prompt for a number. Here two variables, **a** and **b**, are defined. The loop continues if the variable **a** is not a number (undefined is always invalid); however, inside the loop the user's input is stored in variable **b**. This always leaves **a** unchanged, so the loop continues forever.

The second example of Figure 82 is a `for`-loop with the same problem. The loop should add up the values between 1 and 10, but the continue test uses variable **i** while variable **j** is updated in the loop.

The third example of Figure 82 tests and updates the variable **i**, but the direction of the update is wrong. That is, instead of increasing **i** each time, the loop decreases **i**. The first value added would be 1 (as desired), but the next values generated by the update step would be 0, followed by -1, -2, and so on.

Chapter 6 – Conditional Execution and Loops

Each of these values would push the number to be added further away from 10, so the loop would continue infinitely using increasingly larger negative numbers.

By studying these infinite loops next to valid loops, the requirements for valid loops can be identified. First, the variable or condition being tested for loop continuation must be updated somewhere inside the loop. A quick check for **while**-loops and **do-while**-loops is to make sure that the variable being tested appears on the left side of an equal sign (example 1 issue, above). In **for**-loops, make the sure the test condition uses the same variable as the update step (example 2 issue). And lastly, make sure that the loop variable is being updated in the right direction (example 3 issue).

> **Well-Formed Loops**
>
> Always check that your loops are well formed and not infinite. The variable tested in the loop-continuation condition needs to be the variable updated inside the loop. Also, make sure that the loop variable is updated in the correct direction.

Comparing Loops with Numeric Computations

Study the examples carefully to determine the value of **sum**. Remember that (1) the loop may never run, (2) may run forever, or (3) may run for a finite number of times. Thus the first step is to check the starting value, the limit, and the test condition. Make sure that the increment step is changing the variable being tested and that it steps in the right direction. The safest way to check is the following process: list the first value, compute the next value, and compare that second value to the condition. Think through the loop in each step.

for-Loop Examples for Numeric Computations

Now we will study the behavior of some loop examples, both **while**- and **for**-loops. The first step is to determine the start and ending values specified in the loop, and then to list the possible values of the loop variable. Note that some loops will not run, because the test is done at the beginning of the loop and the initial value specified causes the "continuation condition" to fail on the first pass. Let's start with three simple examples of **for**-loops:

Example 1
```
var sum = 0;
for (i = 4; i <= 9; i=i+1)
    sum = sum + i;
```

Example 2
```
var sum = 0;
for (i = 4; i < 9; i=i+1)
    sum = sum + i;
```

Example 3
```
var sum = 0;
for (i = 4; i <= 9; i=i+2)
    sum = sum + i;
```

In **example 1**, the starting value for **i** is 4 and the less-than-or-equal compare allows the last value to be 9. Since **i** is stepping by 1, the possible values are 4, 5, 6, 7, 8, and 9, giving a sum of 39. In **example 2**, the condition is changed to exclude the value 9, so only 4, 5, 6, 7, and 8 are used, giving a sum of 30. In **example 3**, the first example is changed to step by 2. This means that only 4, 6, and 8 are used (since the last step of 10 is larger than 9 and excluded). Thus the sum is 18.

Example 4
```
var sum = 0;
for (i = 9; i > 6; i=i-1)
    sum = sum + i;
```

Example 5
```
var sum = 0;
for (i = 4; i <= 3; i=i+1)
    sum = sum + i;
```

Example 6
```
var sum = 0;
for (i = 4; i <= 9; j=j+1)
    sum = sum + i;
```

In **example 4**, the starting value for **i** is 9 and we are stepping down by 1, with the limit, 6, excluded from the summing set because of the less-than condition. This produces values of 9, 8, and 7, giving a total of 24. In **example 5**, the starting value 4 is larger than the test, so the loop never runs, giving a sum of 0. **Example 6** is the same as **example 1**, except that the step is updating variable **j** but variable **i** is being checked in the condition. This means that **i** is never changed and is always less than 9, so the loop runs forever. Thus **example 6** is an "infinite loop."

Example 7
```
var sum = 0;
for (i = 9; i < 30; i=i+7)
  sum = sum + i;
```

Example 8
```
var sum = 0;
for (i = -3; i < 3; i=i+1)
  sum = sum + i;
```

Example 9
```
var sum = 0;
for (i = 1; i <= 9; i=i-1)
  sum = sum + i;
```

In **example 7**, the starting value for **i** is 9 and we are stepping by 7, with a maximum value of 30. Thus the values used are 9, 16, and 23 (because the next step of 30 fails due to the less-than test). This gives a total of 48. In **example 8** we start with a negative value and step up, with the generated values of -3, -2, -1, 0, 1, and 2 giving a sum of -3. The final example looks like **example 1** except that the step is in the wrong direction. If you were listing values you would find 1, 0, -1, -2, and so on. Since the step is negative, **i** remains smaller than the test until an internal numeric overflow occurs. This loop would be classified as infinite.

while-Loop Examples With Numbers

In order to save space, you can assume that each of the following examples starts with a line that clears the sum variable (`var sum = 0;`). The examples that follow compute the same sequences as the corresponding problems under **for**-loops earlier.

Example 1
```
var i = 4;
while(i <= 9)
{
  sum = sum + i;
  i = i + 1;
}
```

Example 2
```
var i = 4;
while(i < 9)
{
  sum = sum + i;
  i = i + 1;
}
```

Example 3
```
var i = 4;
while(i <= 9)
{
  sum = sum + i;
  i = i + 2;
}
```

In **example 1**, the starting value for **i** is 4 and the less-than-or-equal compare allows the last value to be 9. Since **i** is stepping by 1, the possible values are 4, 5, 6, 7, 8, and 9, giving a sum of 39. In **example 2**, the condition is changed to exclude the value 9, so only 4, 5, 6, 7, and 8 are used, giving a sum of 30. In **example 3**, the first example is changed to step by 2. This means that only 4, 6, and 8 are used (with the last step of 10 being larger than 9 and therefore excluded). Thus the sum is 18.

Example 4
```
var i = 9;
while(i > 6)
{
  sum = sum + i;
  i = i - 1;
}
```

Example 5
```
var i = 4;
while(i <= 3)
{
  sum = sum + i;
  i = i + 1;
}
```

Example 6
```
var i = 4;
while(i <= 9)
{
  sum = sum + i;
  j = j + 1;
}
```

In **example 4**, the starting value for **i** is 9 and we are stepping down by 1, with the limit, 6, excluded from the summing set because of the less-than condition. This generates values of 9, 8, and 7, giving a total of 24. In **example 5**, the starting value 4 is larger than the test, so the loop never runs, giving a sum of 0. **Example 6** is the same as **example 1**, except that the step is updating variable **j** but variable **i** is being checked in the condition. This means that **i** is never changed and is always less than 9, so the loop runs forever. Thus **example 6** is an "infinite loop."

Example 7
```
var i = 9;
while(i < 30)
{
  sum = sum + i;
  i = i + 7;
}
```

Example 8
```
var i = -3;
while(i < 3)
{
  sum = sum + i;
  i = i + 1;
}
```

Example 9
```
var i = 1;
while(i <= 9)
{
  sum = sum + i;
  i = i - 1;
}
```

In **example 7**, the starting value for **i** is 9 and we are stepping by 7, with a maximum value of 30. Thus the values used are 9, 16, and 23 (as the next step of 30 fails because of the less-than test). This gives a total of 48. In **example 8** we start with a negative value and step up, producing values of -3, -2, -1, 0, 1, and 2, which give a sum of -3. The final example looks like **example 1**, except that the step is in the wrong direction. If you were listing values you would find 1, 0, -1, -2, and so on. Since the step is negative, **i** remains smaller than the test until an internal numeric overflow occurs. This loop would be classified as infinite.

Review Questions

1. What are the comparison operators in JavaScript? How do you test if something is exactly the same as something else?
2. What is a block statement and why is it needed?
3. Describe the basic syntax for an `if`-statement. When or where is the `else`-clause used?
4. How are strings compared? That is, what is meant by saying one string value is "larger" than another?
5. How would you compare strings if you don't care whether or not they contain uppercase or lowercase letters?
6. How do you convert a string to all uppercase letters? Lowercase letters?
7. What is the purpose of the `confirm()` function?
8. What are the logical operators in JavaScript and how are they used?
9. What is `NaN` and how does it occur? How is `NaN` tested for (that is, what function is used)?
10. What is the purpose of a loop? How many different loop types are there in JavaScript?
11. What are the three basic steps that are common to all loops in JavaScript?
12. What is the advantage of a `for`-loop (and when would it be used in preference to other loop types)?
13. When would the `while`-loop be preferred to the `for`-loop? Give an example of when a `while`-loop should be used.
14. What is the major difference between the `while`-loop and the `do-while`-loop?
15. What is an infinite loop and how can it occur?

Exercises

1. Ask the user for a number using **prompt()**. If the number is less than 21, write a message saying "Minor" using **alert()**. Otherwise, write a message that says "Adult".
2. Modify the previous exercise as follows. Ask the user for a number, then do the following: if it is not a number, say "Not a number"; if it is a number and less than 21, say "Minor"; and if it is a number greater than or equal to 21, say "Adult". Hint: use the **if-else if** construct.
3. In this exercise you will compare two input numbers and say whether or not the first is larger than the second, or the second is larger than the first, or they are equal. Prompt for two numbers, storing them in variables **a** and **b**, and convert the variables into whole numbers using **parseInt()**. Then display one of three messages: "a larger", "b larger", or "Equal".
4. Add up the following sequence of numbers using a **for**-loop: 3, 9, 15, 21 … 63. That is, start with 3 and increase the value by 6 each time. Stop with any value larger than 63 (but be sure to include 63 in the computation).
5. Repeat the previous exercise with a **while**-loop.
6. Write a loop that requires the user to enter any valid numeric value into a **prompt()** box. As long as no value is given or a non-numeric value is given, ask again. As soon as a numeric value is given, stop the loop and display the value entered using **alert()**. Use a **while**-loop.
7. Repeat the previous exercise using a **do-while**-loop.
8. Write a loop that adds up the numbers from 1 to 75, inclusive. Write it first using a **for**-loop, then with a **while**-loop, and finally with a **do-while**-loop.
9. Write a loop that forces the user to input a numeric value between −5 and 11. Code it with both a **while**-loop and a **do-while**-loop.
10. Write a program that generates a temperature conversion table with two columns: Fahrenheit and Celsius. Start with 0 degrees Fahrenheit, then show 5 degrees, then 10, all the way to 100 degrees. The top part of the table is shown at the right. Be sure to right-align the numbers and show the Celsius temperatures rounded to only 1 decimal place.

F	C
0	-17.8
5	-15.0
10	-12.2
15	-9.4

CHAPTER 7 – FUNCTIONS

A function is a named group of JavaScript statements that can be used over and over by another piece of JavaScript, and a good way to describe their use is that they are tools in your toolkit, to be used when needed (like the library functions you have already seen, such as `alert()`, `prompt()`, and `confirm()`). Think of a function as a black box, one that performs some kind of action or task and generates some type of output. This output might be something displayed on the screen, like the library functions `alert()` and `document.write()`; alternately, the output might be a value returned from a computation, as in the Math library square root program `Math.sqrt()` described below. (A partial list of JavaScript functions is given in Table 18.)

> **Function**
>
> A function is a named group of JavaScript statements that can be referenced and used by that name. Functions simplify code since they can be used again and again.

The key point is that functions perform tasks that are needed in other places. For example, when you click a button, you expect something to happen; that is, there is some action that occurs and some JavaScript that is executed when the button is clicked. JavaScript like this is placed in functions, so that when buttons are clicked these functions are used. Buttons – and writing functions that process events from those buttons – are described in chapter 8 (Web Forms).

Value of Functions

Functions can save you a lot of work when creating a program. Repetitive steps are placed in a function and do need to be reproduced every time you use the function. For example, consider the code for the function shown in Figure 83. This function computes the trigonometric sine value for an angle given in radians. If you did not have a function to make this computation, you would have to reproduce the code shown below every time you wanted to find the sine of an angle. In other words, you would have to copy the 40 lines of code in the function over and over again and just change the numbers.

Note that the function in Figure 83 is probably more complex than any you will ever need to create. The complexity is used here to show the value of functions for repetitive tasks. In actuality, you would not have to create this function anyway, because it is available to you in the Math library (see Math Library below).

Functions also have an advantage in that they can be copied from program to program. For example, once you have verified the accuracy of a sine function, you can use it again later without having to retest it. In fact, many developers place sets of commonly used functions into an external JavaScript file so that those functions can be shared by multiple pages.

```html
<html>
<head>
    <title>Example Trig Function</title>
    <script type="text/javascript">
      // **   Computes sine of x, where x is a value in radians, by
      //    Taylor series: x - x^3/3! + x^5/5! - x^7/7! . . .
      //      Convergence uses the ratio of the absolute change from the
      //    current value to the previous value divided by the previous
      //    value. This speeds convergence (because of truncation errors).

      var maxError = 1.0E-20; // Stop computing test value

      function sin(x) {
        var xPow = x * x * x;
        var answer = x;
        var factorial = 2 * 3;
        var index = 3;
        var i = 1;
        var err = 1;      // Absolute fraction of change previous to current
        var last = x;     // Last value computed; assume x
        do {
          // Compute new value
          var value = xPow / factorial;
          if ((i % 2) === 1)    // Check term number for add or subtract
            answer = answer - value;
          else
            answer = answer + value;

          // Compute convergence error; save last
          // Error is absolute fraction of changed current value to last
          var err = Math.abs((last - answer) / last);
          last = answer;

          // Compute next factorial and power by multiplying twice
          index = index + 1;
          factorial = factorial * index;
          index = index + 1;
          factorial = factorial * index;
          xPow = xPow * (x * x);
          i = i + 1;
        } while (err > maxError)
        document.write("Converged in " + (i - 1) + " loops.");
        return answer;
      }
    </script>
</head>
<body>
  <script type="text/javascript">
    // Compute sine of x using Math library and local function
    // and show the results and the difference
    var angle = prompt("Angle as fraction of PI (eg: 45 deg. = 0.25)", "");
    angle = parseFloat(angle);
    if (!isNaN(angle))
    {
      var x = Math.sin(angle * Math.PI);
      var y = sin(angle * Math.PI);
      var z = Math.abs(x - y);
      alert("x: " + x + "; y: " + y + "; Difference: " + z);
    }
  </script>
</body>
</html>
```

Figure 83. Computing sine of an angle in radians

Function Syntax

The syntax of a function statement is shown below. A function starts with the **function** keyword, followed by the name of the function and then a matching set of parentheses that may or may not contain a list of parameters. This is followed by a block statement, consisting of the opening brace, one or more statements, and the closing brace.

```
function <Function Name> (<Parameters (optional)>)
{
        <statement>;
        <statement>;
        . . . .
        return;            <Return (optional)>
}
```

<Function Name>   This is a valid JavaScript name that you choose for your function. As a JavaScript name, it should meet the syntax and style requirements for names (start with a lowercase letter, etc. as described in chapter 5). Also, since functions perform actions, use a name that connotes action and contains a verb. For example, **getInput()**, **compute()**, **showArea()**, **initializePage()**, etc.

<Parameters (optional)>   This is a list of variable names that are parameters for the function. (Parameters are described below.) Any number of parameters can be used, including none.

<Return (optional)>   Some functions return a value, and if so, the **return** statement is required. Otherwise, the **return** statement is optional. (Return values are also described below.)

Standard Script Functions

As mentioned previously, you have already used several functions (**prompt()**, **alert()**, etc.) in working the various exercises. These functions were planned by the designers of the language and included in the JavaScript standard that is implemented by the various browsers. A partial list of these included functions is given for your convenience in Table 18.

Script Functions	
Function	**Description and Usage**
`alert(<message>);`	Displays a dialog box with <message>. Note that HTML included in the `alert()` function parameter will not be displayed properly in the popup box. Instead, the HTML will be displayed exactly as it appears in the parameter. Note also that a complex alert message can be created by appending variables and strings, as shown below: `alert("Circle of radius " + radius + " has area " + area);`

`confirm(<message>);`	Displays yes/no box. Returns `true` if Yes is clicked and `false` if No is clicked. This function would normally be used inside an `if`-statement, as in the following:
	`var taxTotal = 29.3;`
	`if (confirm("Show Tax Totals?"))`
	   `document.write("Total Taxes:" + taxTotal);`
	A dialog box is shown that has the message `"Show Tax Totals?"`, along with the two buttons OK and Cancel. If the user clicks OK, the screen will include the line for total taxes. If the user clicks Cancel, that line will not appear (try it).

`prompt:`
`var xxx =`
  `prompt(<prompt>,`
  `<default value>);`
	Displays a dialog box with the text of <prompt> and an input field with the given <default value>, and returns the value typed by the user. To leave the default value blank, set it to the empty string (" "):
	  `var radius = prompt("Enter radius: ", "");`
	  `var cent = prompt("Enter Celsius temperature: ", "100");`

`parseInt(<number>);`	Converts a string variable to an integer.
`parseFloat(<number>);`	Converts a string variable to a floating-point number.
`isNaN(<number>);`	Determines whether or not a variable is a valid number. Returns `true` or `false`; if it returns `true`, then what is there is not a number! Use this in your code to make sure the user gives you a valid number in a text box.
`document.write(<message>);`	Writes the message to the page. HTML and complex content can be included by appending text.
`varName.toFixed(<number>);`	Takes a numeric value in the named variable (`varName`) and creates a new string with the value of the number, but with only the specified <number> of digits to the right of the decimal.

Table 18. Script functions

Math Library

In addition to the library functions shown in Table 18, JavaScript includes a complete toolkit of mathematical functions and constants. These are given in Table 19. These functions are packaged in what is called the *Math* library, so to use these functions, type the name `Math` followed by a period and then the name of the function or property.

> **Constants**
>
> Constants are values used in expressions that cannot be changed. Some constants are global in nature, like π, while others might be application-specific, like the tax rate for a given state.

The constants are given in the top half of the table and the functions in the bottom half. Note that the constants are written in all uppercase letters, which follows a popular computer science convention for how names for constants are chosen. "Constant," by the way, means that the value cannot be changed, so if you tried to execute the following line of code, you would find the value of `PI` unchanged. In most languages, the first statement would cause the program to terminate, but in JavaScript, it is just ignored.

```
Math.PI = 5;        // Changes to constants are ignored by JavaScript
```

The second part of the table is a list of functions in the Math library. Most of these functions take just one parameter, while others take two and still others take a varying number of parameters.

Math Library Constants and Functions	
Constant	**Description**
`E`	Euler's Constant, the base for natural logarithms (ln) accurate to 17 digits
`LN2`	Returns the natural logarithm of 2 accurate to 17 digits
`LN10`	Returns the natural logarithm of 10 accurate to 17 digits
`LOG2E`	Returns the base 2 logarithm of E accurate to 17 digits
`LOG10E`	Returns the base 10 logarithm of E accurate to 17 digits
`PI`	Constant for π accurate to 17 digits
`SQRT1_2`	Returns the square root of ½ accurate to 17 digits
`SQRT2`	Returns the square root of 2 accurate to 17 digits
Method	**Description**
`abs(x)`	Returns the absolute value of x
`acos(x)`	Returns the arccosine of x, in radians
`asin(x)`	Returns the arcsine of x, in radians
`atan(x)`	Returns the arctangent of x as a numeric value between -PI/2 and PI/2 radians
`atan2(y,x)`	Returns the arctangent of the quotient of its arguments
`ceil(x)`	Rounds up to the nearest integer
`cos(x)`	Returns the cosine of x with x specified in radians
`exp(x)`	Returns the value of E to the x power
`floor(x)`	Rounds down to the nearest integer
`log(x)`	Returns the natural logarithm (base E) of x
`max(x,y,z,...,n)`	Returns the largest number in the values given
`min(x,y,z,...,n)`	Returns the smallest number in the values given
`pow(x,y)`	Returns the value of x raised to the power of y
`random()`	Returns a random number between 0 and 1
`round(x)`	Rounds off x to the nearest integer value (up if decimal part ≥ 0.5, down otherwise; note that this is reversed for negative values)
`sin(x)`	Returns the sine of x, with x specified in radians
`sqrt(x)`	Returns the square root of x
`tan(x)`	Returns the tangent of an angle, with x specified in radians

Table 19. Math object members

Now let's take a look at some user-defined functions. In the first example in Figure 84, a function is created that calculates the area of a circle from the radius passed in as a parameter. It uses a 17-digit, high-precision value for π (`Math.PI`) along with the power function (`Math.pow()`) to compute the area. In the second example, a function is defined for computing the distance between two Cartesian coordinates, which uses the square root function (`Math.sqrt()`).

```
function areaCircle(radius)
{
   var area = Math.PI * Math.pow(radius, 2);
   return area;       // The area is returned
}

function distance(x1, y1, x2, y2)
{
   var sum = ((x2 - x1) * (x2 - x1)) + ((y2 - y1) * (y2 - y1));
   var d = Math.sqrt(sum);
   return d;          // The distance is returned
}
```

Figure 84. Example use of Math library

Defining Your Own Functions

As you can see, a function specification begins with the `function` keyword, followed by a valid name and an open parenthesis. This is followed by optional parameters (which will be discussed in more detail below) and a closing parenthesis. By convention, all JavaScript functions are placed in a script block located in the `<head>` section of the HTML page. Functions located in the `<head>` section can be used by JavaScript located in either the `<head>` or the `<body>` section of the page.

Figure 85 shows a variation of our first JavaScript program (Figure 61). The left side reproduces the original program, and the right side is the variation that uses a function. Both versions perform exactly the same and show the same sentence "Congratulations!" in an alert box. The only difference is that the actual call to `alert()` has been moved into a function in the second example.

```
<!-- FirstJavaScript.html -->
<html>
  <head>
     <title>My First JavaScript</title>
  </head>
  <body>
    <script type="text/javascript">
     alert("Congratulations!");
    </script>
  </body>
</html>
```

```
<!-- FirstFunction.html -->
<html>
  <head>
    <title>My First Function</title>
    <script type="text/javascript">
      function congratulate()
      {
         alert("Congratulations!");
      }
    </script>
  </head>
  <body>
    <script type="text/javascript">
      congratulate();
    </script>
  </body>
</html>
```

Figure 85. First JavaScript function

There are several things to note as you compare the two sides of the figure. For one, the program has become slightly more complicated. For example, there are now two separate script blocks, where before only one was needed. This is because this simple function was chosen to show how to create functions, and not as an example of how to write such a simple program. In a real-world situation, the function would usually be much more complicated, like the code for computing the sine of an angle expressed in radians as shown in Figure 83. As you look at Figure 83, imagine having to type in that code every time you wanted to compute the sine of an angle. Instead, in the real world you would just use the function as often as needed.

Other notable things about this function:

1. The function is defined in a script block in the `<head>` section. This declaration includes the `function` keyword, the name of the function (`congratulate()`), an opening brace, the `alert()` call, and the closing brace.
2. The function is referenced in a script block in the `<body>` section by using the function name (`congratulate();`), but this time with the semicolon.
3. Pay close attention to the syntax of the function definition. Although most JavaScript statements end in semicolons, this function has only one semicolon, after the `alert()` call. However, when the function is referenced in the `<body>` script, the semicolon is used for the function call.
4. The name of the function is a verb ("congratulate"). Since functions perform some type of action, a verb is usually part of the name. For example: `compute()`, `showResults()`, `getInput()`, `validate()`, etc.

Function Parameters and Static Variables (Shared Data)

Sometimes functions require additional information to perform their computations. For example, if you wanted to compute the trigonometric sine function of an angle, you would have to give that function the angle before it could do the computations.

Additional information is given to functions in the form of "parameters." Parameters are variable names included between the parentheses of the function specification. Note in Figure 83 how the parameter x is included in the function definition (`function sin(x)`). Then, whenever the function is used, you just change the value of the parameter and a different, corresponding value is computed.

The first function covered in this section (Figure 85) used no parameters. The sine function (Figure 83) used one parameter. The choice to add parameters is made based on the number of different pieces of information the function requires to accomplish its work. As in our first example, many functions require no parameters. For example, functions called on a mouse click or other events seldom need any parameters, because the function will usually fetch any needed information from input fields on a form.

Other functions might need several parameters. For example, consider a function that computes the area of a trapezoid. The area of a trapezoid is the height times the average length of the bases. Thus, the function would need three parameters: one for the height and two for the length of both bases (see figures below). In this case, the function declaration might be like the one in Figure 86.

```
<script type="text/javascript">
  function areaTrap(height, base1, base2)
  {
    var a = (1.0 / 2.0) * height * (base1 + base2);
    return a;
  }
</script>
```

Figure 86. Trapezoid area function declaration

As seen in the example, the list of parameters is just a list of variable names separated by commas. However, the names of the variables are chosen to clearly describe their uses in the function (**height**, **base1**, etc.). The values of these variables (parameters) are initialized when the function is called. For example, say the area of a trapezoid is needed with a height of 11, base 1 of 13, and base 2 of 5. The area function could then be used as follows.

```
<script type="text/javascript">
  // Call function with values
  var area = areaTrap(11, 13, 5)
  document.write("A trapezoid with height 11 and bases of " +
      "13 and 5 has an area of " + area + "<br />");

  // Call function with variables
  var ht = 8;
  var b1 = 4;
  var b2 = 6;
  area = areaTrap(ht, b1, b2)
  document.write("A trapezoid with height " + ht + " and bases of " +
      b1 + " and " + b2 + " has an area of " + area + "<br />");
</script>
```

Figure 87. Trapezoid area function references

Compare the function declaration of Figure 86 to the function references in Figure 87. Since the **height** is the first parameter, 11 is the first value in the parentheses. This is then followed by the values for **base1** and for **base2**. Then, when the function begins processing, the variable names specified in the declaration have the corresponding values that were specified when the function was called.

> **Function Parameters**
>
> Function parameters are variable names separated by commas inside the parentheses of the function declaration. When the function is used, values for each of them must be specified in the same order in which they were defined. In other words, the parameter order in the usage must match the parameter order in the declaration.

JavaScript allows parameters for a function to be values, variables, or even mathematical expressions. In the first use of the function, just numbers are passed, but in the second example, variables are first declared and then passed. Under the hood, JavaScript will take the values used in the reference to the function, create the corresponding variables with the names given in the function definition, and then insert values into them. This is all done before the first line of the script is executed within the function. In the first example, where 11, 13, and 5 are passed as values to **areaTrap()**, the result is the same as if the function had had three variable declarations placed before the computation of the area. It is as if the code for the first case were as follows:

```
var height = 11;  // Equivalent definition of first parameter
var base1  = 13;  // Equivalent definition of second parameter
var base2  =  5;  // Equivalent definition of third parameter
var area = (1.0 / 2.0) * height * (base1 + base2);
return area;
```

In the second case, when the function was called with variables, JavaScript would have opened each of the variables in the call (`area = areaTrap(ht, b1, b2)`) and obtained the values in them (8, 4, and 6 respectively). Then JavaScript would define new variables inside `areaTrap()` for `height`, `base1`, and `base2`, with the same corresponding values. The result is that during the execution of the function there will be two locations in memory for storing the value for height (`ht` in the `<body>` JavaScript, and `height` in the `areaTrap()` function).

In summary, function parameters can be thought of not only as variables defined inside the function, but as variables that take on the values passed when the function is called. The important thing to remember is that the parameters are given values in the order they are defined.

Function Return Values

Functions often return values as well (see example below). If the function does not return a value, no `return` statement is needed. For example, the function called by a button usually has no `return` statement (see chapter 8). However, consider the following example taken from Figure 86:

```
function areaTrap(height, base1, base2)
{
  var a = (1.0 / 2.0) * height * (base1 + base2);
  return a;
}
```

The above function is passed in three variables (`height`, `base1`, and `base2`). From that, an area will be computed, after which the computed value will be sent back to the requesting script in the `<body>` section using the `return` keyword. Then the value of the function is placed in the variable `area` in this line:

```
var area = areaTrap(11, 13, 5)
```

Scope of Variables (Persistence)

When a variable is defined inside a function by using the `var` statement or by defining parameters, those variables are visible only to the function itself and to no other piece of JavaScript. Furthermore, the same variable *name* might be used in other functions or JavaScript blocks outside that function, but these names would still refer to different locations in memory. Since a function's variables are visible only to it, it does not matter if variable names used *outside* the function might duplicate variable names *inside* the function.

The memory used to store data for variables inside a function is allocated when the function is called and then released back to the memory "pool" when the function exits. This means that the variable `area` in `areaTrap()` will be undefined each time the function is called until the function is initialized (that is, before the function is actually run each time). In other words, the variable `area` does not retain any information once the function completes. In computer science phraseology, we say that `area` does not *persist* between executions of the function.

Static (Persisted) Variables

Since variables defined in a function do not persist after the function is complete, the question arises as to how or where data can be stored that can be referenced from one function execution to another. A related question is how or where data would be stored that could be shared by multiple functions and remain in memory until the page is closed.

The answer to both of these questions is the same: define variables outside any function in the JavaScript block that is located in the `<head>` section of the page. Variables defined here are often called *page variables*. As an example, say that a JavaScript application needs to ask the user for their name, and then that name needs to be used in different functions or by other script blocks. In Figure 88, a function, **getUserName()**, is defined that asks the user for their name (using the `prompt()` function) and then stores the returned name in the variable **curUserName**. This function would be called once to get the user name; then, when the name is needed anywhere else – as in **showUser()** – the variable **curUserName** is used rather than having to call the function again or request the information again from the user. Event handlers frequently use this capability and are described briefly below (and covered in detail in the next chapter).

```
<html>
  <head>
    <title>Persisted Variables</title>
    <script type="text/javascript">
      var curUserName;     // Name of current user
      function getUserName()
      {
        curUserName = prompt("Enter user name", "");
      }
      function showUser()
      {
        alert("Current user is " + curUserName);
      }
    </script>
  </head>
  <body>
    <script type="text/javascript">
      getUserName();   // Get current user
      showUser();      // Show that stored name
    </script>
  </body>
</html>
```

Figure 88. Example of persisted data

However, using a global variable such as this can cause another problem, a problem called *variable masking*. This happens when a function defines a local variable with the exact same name as a global variable. In this case, the global variable is masked (hidden) and changes would be made to the local variable with that name in the function instead. Consider this script block placed in the body shown in Figure 89.

```
<script type="text/javascript">
  var temp = 212; // Fahrenheit temperature
  function resetTemp()
  {
    var temp        // Local variable with same name
    temp = 32;      // Change variable with name "temp"
    alert("Temp inside reset: " + temp);
  }
  resetTemp();      // Call function to reset the temp
  alert("Temp after reset: " + temp);
</script>
```

Figure 89. Masking global variables

A global variable `temp` is defined as a global variable with a value of 212. Then the function `resetTemp` is called, which defines a local variable `temp` and sets its value to 32. The `alert()` inside the function shows a value of 32, while the `alert()` after the function call shows the original variable value of 212. Here, the locally defined variable `temp` hid the global variable of the same name.

Although the local variable in the above example hid the global variable, that global variable can still be accessed by using the global `window` object, as shown in Figure 90.

```
<script type="text/javascript">
  var temp = 212; // Fahrenheit temperature
  function resetTemp()
  {
    var temp;         // Local variable with same name
    temp = 32;        // Change variable with name "temp"
    window.temp = 0;  // Change global with name "temp"
    alert("Temp inside reset: " + temp);
  }
  resetTemp();        // Call function to reset the temp
  alert("Temp after reset: " + temp);
</script>
```

Figure 90. Accessing global variables masked by a local variable

In this case, the local variable `temp` is set to 32, and the global variable is set to 0 by using the global `window` object (`window.temp`). You can always use this object to access any global variables you have defined. This is all well and good for this example, but using local and global variables with the same name can make your code confusing and hard to read. For this reason, you should usually not use the same name for both global and local variables.

Functions as Event Handlers

Functions can also be used to handle actions at the computer. For example, a function is usually used to respond to a button click. Functions used in this way are, like all functions, defined in the `<head>` section of the document. This will be covered in more detail in the next chapter.

Other Examples of Function Definitions

The following examples illustrate other types of functions: some that take no parameters, others that take one, and one that takes three.

```
// Convert Fahrenheit to Celsius
function fToC(f)
{
    var c = (5.0/9.0)*(f - 32);
    var answer = "<h2>"+ f + "F = " + c + "C</h2>";
    document.write(answer);
}
// Convert Celsius to Fahrenheit
function cToF(c)
{
    var f = (9.0/5.0)*c + 32;
    var answer = "<h2>" + c + "C = " + f +"F</h2>";
    document.write(answer);
}
// Compute Area of a Trapezoid
function areaTrap(h, b1, b2)
{
    var area = (1.0 / 2.0) * h * (b1 + b2);
    return area;
}
```

```
// Page Load Event Handler
function pageLoad()
{
    // Position cursor on first name
    form1.txtFirst.focus();
}
// Hello Button Event Handler
function hello()
{
    // Fetch user input
    var first = form1.txtFirst.value;
    var last = form1.txtLast.value;
    alert("Hello " + first + " " + last);
}
```

The High-Low Game Example

The example for this section is the high-low guessing game. This section ties together material from this chapter and chapters 5 and 6 by combining functions with loops and **if**-tests. In this game, the computer picks a number between 1 and 10 and asks you to guess the number. If your guess is larger than the picked number, the computer responds with the message "High". If your guess is smaller than the picked number, the computer responds with "Low". If your guess is correct, the computer tells you that you won and how many guesses it took you to find the number. The complete code is shown below and will be discussed in the following paragraphs.

```
<html>
  <head>
    <title>While Loop to Fetch Valid Input</title>
    <script type="text/javascript">
      // ** Generates random integer between min and max, inclusive
      function randomInt(min, max)
      {
        return Math.floor(Math.random() * (max - min + 1)) + min;
      }

      // ** Fetches a number from the user between min and max, inclusive
      function getNum(min, max)
      {
        var message = "Enter a value between " + min + " and " + max;
        var num = prompt(message, "");
        num = parseInt(num);
        while (isNaN(num) || num < min || num > max) {
          num = prompt("Incorrect. " + message, "");
          num = parseInt(num);
        }
        return num;
      }

      // ** Plays one single game of High-Low
      function playOnce()
      {
        var answer = randomInt(1, 10); // The value to be guessed
        var guess = getNum(1, 10);     // This is their guess
        var count = 1;
        while (guess !== answer)        // Loop until they guess correctly
        {
          if (guess < answer)           // If low, say so
            alert("Low");
          else                          // If high, say so
            alert("High");
          guess = getNum();             // Get next guess
          count = count + 1;
        }
        alert("You won in " + count + " tries.");
      }
    </script>
  </head>
  <body>
    <script type="text/javascript">
      playOnce();
    </script>
  </body>
</html>
```

Figure 91. High/low game

Generating Random Numbers with `randomInt(min, max)`

The `Math.random()` function generates a random fractional value greater than or equal to 0 but less than 1. The `randomInt(min, max)` function uses `Math.random()` to generate a random integer between the `min` and `max` parameters, by multiplying the output from `Math.random()` by max - min + 1 (in other words, the range between min and max plus 1). The fractional part of this number is discarded by rounding down using the `Math.floor()` function, which results in an integer between 0 and 9. Finally, the `min` value is added (1 in this case), resulting in a value between 1 and 10 *inclusive* (that is, including the end points). The final value is returned at the end of the function.

Fetching User Input: `getNum(min, max)`

The `getNum(min, max)` function requests the user to input a value between the min and max parameters, inclusive. The code for `getNum(min, max)` in Figure 91 mirrors the code shown in the previous chapter in Figure 79, except that the loop has been moved to a function so the user can be prompted for different ranges of values. Instead of just requesting an exact range from the user, the prompt uses the input parameters given to the function. Also, the `while`-loop continuation test uses `min` and `max` as well, instead of hard-coding the numbers 1 and 10 as in Figure 79. Finally, the validated value is returned to the calling script.

Playing the Game: `playOnce()`

The `playOnce()` function is the heart of the game. It starts by generating the random number using the `randomInt()` function and storing that value in the variable `answer`. Next, it requests a value from the user by using the `getNum()` function and stores that value in the variable `guess`. The final step of initialization is to define a `count` variable and set it equal to 1. After initialization, it starts a `while`-loop that continues as long as the user's guess is not equal to the answer, and inside this loop `if`-statements are used to generate the proper message to the user. Note, however, that the continuation test on the loop guarantees that the answer is incorrect inside the loop (since if it were correct the loop would have been exited). Therefore, inside the loop only one test is made for a low value, because if the answer is wrong and it is not low, then it must be high. Once the proper message is shown inside the loop, the `count` variable is incremented, and once the loop completes, the user has correctly guessed the random integer and the count is shown.

Summary

Study the example carefully and try to reproduce it without looking at the solution. This will help firm up your understanding of both loops and `if`-statements. As a final exercise, change the range of values for the game (like 1 to 100) and try to play it.

Review Questions

1. What is the purpose of a user function? Where are they most frequently used?
2. Describe the advantages of using functions.
3. What is the Math library? List some of the functions and constants contained in that library.
4. Give examples of functions supplied with JavaScript that you have already been using.
5. In what part of the HTML page are user functions normally placed?
6. What Math library function is used to round off a number? To take the square root of a number?
7. How is a function used once it has been defined? (See Figure 85 for an example.)
8. Write just the function specification (first line of the function) for a function named `rectangleArea()` that takes two parameters: `length` and `width`.
9. Write just the function specification for a function named `areaTriangle()` that takes three parameters: the three lengths of the sides (`a`, `b`, and `c`). Do not write the function, just the function declaration (first line of the function).
10. What function in the Math library is used to generate random numbers? How is it used?
11. What are function parameters? How are they used?
12. When is the `return` statement needed?
13. If a function defines a variable, how long is that variable available (i.e. how long does it persist)?
14. What are *static* (or *persisted*) variables and why are they needed?

Exercises

For these exercises, refer to Figure 86 and Figure 87 for help, which illustrate the computation of the area of a trapezoid.

1. In the `<body>` section of the page, write a script block to prompt the user for the radius of a sphere and store that value in a variable. Then create a function called `volumeSphere()` in the `<head>` section that has one input parameter (`radius`) and computes the volume and returns it. In the `<body>` script, display the returned volume using the `alert()` function. (For reference, the formula for a sphere's volume is $v = (4/3) \cdot \pi \cdot r^3$.)
2. In the `<body>` section of the page, write a script block to prompt the user for the length, width, and height of a box and store those values in variables. Then create a function called `volumeBox()` in the `<head>` section that has three input parameters – `length`, `width`, and `height` – and computes the volume and returns it. In the `<body>` script, display the returned area using the `alert()` function.
3. Write a piece of JavaScript that creates a random integer between -10 and 10, inclusive. Do not use the `randomInt()` function given in Figure 91. Instead, write your own code to generate the number. Test your answer.
4. Modify the High/Low game in Figure 91 so that, after a win, it will ask the user if they want to play again using a prompt that looks something like the following:

   ```
   Play again (Y/N)?
   ┌─────────────┐
   │             │
   └─────────────┘
   ```

   If the user types either an uppercase or lowercase letter "Y", restart the game. Otherwise, end the game. Hints:
   - Use a `do-while`-loop that surrounds the entire game and place that code in a function called `play()`. Call `play()` on the body load event.
   - After the end of the game and at the end of the loop, prompt for the play-again variable. Convert the variable to uppercase and compare it to an uppercase "Y".
5. Create a dice-rolling program that simulates the casino game where 2 dice are rolled and you total the number of spots on both dice. The rules of the game are as follows:
   - If you throw a total of 7 or 11 on your *first* throw, you win.
   - If you throw a total of 2 ("snake eyes") or 12 ("box cars") on your *first* throw, you lose.
   - If you roll any other total, that total becomes your "point" and you continue to roll.
     - If you roll 7 or 11 now, you lose.
     - If you roll the same total as your "point," you win.

   Write a function called `roll()` that generates and returns a random integer from 1 to 6. (This represents the number of spots visible on 1 die.) Then write a function called `rollTwo()` that calls `roll()` twice and adds the results together, which is then returned as the value of `rollTwo()`. Next, write the main game function and call it `playDice()`. This function will enforce the rules of the game, list each roll, and also display the final result of the game. It will first call `rollTwo()` to get a total and test it for a win or a loss; if not a win or loss, it should go into a loop that repeatedly calls `rollTwo()` until there is either a win (match "point") or a loss (7 or 11). For output, use `document.write()` to show the results of each roll. (You can do this in `rollTwo()`.) Then state the win or loss result at the end.
6. Modify the game in exercise 5 by asking the user if he or she wants to play again at the end of the game (see exercise 4). If they keep playing, keep track of the wins and losses and show a total when they eventually say "no" to the "play again?" question.

CHAPTER 8 – FORMS AND ACCESSING HTML ATTRIBUTES

Defining the Form

A form should be defined in the `<body>` section of an HTML page using the `<form>` and `</form>` tags. Some HTML editors like Visual Studio will fuss if you do not specify an *action* attribute, as shown below; however, this attribute is not needed until you are writing server-side code. One more thing: since the direct addressing technique described below requires it, specify an *id* property for the form as well.

```
<form id="form1" action="">        <!--Action is optional-->
```

Inside the form element you will add input controls and other HTML statements, using styles to achieve an attractive format. Frequently you will also use a `<table>` element to align input controls with their labels. Some of the controls that you might use are listed in Table 21 and Table 22.

Form Controls

HTML includes a variety of input controls that can be added within the `<form>` element. The specification for each control should include an `id="..."`, where the value inside quotes is the name of the control. This name should be a valid JavaScript name, starting with the type of the control followed by the rest of the control, as shown in the "Label Prefix" column of Table 21 and Table 22. Some examples: `txtFahr` – Fahrenheit conversion text box; `chkEmployed` – checkbox for employment status; etc.

Events

An "event" in the web world means that an external action has occurred at the computer that may require attention by the computer. This action may be in the form of input from the user, like a mouse or keyboard operation; alternately, it may be the completion of some process previously initiated by the computer or the user (like a reply from a web service, expiration of a timer, or the loading of the page).

All events arriving at the browser are "handled," if not in code included in the web page, then by the browser itself. If no code is specifically written to do something with ("handle") the event, the browser will normally take no action, thus discarding the event. For example, if you click in the open space of the form, nothing usually happens visually even though an event has happened.

However, there are many times that the web page needs to handle an event, as when a button on the page is clicked. Adding code for events is the way the functionality of the page is extended and the user's experience is enhanced. Events thereby allow the page to display different information based on interaction and input from the user. This is what is meant by "dynamic HTML."

Some web events are shown in Table 20. However, there are many more kinds of events that can be handled than are in the table. Furthermore, some of the events in the table can be defined for many HTML elements; any HTML element can have an *onclick* event, for example.

Some Web Events		
Control	**Event**	**Usage**
`<body ...`	*onload*	Called when the page first loads and (in most browsers) when the page is refreshed.
`<input type="button" ...`	*onclick*	Calls a user function or library function when the button is clicked.
`<select ...`	*onchange*	Called when the user changes the currently selected entry of a list box.
`<input type="radio" ...` `<input type="checkbox" ...`	*onclick*	Called when the radio button or checkbox was clicked, implying the value will be changed. **NOTE:** The event handler function executes *before* the actual state of the **checked** property of the radio or checkbox is changed. For example, if the checkbox is unchecked when you click the box, the **checked** property will be **false** when tested in the event handler!

`<a>`
`<div>`
`<p>`
`<h1>`
etc.
 	
(Basically, most HTML elements)
	onclick	Any HTML element can have an **onclick** event. If it does, the function is called when anything inside that element is clicked. This allows any portion of the page to be a button of sorts.

	onmouseover	Script to run when the mouse is over an element. Use this to change the style of the element to highlight that the mouse has moved over the element.
	onmouseout	Script to run when mouse is no longer over an element. Use this to restore the style of the element back to what it was before the mouseover.

Table 20. Some web events

Event Handlers

Event handlers are user code – usually written in JavaScript – that take a specific action based on the type of the event and/or the contents of form controls (see Table 21 and Table 22). Since the JavaScript associated with event handlers is not used for formatting or content when the page is loaded, *the code for event handlers is usually placed in the `<head>` section.*

Event handlers are specified using JavaScript functions. The function's name is your choice, but it should relate to the event being handled. (Some developers include the name of the control generating the event and the type of event being handled, as shown in the examples below.) Whatever your naming style, your event handler function names should clearly indicate their usage.

```
function btnToCent_onclick()
function btnSendEmail_onclick()
function form_load()
```

Source: Centigrade button; **Event:** click
Source: email button; **Event:** click
Source: page; **Event:** load

Most event handler functions do not include parameters, but they certainly can include them. In fact, you can add parameters so that the same event handler could be used for multiple buttons. In that case, a parameter would be added to the function that would indicate the type of operation to be performed in the handler.

Here is an example of a button handler that does a Fahrenheit-to-Celsius conversion using an input value obtained from a text box. (The input value is validated first before the conversion.) In the example, a couple of functions are used that you have not seen before: **getElementById()** and **focus()**. These functions will be covered towards the end of the chapter. For now, note how a function is used for the button.

```
// Button handler: convert Fahrenheit to Celsius
function btnToCent_onclick()
{
  var txtFahr = document.getElementById("txtFahr");     // Shortcut to txtFahr
  var txtCent = document.getElementById("txtCent");     // Shortcut to txtCent
  var fahr = txtFahr.value;

  if (isNaN(fahr))
  {
    alert("Fahrenheit temperature is not a number");
    txtFahr.value = "";
    txtFahr.focus();
  }
  else
  {
    var fahr = txtFahr.value;
    var cent = (5.0/9.0)*(fahr - 32.0);
    txtCent.value = cent;
  }
}
```

Button Events

Although buttons will be covered in more detail later, note the HTML shown below to define a button. The button has an *id* of **"btnXXX"** and a label (*value*) on the button of **"Button Name"**. To define what to do on a click, the *onclick* attribute is defined with a value of **"btnXXX_onclick()"**. The key thing to note is the attribute that identifies the event handler. The attribute consists of the word *on* followed by the name of the event (*click*), or *onclick*. This attribute is then assigned a value, which is actually a miniature piece of JavaScript; in most cases, the piece of JavaScript is just the name of a function, followed by a pair of parentheses and a semicolon.

```
<input id="btnXXX" type="button" value="Button Name" onclick="btnXXX_onclick();" />
```

Load Event

You can do special processing when a form is first loaded, which is done by handling the *onLoad* event. Again, the attribute consists of the word *on* followed by the name of the event (*Load*). This event is captured by adding the *onLoad* attribute to the **<body>** tag, as shown below. In this code, **form_load()** is a JavaScript function in the **<head>** section of the HTML file.

```
<body style="text-align: center" onload="form_load();">
```

Use the load event to allocate or acquire resources for the form and to do any other one-time initializations of the page. This might include setting up a series of graphics for a portfolio viewer, connecting to a web service, etc.

			HTML Input Controls (1 of 2)
HTML Tag	Type (*type*)	Label Prefix	Usage and Notes
`<input>`	`button`	`btn`	A button used for action within the local browser. (That is, it executes JavaScript in the local page.) Buttons do not require an *id* property if the button attributes are not going to be changed by JavaScript. The *value* property of a button is the label on the button. Lastly, buttons will always have an *onclick* event. `<input type="button" value="Say Hello" onclick="hello();" />`

`<input>`	`text`	`txt`	A single-value text box. The most commonly referenced property of the text box in JavaScript is the *value* property, which is the content entered by the user into the text box. Note that, if you specify a *value* property in the HTML, that value will be displayed in the box when the form loads. Examples:
			`<input type="text" id="txtName" value="" />`
			`<input type="text" id="txtState" value="MI" />`
			
			To reference the content typed by the user, use the dot notation on the form ID, followed by the text box ID and the *value* property:
			`var name = form1.txtName.value;`
			`alert("Hello " + name);`

`<input>`	`checkbox`	`chk`	A checkbox that has two values (checked or not). To test for which value is there from within JavaScript, reference the **checked** property. The most commonly referenced property of the checkbox is its **checked** property, and it will usually be used inside an `if`-statement.
			`if (form1.chkDVD.checked)`
			`  document.write("DVD Chosen.");`

`<input>`	`radio`	`rad`	A "radio button" that is used to select one of a set of values. To make a set of radio buttons function as a set, set the **name** property to the same value on each button. Then check each button in an `if`-statement. Note that the first button is preselected.
			`<input type="radio" id="radS08" name="CPU" checked="checked" value="800 MHz" />`
			`<input type="radio" id="radS12" name="CPU" value="1.2 GHz" />`
			`<input type="radio" id="radS24" name="CPU" value="2.4 GHz" />`
			
			To test for which value is in any one of the buttons from within JavaScript, reference the **checked** property or pass a parameter to an *onclick* event handler that will handle the radio buttons.
			`function showSpeed()`
			`{`
			`  if      (form1.radS08.checked)`
			`    document.write("Speed = 800 MHz");`
			`  else if (form1.radS12.checked)`
			`    document.write("Speed = 1.2 GHz");`
			`  else    // Speed = 2.4 GHz`
			`    document.write("Speed = 2.4 GHz");`
			`}`

Table 21. HTML input controls (1 of 2)

HTML Input Controls (2 of 2)

HTML Tag	Type (*type*)	Label Prefix	Usage and Notes
`<select> </select>`		lst	Used for a list box. Items in the list are nested within the `<select>` element by using one or more `<option>` tags. Note that the *id* property for the list is set here and is not needed in the individual options.

`<option> </option>`			Used for list box options. Specify the return value for the selected item by setting the *value* property, and to mark the item as selected by default, set *selected*="selected".
			
			The example below shows how to access three significant properties of the list. The first item obtained in `showValues()` is the value of the list. Note that there is no *value* property on the `<select>` HTML element, but the value is specified on the `<option>` element and is the value of the selected item.
			
			The next item obtained is the index of the item selected. Note that this is a value from 0 to 1 less than the number of items in the list (as with most computer languages, items in HTML lists start numbering from 0).
			
			The last item obtained is the actual text given in the option (between `<option>` and `</option>`). The *value* property requires that you index into the list options to find the text using arrays (see chapter 9).
			
			Finally, note how the *onchange* property is used to show the values in the list. This event is not often used but would be used when you need to change something on the screen when they select a different option. (For example, you might reveal a different part of the screen.)
			
			``
			<script type="text/javascript" language="javascript">
			function showValues()
			{
			    var selValue = form1.lstSpeed.value;
			    var selIndex = form1.lstSpeed.selectedIndex;
			    var selText = form1.lstSpeed.options[selIndex].text;
			    document.write("Speed: " + form1.lstSpeed.value + "
			");
			    document.write("Index: " + selIndex + "
			");
			    document.write(" Text: " + selText + "
			");
			}
			</script>
			. . .
			<select id="lstSpeed" size="1" onchange="showValues();">>
			  <option value=".8" selected="selected">800 Khz</option>
			  <option value="1.8">1.8 MHz</option>
			  <option value="3.2">3.2 MHz</option>
			</select>
			
			<input type="button" value="Show Speed" onclick="showValues();" />
			``

Other HTML Input Commands Not Covered in This Text

HTML Tag	Type	Label Prefix	Usage and Notes
`<input>`	Reset	btn	A button used to automatically clear other controls on the form.
`<input>`	Submit	btn	A button used to submit all the data to the web server.
`<input>`	File	txt	An input text box for the user to type in a full pathname for a file, plus a "browse" button that will pop up a "Choose File" dialog to search for that file. The contents of the control are in the *value* property.
`<input>`	Password	txt	A single value text box that displays typed characters as asterisks or round dots. The contents of the control are returned in the *value* property.
`<input>`	Hidden	hid	This control is invisible on the form but can be used inside JavaScript or server code to store data for reuse between events or POSTings.
`<textarea> </textarea>`		tar	Set the number of columns and/or rows in the textarea by setting *cols*="..." or *rows*="...". This means that the control will display only *rows* lines of text, each line of which can contain only *cols* characters. The control can, however, contain a lot more data than that (which, to see all of it, must be scrolled through).

Table 22. HTML input controls (2 of 2)

Setting Tab Order on Input Controls

You can specify the order in which the tab key moves focus (selection) from input control to input control. Just set the *tabindex* HTML attribute on each input control to a numeric value (other than 0) and the focus will move in ascending order of *tabindex*. When the tab key is pressed in the control with the highest *tabindex*, focus then moves to input areas in the browser and eventually back to the control with the lowest-numbered *tabindex*.

Accessing Form Content

There are two ways that you can access HTML elements inside JavaScript. The first method uses input elements inside a `<form>` element, and the other one works from the *id* attribute and can be used with almost any type of element. Each of these will be covered in this section.

Accessing Input Controls with the "Dot" Notation

The XHTML standard is for all input controls to be nested inside a form element. By giving both the elements inside the form and the form itself separate *id* properties, you can use these *id* names to access the contents of the controls. The form is frequently given the name "form1," as in this example: `<form id="form1">`.

With this structure, you can directly access all the attributes of the controls using the names of the attributes. These attributes may be properties or functions. Here are a few examples of accessing various properties of a text box:

```
var a = form1.txtA.value;                    // (1) Grab the input value from A
form1.txtA.focus();                          // (2) Set focus to A (function call)
form1.txtA.style.backgroundColor = "pink";   // (3) Change background color on A
form1.txtA.className = "inBox";              // (4) Set the CSS class for A
form1.btnAdd.disabled = "disabled";          // (5) Disable the button
form1.btnAdd.title = "Click here to add.";   // (6) Change the popup on hover over button
form1.txtSum.readOnly =true;                 // (7) Make sum box read-only
```

Note that several properties of the **txtA** control are being accessed using their property names. On line (3) above, the background color style property of the text box is being changed (see "Accessing Style Attributes from within JavaScript" below for more details on changing style). This notation derives from the fact that both the form and the text box are what other languages call "objects" (see chapter 9). That is, they are complex things with multiple components. Components of **form1** are nested "things," which are the controls nested in the form, and components of **txtA** are either even smaller nested "things" (like the *value* and *style* properties) or actions, like the *focus()* method.

Figure 92 should help clarify the object structure. Consider the example of a simple adding machine form. The form has two input text boxes (**txtA** and **txtB**), one output box (**txtSum**), and one button (**btnAdd**). The form would then have four major components, one for each of the four controls. Each of the controls has a variety of properties, depending upon the type of control.

In the figure, only a few of the properties are being shown for each control. For example, buttons have an *onclick* property, which text boxes could have but probably would not. Buttons, on the other hand, would not have a *readonly* attribute because buttons do not contain modifiable content.

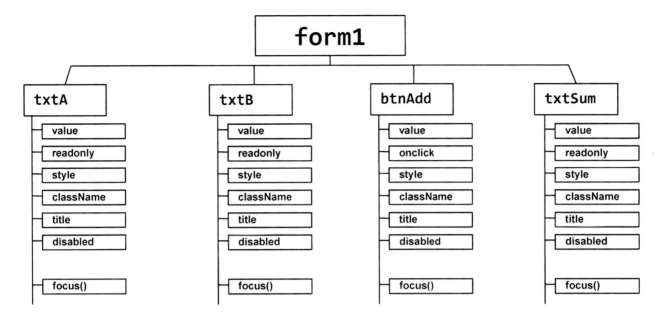

Figure 92. Sample form object structure

Buttons

Usually a JavaScript function is called when a button is clicked. (In fact, buttons will be the main tool for running the JavaScript examples in the remainder of this chapter.) A button is an area of the form that can be clicked to cause a response from the browser, typically signaled by a unique type of border and shading. Also, when the mouse is over a button the browser will typically change the shading on the button, although you can change this behavior if desired (using the *onmouseover* event).

The label on the button is defined by setting the *value* attribute equal to the label name. Since buttons are of no use unless they handle click events, all buttons will also have an *onclick* attribute set to a function name for processing the event. Note that the value of *onclick* should include the semicolon after the last parenthesis on the function call. In the example below, the label on the button is "Compute" and the function called is *compute()*.

```
<input type="button" value="Compute" onclick="compute();" />
```

Style attributes might be specified as well (*style* or *class*) when needed to achieve a desired visual effect. Also, you might include *onmouseover* and *onmouseout* if you wanted to change the appearance of the button when the mouse is over the button (see example in Figure 98).

Almost every HTML input control will have an *id* attribute, because you will need to access that control inside JavaScript for input or output. Buttons, however, are a little bit different in that clicking them causes immediate action. Therefore, the only time you will need an *id* attribute on a button is when you want to change something about the button in JavaScript, like the label on the button or the button's style.

Text Input and Output with a Form

In forms, there are two ways to offer the user a way to enter text or show him or her text output: (1) the input text box control, and (2) the text area control. The input text box uses the `<input type="text" . . .>` element and is useful for obtaining up to one line of input. If you need multiple lines of user input, then the `<textarea . . .>` element should be used. Each of these is covered in this section.

Text Box

Figure 93 is a copy of an example first shown in the introduction. It illustrates how to use a form to prompt for the radius of a circle, and from that radius, display the area of the circle. Two input text boxes are used, as shown at the right: one for the input radius (`"txtRadius"`) and one for the resulting area (`"txtArea"`). The single button on the page runs the `compute()` function that fetches the input radius, makes it a fractional number (`parseFloat()`), computes the area, and then returns the result to the form.

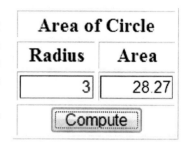

```html
<html>
    <head>
        <title>Area of a Circle Using a Form</title>
        <style type="text/css">
            .inBox
            {
                width:60;
                border-style:groove;
                border-width:1;
                border-color:green;
                text-align:right;
            }
        </style>
        <script type="text/javascript">
            function compute()
            {
                var radius = form1.txtRadius.value;     // Get input value from form
                radius = parseFloat(radius);            // Try to make it a number
                var area = Math.PI * radius * radius;   // Compute area
                form1.txtArea.value = area.toFixed(2);  // Display area with 2 decimal places
            }
        </script>
    </head>
    <body onload="form1.txtRadius.focus();">
        <form id="form1">
            <table border="1">
                <tr><th colspan="2">Area of Circle</th></tr>
                <tr><th>Radius</th><th>Area</th></tr>
                <tr>
                    <th><input type="text" class="inBox" id="txtRadius" /></th>
                    <th><input type="text" class="inBox" id="txtArea" readonly="readonly" /></th>
                </tr>
                <tr><th colspan="2">
                    <input type="button" value="Compute" onclick="compute();" /></th></tr>
            </table>
        </form>
    </body>
</html>
```

Figure 93. Circle area using a form

The key to using a text box for reading or writing is to reference its *value* attribute. Inside JavaScript, the *value* property of a text box is the contents of the text box as seen on the screen. If you want the text box to have content when the form is first displayed, then set the *value* attribute to the desired content within the HTML defining the text box. To read the contents of a text box, reference the *value* attribute in code. To write a result back to the form, simply modify the *value* property of the control (for example: form1.txtArea.value = area.toFixed(2);). One additional note is that the user cannot type in the text box **txtArea** because the read-only property is set (*readonly*="readonly").

Text Area

The <textarea> HTML element is used to fetch or display multiple lines of text from or to a form. The size of the <textarea> element is changed by setting the *rows* and *cols* attributes. Figure 94 creates a simple form with a <textarea> element and two buttons: the first button sets whatever text is in the box to all uppercase, and the second button clears the content.

As with the input box, the content of the text box is obtained in JavaScript by referencing the *value* attribute. However, if you want the <textarea> element to have content when the form is first displayed, place that content between the beginning and ending tags of the <textarea> element. Note, however, that any content between the opening and ending tags is included as-is. Unlike regular HTML, if you add spaces or indent the content that extra space will be included in the output (try it). For this reason, the quote in the example is left justified in the form, instead of being indented between the tags.

```
<html>
  <head>
    <title>Text Area Example</title>
    <script type="text/javascript">
      function setUpper() {
        form1.txtQuote.value = form1.txtQuote.value.toUpperCase();
        form1.txtQuote.focus();
      }
      function clearAll() {
        form1.txtQuote.value = "";
        form1.txtQuote.focus();
      }
    </script>
  </head>
  <body onload="form1.txtQuote.focus();">
    <div style="text-align:center">
      <h2>Example of Text Area Input</h2>
      <form id="form1" action="">
        <textarea rows="3" cols="30" id="txtQuote">
Four score and seven years ago our fathers brought forth on this continent,
a new nation, conceived in Liberty, and dedicated to the proposition that
all men are created equal.
        </textarea><br />
        <input type="button" value="Set Uppercase" onclick="setUpper();" /><br />
        <input type="button" value="Clear Content" onclick="clearAll();" />
      </form>
    </div>
  </body>
</html>
```

Figure 94. Text area example

Adding Options to a Form

There are three ways to offer a user a set of options on a form:

1. **Checkboxes:** Allow user to either accept or reject an option, by checking a box or not.
2. **Drop-Down Lists:** Allow user to pick one of several items in a list.
3. **Radio Buttons:** Allow user to pick one of several items by clicking the desired circle.

Checkboxes are always referenced using *if*-statements that will take one of two different paths through the code. Drop-down lists and radio buttons allow the user to select from multiple elements (two or more) and may or may not include several *if*-statements in the code.

These three different controls have to be handled somewhat differently in code. Checkboxes are the simplest in both HTML and in JavaScript; radio buttons require a fair amount of JavaScript to handle, but the HTML for them straightforward; and finally, drop-down lists take a fair amount of HTML to define, but have the simplest JavaScript. This section discusses when to use each of these controls and how to handle them in JavaScript.

Checkboxes

The primary attribute used on a checkbox is **checked**. If the box is **checked**, then in JavaScript the **checked** property is **true**, and if not **checked**, is **false**. The example below allows you to choose the extended warranty (or not). When the button is clicked, the **checked** property is tested and an appropriate alert shown.

```html
<html
  <head>
    <title>Checkbox Example</title>
    <script type="text/javascript">
      function displayChoice() {
        if (form1.chkWarranty.checked)
          alert("Extended warranty is selected.");
        else
          alert("Extended warranty is not selected.");
      }
    </script>
  </head>
  <body>
    <h1>Warranty Options</h1>
    <h2>Select Warranty or Not</h2>
    <form id="form1">
      <input type="checkbox" id="chkWarranty" />
        <strong>Include extended (70,000-mile) warranty?</strong><br />
      <input type="button" value="Display Choice" onclick="displayChoice();" />
    </form>
  </body>
</html>
```

Figure 95. Checkbox example

Drop-Down Lists

The drop-down list is the easier of the two ways to get multiple options from the user – from the standpoint of JavaScript, anyway – but the HTML is a bit detailed. First of all, there can be varying numbers of items in a list, so the HTML syntax needs a way to specify lists of varying lengths. This is accomplished by nesting two or more `<option>` elements inside the `<select>` element. Attributes of the list such as *style* and *id* are defined in the `<select>` element, and the specifics of each line in the list are defined with the `<option>` element.

Figure 96 illustrates a set of options for the engine of a Ford F150 pickup, taken from the Ford company site. The site lists three choices for the engine, but the list has four options; an extra option is added to the top of the list which instructs them to select an option. By using this "unselected" option, any JavaScript code can tell if a selection has not yet been made (`selectedIndex` of 0) and can ask the user to make a selection before continuing.

```
<!DOCTYPE html PUBLIC "-//W3C//DTD XHTML 1.0 Transitional//EN"
  "http://www.w3.org/TR/xhtml1/DTD/xhtml1-transitional.dtd">
<html xmlns="http://www.w3.org/1999/xhtml" >
  <head>
    <title>Radio Button Example</title>
    <script type="text/javascript">
      function displayChoice()
      {
        if (form1.lstEngine.selectedIndex === 0)
          alert("Engine has not yet been selected.");
        else
          alert("Engine: " + form1.lstEngine.value);
      }
    </script>
  </head>
  <body>
    <h1>Ford F150 Options <a href="http://www.ford.com/trucks/f150/trim/"
      style="font-size:medium; color:Blue;">(Ford site)</a></h1>
    <h2>Select Engine Type</h2>
    <form id="form1">
      <select id="lstEngine">
        <option value="Not SelectedL" selected="selected">Select engine below</option>
        <option value="3.5L">3.5L V6 EcoBoost™ Engine</option>
        <option value="3.7L">3.7L V6 FFV Engine</option>
        <option value="5.0L">5.0L V8 FFV Engine</option>
      </select><br />
      <input type="button" value="Display Choice" onclick="displayChoice();" />
    </form>
  </body>
</html>
```

Figure 96. Drop-down list example

Drop-down list options are added with the `<option>` element, as noted previously. The part that is displayed in the list is placed between the beginning and ending tags of the element, and in addition, a **value** attribute is included with `<option>`, so that when an option is selected that option's **value** attribute becomes the **value** attribute within JavaScript for the `<select>` element.

Note that the JavaScript **value** attribute is hidden from the user of the browser and is only available to JavaScript. This is handy because you can have a variety of things stored in the value that are not the same as the displayed text of the option.

In addition to the *value* attribute, the `<select>` element has an attribute called *selectedIndex* which is an index into the list of items. However, it is again important to note that, in the computer world, lists of items start with 0 and not 1. For example, the first option of four options would be numbered 0 and the last option of four options would be numbered 3 (for four values total of 0, 1, 2, and 3).

The *selectedIndex* attribute can be used for extra checks with `if`-statements and also for more advanced scripts. In the example, a *selectedIndex* of 0 means that the first element in the list has been selected. However, the first element in the list is not a real engine type but an instruction to select an engine. Therefore, when 0 is the index the user is instructed to select a real engine type before continuing. Otherwise, the engine type is shown in an alert box.

Radio Buttons

Radio buttons are individual controls that do not have any displayable text content, but instead are simply circles that can be clicked; it is up to the developer of the web page to add text to indicate the use for a radio button. If you study the form in Figure 97, you will note that each radio button is followed by a separate HTML `<strong>` element text item describing the button. Also note that none of the buttons are selected initially.

Defining Radio Buttons

Since a form could have multiple groups of radio buttons that need to operate as single groups, there must be some way to group each set of buttons so they will operate independently of other groups. (For example, if you go to the Ford website you will see that there are options for cab, box, and engine.) To group radio buttons, you set the *name* attribute on all buttons of a set to the same thing (for example: *name*=`"Engine"`). To create a set of radio buttons, define them together in the form with some label before or after them. An example is shown in Figure 97.

```html
<html>
  <head>
    <title>Radio Button Example</title>
    <script type="text/javascript">
      var engineIndex = 0;
      var engineType = "Not Selected";

      function setEngine(index, engine) {
        engineIndex = index;
        engineType = engine;
      }

      function displayChoice() {
        if (engineIndex === 0)
          alert("Engine has not yet been selected.");
        else
          alert("Engine: " + engineType);
      }
    </script>
  </head>
  <body>
    <h1>Ford F150 Options <a href="http://www.ford.com/trucks/f150/trim/"
      style="font-size:medium; color:Blue;">(Ford site)</a></h1>
    <h2>Select Engine Type</h2>
    <form id="form1">
      <input type="radio" name="Engine" onclick="setEngine(1, '3.5L');" />
        <strong>3.5L V6 EcoBoost™ Engine</strong><br />
      <input type="radio" name="Engine" onclick="setEngine(2, '3.7L');" />
        <strong>3.7L V6 FFV Engine</strong><br />
      <input type="radio" name="Engine" onclick="setEngine(3, '5.0L');" />
        <strong>5.0L V8 FFV Engine</strong><br /><br />
      <input type="button" value="Display Choice" onclick="displayChoice();" />
    </form>
  </body>
</html>
```

Figure 97. Radio button example

Referencing Radio Buttons in JavaScript

Unfortunately, radio buttons do not have *value* attributes, nor are there **selectedIndex** attributes for JavaScript to examine, so the difficulty here is determining which radio button is selected when the button is clicked. The simplest approach, as covered here, is to use parameters passed to a function when a radio button itself is clicked. The parameter passed will indicate the button clicked. Another way of handling radio buttons, using arrays, is given in chapter 9 (see Figure 111). In that example, all radio buttons having the same name are scanned to determine which button is selected.

The solution shown in Figure 97 uses the fact that, when you click a radio button to select it, it fires the click event. By adding a function to handle that event, information about the specific button is captured, and the information captured is passed as parameters to the function and subsequently stored in persistent variables. Note that the same function handles the event for all the buttons in the set. That function has two parameters and is defined as follows:

```
function setEngine(index, engine)
```

The **index** parameter is an integer value from 1 to the number of radio buttons, and the **engine** parameter is a text description of the engine that will be displayed when requested.

Each radio button then calls this function, passing different information for these two parameters. The first button passes 1 and "3.5L", the second button passes 2 and "3.7L", and so on. The `setEngine()` function saves the values of these parameters in the global variables `engineIndex` and `engineType`, which are defined outside of any function. By defining these values outside of a function, they are available to all functions in the script block and persist until the page is closed.

In an attempt to duplicate the capabilities of the drop-down list from before, the values chosen for the index and engine mirror the values used by the options of the drop-down list. To handle the condition of a radio button not being selected, the variable `engineIndex` is given a value of 0 when it is defined. In this way, if no radio button is ever clicked, then `engineIndex` has a value of 0, indicating that an option needs to be selected. This mirrors the `selectedIndex` value of 0 for the first option in the drop-down list earlier, which indicated a similar problem.

In a similar fashion, the initial value assigned to `engineType` is `"Not Selected"`. This likewise corresponds to the *value* attribute of the first option in the drop-down list we saw previously. By defining and setting the variables in this way, the logic of showing the results is virtually identical for the drop-down list and the radio buttons. When the results are shown with the Display Choice button, the stored value for `engineIndex` is used to show the error message when no button has been selected, and the stored value for `engineType` is used when an engine is selected.

Accessing Non-control HTML Elements

The "dot" notation can only be used for input controls nested inside a form. But you can also access all HTML elements – including input controls – by assigning *id* attributes to those elements and having the browser search for elements with those *id*s.

Consider the simple program in Figure 98 that contains a table and a button. When the button is clicked, it calls the function `changeRow()`. The `changeRow()` code first obtains a pointer to the row by using the `getElementById()` method, and in that method call, it passes in a single parameter, the *id* ("trData"), that is assigned to the row. (As the subtitle shows, the `getElementById()` function is referenced using the dot notation after the `document` object.)

```
<html>
  <head>
    <title>Change Row in JavaScript</title>
    <style type="text/css">
      .yellowRow { background-color: Yellow; }
      .whiteRow  { background-color: White;  }
    </style>
    <script type="text/javascript">
      // Swaps the class name on row with id "trData" between yellowRow and whiteRow
      function changeRow() {
        var trRow = document.getElementById("trData");   // Get pointer to row
        if (trRow.className === "yellowRow")             // If pointer found (should work)
          trRow.className = "whiteRow";                  //   change CSS class (make white)
        else                                             // Otherwise
          trRow.className = "yellowRow";                 //   change CSS class (make yellow)
      }

      // Changes background color of control in parameter 1 to color in parameter 2
      function setColor(control, color) {
        control.style.backgroundColor = color;           // Control passed using this keyword
      }
    </script>
  </head>
  <body>
    <table border="1">
      <tr><th colspan="3"
          onmouseover="setColor(this, '#C0D0FF');" onmouseout="setColor(this, '');">
          Address Book</th></tr>
      <tr><th>Name</th><th>Address</th><th>Phone</th></tr>
      <tr id="trData"><td>Joe Parks</td><td>1234 E 5th</td><td>800-555-1212</td></tr>
    </table>
    <input type="button" value="Change Row Color" onclick="changeRow();"
        onmouseover="setColor(this, 'Pink');" onmouseout="setColor(this, '');" />
  </body>
</html>
```

Figure 98. Accessing HTML controls inside JavaScript

The `getElementById()` function, when called, returns a "pointer" to the second row in the table, the one with attribute `id="trData"`. Now, if you are careful to spell the `id` correctly when it is passed to `getElementById()`, then the variable `trRow` that is returned is an object (see chapter 9) that gives you access to all the attributes of the row.

The variable `trRow` is placed inside an `if`-statement, but this test will only work if a valid element was found by `getElementById()`, as you might guess. If, due to a spelling mistake or other error, the element was not found, then the attempt to change the style of the element will fail and the script will stop execution at that point (without any warning).

If the element was found, then we use the dot notation to access its CSS class using the property `className`. (The `className` property in the JavaScript corresponds to the `class` attribute in the HTML row.) The class name is then set to the CSS class name `"yellowRow"`, which is defined in the internal stylesheet.

Changing Style on Mouse Over

This example also shows how to change the style on any HTML element when the mouse is over the element. The technique uses the *onmouseover* attribute to set a new background color and uses the *onmouseout* attribute to restore the original color. Both of these events call the `setColor()` function, but with different colors.

These two events have been added to both the `<th>` element in the top row of the table as well as the button after the table. When the mouse is over the top row, the background color is changed to light blue, and when the mouse is over the button, the background color is set to pink. On both the first table row and the button, the background color is restored to its original setting by setting the color to the empty string. This is particularly important with buttons since, by default, buttons have a special shaded color. For more information on changing style attributes, see the next section.

Using the `this` Keyword

In the above example, both the *onmouseover* and *onmouseout* events on the table heading and the button use the `setColor()` function. This function takes two parameters, the first being the actual input control itself using the `this` keyword. The construct basically says, "Pass *me* to the handler." With this construct, multiple and varied HTML elements can use the same function to achieve background color highlighting. It works for all HTML controls because all HTML controls support the *style* attribute.

Passing Strings inside Strings

The second parameter to `setColor()` is the new color to use, passed as a string. This color can be a standard color name, a hex color code (`#C0D0FF`), or a set of values using the `rgb` syntax (`rgb(192,208,255)`). Note, however, the syntax of how the name is passed in (*onmouseover*=`"setColor(this, 'Pink');"`). The color string is set off using single quotes because the string value is inside the value of the *onmouseover* attribute, which is using double quotes. Thus, when you want to pass a string value inside a quoted value, use single quotes to set it off. (This is the same technique as covered for strings in JavaScript in chapter 5 (see Figure 72).)

Using `getElementById()` for Input Controls

The `getElementById()` function can also locate input elements in the HTML, like text boxes, buttons, and the like. Below is a modest rewrite of a couple of the above examples, replacing the dot notation with `getElementById()`:

```
var boxA = document.getElementById("txtA");
if (boxA)
{
    var a = boxA.value;                    // Grab displayed value in A
    boxA.focus();                          // Set focus to A
    boxA.style.backgroundColor = "cyan";   // Change background color for A
    boxA.className = "inBox";              // Set the CSS class for A
}
var btnA = document.getElementById("btnAdd");
if (btnA)
{
    btn.disabled = "disabled";             // Disable the button
    btn.title = "Click here to add";       // Change the popup on hover over button
}
```

Testing Pointers returned from `getElementById()`

In the example, note the second line of code (`if (boxA)`). This `if`-statement tests for the existence of the pointer to the HTML element searched for by `getElementById()`. The test will take the `true` path only if the text box was found by `getElementById()` (that is, when **boxA** is not **null**; see next paragraph for more information). By using a statement block, the test will skip all references to **boxA** when `getElementById()` could not find the element. This test, then, is a way of insuring that you did not misspell the name of the text box or make some other such error. If this test were not made and **boxA** were also not defined, the JavaScript would cause an error on any reference to it (as in `boxA.focus();`) and the script would terminate immediately at that point.

About the **null** value for variables in JavaScript: **null** is a value that tells JavaScript that the variable has not been given a specific value so far in the code. Thus **null** means uninitialized or non-existent. **null** as a keyword can also be used in an `if`-statement (as in "`if (boxA === null)`").

Accessing Style Attributes from within JavaScript

All HTML elements have *style* attributes, and the styles of HTML elements can be modified by JavaScript. In the following example, the background color of **txtA** is changed by using dot notation and the **style** property of the control:

```
form1.txtA.style.backgroundColor = "cyan";     // Change background color on A
```

Note that the syntax of the style property may not be what is expected. When the background color is set in either an inline style or a stylesheet, the property is hyphenated as **background-color** (as shown below) and not written as **backgroundColor**.

```
style="background-color:cyan; text-align:right; font-weight:bold;"
```

Specifically, when defining styles that consist of two words, the words are separated by a dash in CSS. Since JavaScript defines the dash as a minus sign, the example above would not be syntactically correct if we used **background-color** and wrote the line as shown below:

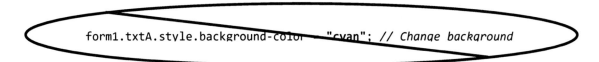

```
form1.txtA.style.background-color = "cyan"; // Change background
```

If you attempted to change the background color in this way, JavaScript would look for a property named *background* (which it would not find) and then subtract from it a variable called **color**. For this reason, JavaScript renames the multi-word style attributes in "camel case," where the dash is removed and each word after the first is written with a capital letter. For example: **backgroundColor**, **textAlign**, **fontWeight**, **listStyleType**, etc. Single-word style attributes would remain the same, though (**color**, **width**, **height**, etc.).

Showing and Hiding HTML Elements

JavaScript can also be used to show or hide HTML elements in two different ways. First, you can change the *display* property of the style associated with the HTML element. When *display* is set to **"none"** on an HTML element, that element is not displayed, and when the *display* property is changed from **"none"** to an appropriate value, the element will again become visible. The demonstration of this is long, though, and therefore split across two figures (Figure 99 and Figure 100). It illustrates showing and hiding divisions, tables, and table rows, and it also shows how to change the contents of just one table cell. The paragraphs that follow describe each of the steps in the example.

In addition to using the *display* property, HTML elements can also be shown and hidden by changing the *visibility* property associated with them. When *visibility* is set to **"hidden"**, the element is not shown but the space it occupied on the screen is still used, just blank. When *visibility* is then set to **"visible"**, the item is again displayed. Since the space occupied by the element remains allocated, this section will only cover showing and hiding by modifying the *display* property. However, the example in Figure 99 using the *visibility* property is available in the online files. There are, then, two solutions for Figure 99: the first using *display*, and the second using *visibility*.

(Note also that the online solutions to Figure 99 include external CSS stylesheets and other additional features. Specifically, detailed help instructions are shown, and these instructions can be hidden or shown using a "minimize" or "maximize" button. The examples also use the current time of day when updating the single table cell.)

Using Pointers to HTML Elements

Due to the need to reference each HTML element several times within the JavaScript, pointers are created to these elements so `document.getElementById()` will not have to be used repeatedly throughout the code. This shortens the code and makes it easier to follow. To create the pointers, first they must be declared with the **var** keyword at the top of the script section. Seven of these pointers are declared (`dvDiv` through `tdCell`), and then these are all given the value **null** just so they will be initialized. By defining the pointers outside any function (at the script level), they can be referenced from all functions in the script section.

Next, the *onLoad* event is handled in the `<body>` element and calls the function `initPage()`. This function uses `document.getElementById()` to initialize each of the element pointers.

HTML for the Example

The HTML defines four buttons, each for changing a different part of the form. Each of the functions called by the buttons then uses the element pointers instead of having to use `document.getElementById()` each time. Next the buttons are followed by a table, with three rows and two columns. Note that an *id* attribute is defined for each of the following: the table itself, the last row of the table, and the second cell of the second row of data. These *id* attributes are then used by the `document.getElementById()` calls above to create the pointers. Finally, there is a `<div>` with an *id* attribute so that the entire division can be referenced.

Showing and Hiding a Division (Div)

The `showHideDiv()` function changes the display property on the `<div>` and also changes the label on the button to correspond to the new state of the `<div>`. The code first checks the current state of *display* and then uses that value to determine the new state. If the value is **"none"**, it is changed to **"block"**; otherwise (in the **else** clause), the `<div>` is assumed to be displayed and *display* is set to **"none"**.

Note that to restore visibility on a `<div>`, *display* is set to **"block"**. Setting *display* to **"block"** should not be used on other items, because different values are needed (as shown in the example). Finally, note that the label on the button is changed at the same time as the *display* property.

Showing and Hiding a Table and Table Rows

To show or hide a `<table>`, follow the same steps as for a `<div>`, except that instead of changing the *display* attribute to **"block"** to show the table again, the *display* attribute is set to **"table"**. In a related fashion, to show a table row, set the *display* attribute to **"table-row"**.

Changing a Table Cell

Changing a table cell is slightly different than changing a style attribute. In this case, you want to change, in effect, what lies between the `<th>` and `</th>` (or `<td>` and `</td>`) tags. To change the content of an HTML element, you reference the *innerHTML* attribute of the element within the JavaScript. In the above example, the contents of the cell are set to the current time, so that a different value is displayed each time the button is clicked.

```html
<html>
  <head>
    <title>Showing and Hiding Elements</title>
    <link rel="stylesheet" type="text/css" href="Styles/ShowHide.css">
    <script type="text/javascript">
      // To shorten the code, generate pointers to HTML items
      var dvDiv = null;    // Pointer to hidden div
      var dvBtn = null;    // Pointer to div button
      var tbTbl = null;    // Pointer to table
      var tbBtn = null;    // Pointer to table button
      var trRow = null;    // Pointer to table row
      var trBtn = null;    // Pointer to row button
      var tdCel = null;    // Pointer to table cell
      function initPage() {
        // Generate pointers
        dvDiv = document.getElementById("hideDV");
        dvBtn = document.getElementById("btnShowHideDiv");
        tbTbl = document.getElementById("tblDemo");
        tbBtn = document.getElementById("btnShowHideTbl");
        trRow = document.getElementById("trBill");
        trBtn = document.getElementById("btnShowHideRow");
        tdCel = document.getElementById("email");
      }
      function showHideDiv() {
        if (dvDiv.style.display === "none") {
          dvDiv.style.display = "block";
          dvBtn.value = "Hide Instructions";
        }
        else {
          dvDiv.style.display = "none";
          dvBtn.value = "Show Instructions";
        }
      }
      function showHideTbl() {
        if (tbTbl.style.display === "none") {
          tbTbl.style.display = "table";
          tbBtn.value = "Hide Table";
        }
        else {
          tbTbl.style.display = "none";
          tbBtn.value = "Show Table";
        }
      }
      function showHideRow() {
        if (trRow.style.display === "none") {
          trRow.style.display = "table-row";
          trBtn.value = "Hide Row";
        }
        else {
          trRow.style.display = "none";
          trBtn.value = "Show Row";
        }
      }
          function editTheCell() {
            var now = new Date;
            var time = now.getHours() + ":" + now.getMinutes() + ":" +
                       now.getSeconds();
```

Figure 99. Showing and hiding HTML elements (1 of 2)

```
      function editTheCell() {
        var now = new Date;
        var time = now.getHours() + ":" + now.getMinutes() + ":" +
                   now.getSeconds();
        tdCel.innerHTML = time;
      }
    </script>
  </head>
  <body onload="initPage();">
    <h3>Showing and Hiding HTML Elements Using JavaScript</h3>
    <form id="form1" action="">
      <input class="btn" id="btnShowHideDiv" type="button" value="Show Instructions"
        onclick="showHideDiv();" />
      <input class="btn" id="btnShowHideTbl" type="button" value="Hide Table"
        onclick="showHideTbl();" />
      <input class="btn" id="btnShowHideRow" type="button" value="Hide Row"
        onclick="showHideRow();" />
      <input class="btn" id="btnChangeCell" type="button" value="Change Cell"
        onclick="editTheCell();" />
      <br /><br />
    </form>
    <table border="2" id="tblDemo">
      <tr><th colspan="3">Employee List</th></tr>
      <tr><th>Name</th>      <th>Phone         </th><th>Email              </th></tr>
      <tr><td>Joe Smith </td><td>(800)555-1212</td><td>joeS09@yahoo.com    </td></tr>
      <tr><td>Mary Jones</td><td>(800)555-1234</td><td id="email">mjones@chartermi.com</td></tr>
      <tr id="trBill">
        <td>Bill Watson</td><td>(800)555-4321</td><td>bWatson@gmail.com  </td></tr>
    </table>
    <!-- Note: You must specifically set the style attribute to hide the div. -->
    <!--       You cannot use the class attribute to hide it.     -->
    <div id="hideDV" style="display:none">
      <h2>Instructions</h2>
      You could place instructions here but leave them hidden unless someone asked for them.
    </div>
  </body>
</html>
```

Figure 100. Showing and hiding HTML elements (2 of 2)

Input Validation

The number one objective for using JavaScript with HTML is validating user input. Input errors on web pages are usually of two types: (1) no input is given or (2) the input is not valid. Also, invalid input frequently occurs when the user is asked for numbers but supplies non-numeric information, like names or symbols. In this section, we will look at several techniques for validating user input.

User Input Format

All input from the user will be is string format, regardless of its source. Thus the value obtained from a text box (var a = form1.lstSpeed.value) or from the **prompt()** function (var a = prompt("Enter age", "");) will be in string format, so these validation methods are therefore based around working with string input.

Missing Information

The easiest way to find out if user input is missing is to compare the input result to the empty string. Consider the following code segments:

```
var name = form1.txtName.value;         if (form1.txtName.value === "")
if (name === "")                            alert("Name is required.");
    alert("Name is required.");
```

In the first example, the input value is placed in a local variable and that variable is compared to the empty string (""). In the second example, the input string is tested directly. In either case, if there is no input, the input is the empty string, and the `if`-statement displays the error message.

An alternate approach takes advantage of the fact that the input is always a string:

```
var name = form1.txtName.value;         if (form1.txtName.value.length === 0)
if (name.length === 0)                      alert("Name is required.");
    alert("Name is required.");
```

Here we use the property of strings called `length`. The `length` gives the count of characters in a string, and this count will be 0 when no input is supplied. (Remember that to compare equality – as in all the examples above – the triple equal ("`===`") sign is used!)

Invalid Numbers

Number validation generally means using the `isNaN()` function. The `isNaN()` function takes a single input value and returns `true` if the name is *invalid* and `false` if the input is *valid*. Returning true on bad data sometimes makes the code appear to be a double negative, so be careful when using this function to avoid inverting the logic. Consider the following code segment:

```
var height = parseFloat(form1.txtHeight.value);
if (isNaN(height))
{
    alert("Height is not a number or is not given!");
    txtHeight.focus();
}
else
{
    // All clear; compute
       . . .
}
```

The `isNaN()` function on some browsers will return `false` on an empty string. That is, it will indicate that an empty string is a valid number. However, `parseInt()` and `parseFloat()` will convert the empty string into `NaN` (not a number). Therefore, it is best to first convert the input to a number using `parseInt()` or `parseFloat()` before testing with `isNaN()`, as shown in the above example.

If the variable in the above example is not a number after conversion (that is, it is empty or has invalid characters), `isNaN()` returns `true` and the warning is displayed. To make the user's life easier, the cursor is placed afterwards in the offending input box using the `focus()` method. Alternately, if `height` is valid, `isNaN()` returns `false`. Then the `else`-clause is taken and the computation would continue.

Separating Missing Data from Invalid Numeric Format

To generate a different message depending upon the type of the error, you will need to test both invalid data conditions and show the appropriate error message depending upon the cause:

```
var height = form1.txtHeight.value;
if (height === "")
{
    alert("Height is not given!");
    txtHeight.focus();
}
else if (isNaN(height))
{
    alert("Height is not a number!");
    txtHeight.focus();
}
else
{
    // All clear; compute
    height = parseFloat(height);
        . . .
}
```

In the above code, the `if`/`else-if` syntax is used to test both conditions and then compute only if neither error condition exists.

Testing Multiple Input Values and Highlighting Errors

All of the above examples assumed that you had only one input variable to be used in the computations. The question arises, then, of how to handle checking of multiple input values and only doing the computation when all the input is valid. Assume, for example, you have a program to compute the volume of a box that has the three dimensions of height, width, and length. All of these must be valid for the volume to be computed, of course.

One approach would be to create a test for all input and do the computation only when they are all valid. If any error were found, then you could pop up an alert box on each input box. This technique would work, but could be quite obnoxious, because the user would have to dismiss three alert boxes if all numbers were invalid.

Another approach is to show one error message that lists all fields that are in error as a single message, and then doing the computation only if all are valid. This is certainly a better approach; however, even this approach can be improved by adding two other steps. The first is to place the cursor in the first field that is in error (or, when all data are valid, the first field), and the second would be to show a red asterisk (*) in front of all fields that are in error. (This second approach is also shown in the example.)

The Input Form

An input form is shown in Figure 101. Note that there are three input fields (length, width, and height) and one output field (volume). There are also two buttons: the first button, which computes the volume, possibly shows three alert boxes, and does not do any cursor positioning (except for placing the cursor in the length box when it is done); and the second button, which shows only one alert box, positions the cursor, and highlights the fields in error.

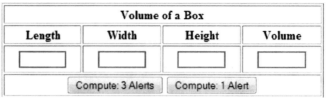

Figure 101. Sample form for volume of a box

Since the entire program is quite long, it will be shown in pieces. First is the CSS in the `<head>` section in Figure 102, followed by the `<body>` section shown in Figure 103, and then followed by the various pieces of JavaScript in later figures.

```css
<style type="text/css">
  .inBox
  {
    border-color:    green;
    border-style:    solid;
    border-width:    1;
    text-align:      right;
    width:           60px;
  }
  .hidden
  {
    color:           red;
    display:         none;
    font-size:       large;
    font-weight:     bold;
  }
  .bigCell
  {
    width:           100px;
    height:          35px;
  }
</style>
```

Figure 102. CSS for volume of box example

```html
<body onload="pageLoad();">
  <form id="form1">
    <table border="1">
      <tr><th colspan="4">Volume of a Box</th></tr>
      <tr><th>Length</th><th>Width</th><th>Height</th><th>Volume</th></tr>
      <tr>
        <th><span id="spnLength" class="hidden">*</span>
            <input type="text" id="txtLength" class="inBox" /></th>
        <th><span id="spnWidth"  class="hidden">*</span>
            <input type="text" id="txtWidth" class="inBox" /></th>
        <th><span id="spnHeight" class="hidden">*</span>
            <input type="text" id="txtHeight" class="inBox" /></th>
        <th><input type="text" id="txtVolume" class="inBox" readonly="readonly" /></th>
      </tr>
      <tr><th colspan="4">
        <input type="button" value="Compute: 3 Alerts" onclick="compute3();" />
        <input type="button" value="Compute: 1 Alert" onclick="compute1();" />
      </th></tr>
    </table>
  </form>
</body>
```

Figure 103. Body of HTML for volume of a box

The HTML for the input form shown above requires a few comments. First, the load event is captured and handled by the **pageLoad()** function, which positions the cursor in the **length** text box. Next, the text boxes are formatted using the CSS class **inBox**. This class draws a green border on the text boxes, sets the width, and makes the boxes right-justified. After this, the red asterisk has the CSS class **hidden** applied to it, thereby setting *display* to *"none"* and making the asterisk red. (Later on in the code, the *display* attribute will be changed to *"inline"*.) Finally, the volume text box is marked as read-only.

The pageLoad() Event Handler

The event handler for page loading has only one line of code, as shown below. This moves the cursor to the first input control on the form, which is the **length** box.

```
form1.txtLength.focus();
```

The Three Alert Code

When you click the left button, it calls the function **compute3()**, as shown below. This function first converts all the input values to numbers using **parseFloat()**. If the input is an empty string or cannot be converted to a number, its value will be **NaN**; then, each of these converted values is checked inside a single **if**-statement using the **isNaN()** function, and if none of the **isNaN()** tests indicate an invalid number by returning **true**, then the computation is done and the result put into the **volume** text box.

If any of the boxes is in error, the **else**-clause is taken and each of the input variables is tested again, one at a time, to display an error message. This duplicates some of the testing of the input values but makes the code a little easier to read.

Note how the cursor is positioned during the individual field checks. When an error is encountered, the cursor is moved to the field in error, but since the fields are being processed in reverse order of their appearance in the form, the first field in error will have the focus (which is the desired result).

```
// Compute volume showing up to 3 alerts
function compute3()
{
    var length = parseFloat(form1.txtLength.value);
    var width  = parseFloat(form1.txtWidth.value);
    var height = parseFloat(form1.txtHeight.value);
    if (!isNaN(length) && !isNaN(width) && !isNaN(height))
    {
        var volume = length * width * height;
        form1.txtVolume.value = volume;
    }
    else {
        // Errors found; highlight each with a separate message (annoying)
        if (isNaN(height)) {
            alert("Height is invalid or not specified.");
            form1.txtHeight.focus();
        }
        if (isNaN(width)) {
            alert("Width is invalid or not specified.");
            form1.txtWidth.focus();
        }
        if (isNaN(length)) {
            alert("Length is invalid or not specified.");
            form1.txtLength.focus();
        }
    }
}
```

The One Alert Code

When you click the button on the right, it calls the function **compute1()**, as shown below. This function uses separate methods to do most of its work. The first method, **showErrors()** (shown a bit later), changes the style of the red asterisk so that it appears on any fields in error. The other function, **validateInput()** (also shown a bit later), returns a string containing a summary of the errors, if any.

```
// Compute volume showing zero or one alert
function compute1()
{
    showErrors();     // Flag invalid fields with a red *
    var errMsg = validateInput();
    if (errMsg.length > 0)
        alert(errMsg)
    else {
        var length = parseFloat(form1.txtLength.value);
        var width  = parseFloat(form1.txtWidth.value);
        var height = parseFloat(form1.txtHeight.value);
        var volume = length * width * height;
        form1.txtVolume.value = volume;
    }
}
```

Since **validateInput()** returns an empty string when there are no errors, the **length** property of the string is used to check if errors had been encountered or not. If errors were encountered, the errors are shown with a single alert box, but if there were no errors, the input values are fetched from the form and converted to numbers. Then the volume is calculated and the result placed in the **volume** text box.

The `showErrors()` Function

The `showErrors()` function examines each input text box one at a time, testing for an empty string or `NaN` in a single `if`-statement and displaying an asterisk on either error condition. In other words, the two conditions are connected with the logical "or" function so that if either condition is true, the first path is taken. If neither condition is true (no errors), then the `else`-clause is taken. When the first (error) path is taken, the display of the red asterisk is set to `"inline"`; on the no-error path, the display is set to `"none"`.

Note that we do not use the "dot" method to locate the `<span>` element containing the red asterisk. This is because you can only use the dot method when referencing input controls. Instead, a pointer is obtained to the control using the `document.getElementById()` function, which takes as input the name of the HTML element. With this pointer, the code can access the *style* property, and then within the *style* property, it can access the *display* property.

```
// Display red asterisk above invalid fields by changing the display attribute
// (Note that the dot method works only for HTML elements that are input controls)
function showErrors()
{
    var spanBlock;
    spanBlock = document.getElementById("spnLength");
    if (spanBlock)
    {
        if (form1.txtLength.value.length === 0 || isNaN(form1.txtLength.value))
            spanBlock.style.display = "inline";
        else
            spanBlock.style.display = "none";
    }
    spanBlock = document.getElementById("spnWidth");
    if (spanBlock)
    {
        if (form1.txtWidth.value.length === 0 || isNaN(form1.txtWidth.value))
            spanBlock.style.display = "inline";
        else
            spanBlock.style.display = "none";
    }
    spanBlock = document.getElementById("spnHeight");
    if (spanBlock)
    {
        if (form1.txtHeight.value.length === 0 || isNaN(form1.txtHeight.value))
            spanBlock.style.display = "inline";
        else
            spanBlock.style.display = "none";
    }
}
```

The `validateInput()` Function

The `validateInput()` function returns different error messages depending upon the types of errors found, and it also sets the focus to the first control in error as it goes through. The code works as follows. The program starts by assuming the control in error is the first control – the `length` text box – and if it finds no errors in `length`, it will assume that the control in error is the next text box `width` instead; but if it *does* find an error in `length`, the focus will remain on the `length` box. After this testing turns to the `width` and `height` boxes and proceeds similarly. After the processing is all done, the length of the error message is checked, and if it is 0, the focus is placed back on the first control, the `length` text box.

```javascript
// Function that will display a summary of all errors in a single alert box.
// If there are no errors, nothing is displayed.
// The function also positions the cursor at the field in error, if any,
// and if none are in error, it positions it at the first field.
function validateInput() {
    var errorSummary = "";   // Start with empty string

    form1.txtLength.focus();                        // Assume Length field is in error
    if (form1.txtLength.value === "")
        errorSummary = errorSummary + "Length is not specified.\n";
    else if (isNaN(form1.txtLength.value))
        errorSummary = errorSummary + "Length is not valid.\n";
    else
        form1.txtWidth.focus();                     // Assume width field is in error
    if (form1.txtWidth.value === "")
        errorSummary = errorSummary + "Width is not specified.\n";
    else if (isNaN(form1.txtWidth.value))
        errorSummary = errorSummary + "Width is not valid.\n";
    else
        form1.txtHeight.focus();                    // Assume height field is in error
    if (form1.txtHeight.value === "")
        errorSummary = errorSummary + "Height is not specified.\n";
    else if (isNaN(form1.txtHeight.value))
        errorSummary = errorSummary + "Height is not valid.\n";
    if (errorSummary.length === 0)
        form1.txtLength.focus();                    // Back to Length field if no errors
    return errorSummary;
}
```

Review Questions

1. What HTML element is used to define forms?
2. What is an event?
3. What are event handlers?
4. What is the *onload* event and why is it needed?
5. What type of form control(s) can be used to fetch text data?
6. Define a checkbox with an *id* of "chkTaxable" that is checked by default when the page is displayed.
7. How do you obtain data from checkboxes used in JavaScript?
8. Create a drop-down list with three options.
9. How are drop-down lists used in JavaScript? (That is, what is their purpose?)
10. Create three radio buttons in one group and two radio buttons in another group. Be sure to label each button with bold text.
11. Describe the basic strategy for handling radio buttons in JavaScript (using the shared *onclick* event handler).
12. How would you change the background color on a heading using JavaScript?
13. Describe how to validate input numeric data.
14. What is the primary difference that results from setting an element's *display* property to "none" as opposed to setting the *visibility* property to "hidden"?

Exercises

1. Figure 86 and Figure 87 illustrate the computation of the area of a trapezoid. Create an input form that prompts for the height, the first base length, and the second base length of the trapezoid, and has an output box for the area. Use the `areaTrap()` function to compute the area and write the area to the output field.

2. Create a form like the one at the right for converting temperatures between Fahrenheit and Celsius (in both directions). To convert from Fahrenheit to Celsius, you should be able to type a number in the left input box and click the button below the left box, which will compute the Celsius temperature and write that value in the right input box. To convert the other way, you should be able to start with a value in the right box and click the button below it. Validate user input by having four messages: if the Fahrenheit temperature is not specified and the button below the Fahrenheit temp is clicked, indicate that no value is given; if a value is given but invalid, display a different message; and similarly, have messages for missing or invalid Celsius temperatures.

3. Create a form like the one at the right for computing the distance between two Cartesian coordinates. The formula, derived from the Pythagorean Theorem, is shown below. As an exercise in HTML and CSS, try to exactly match the border and background colors shown in the figure.

$$d = \sqrt{(x_2 - x_1)^2 + (y_2 - y_1)^2} \quad d = \sqrt{(x_2 - x_1)^2 + (y_2 - y)^2}$$

4. Change the High/Low game in Figure 91 to ask at the end of the game whether you want to play again or not. If the user types "Y" or "Yes" to the question "Play again?", generate a new number and start over. (Hint: surround the existing program with either a `while`-loop or a `do-while`-loop, and add a separate function called `play()` that calls `playOnce()` each time another play is requested.)

5. Convert the High/Low game in Figure 91 to use an input form. The form should have an input field for the user's guess, a read-only field to show the current number of guesses, and a button to check the guess. You can continue to show the high/low/win status with alerts. Add a second button to start over and create a new game, which would generate a new random number and set the number of guesses back to zero.

6. Write a page that has a heading and one button. Have the button change the background color on the heading.

7. Create a page with one button that is highlighted when the mouse is over the button. You can change the background color, the font size, or whatever else you like, as long as there is a clear change when the mouse is over the button. Do not use the `setColor()` function; instead, do all the work in the event handlers for mouse over and mouse out.

8. Create a page with two headings and a button. Have both headings visible when the page loads, but hide the second heading when the button is clicked and then redisplay it when the button is clicked again. Change the text on the button to correspond to the visibility state of the second heading.

9. Add input validation to the page you created above to compute the area of a trapezoid, and show the user just one error message that summarizes the errors, no matter how many are present. Include the red asterisk on invalid fields, and only do the computation if all input is valid.

Order Form Project

Overview

This project will solidify your understanding of JavaScript computations and HTML forms. In this project you will create a simple order form that should look quite similar to the following, including the list of items and the price of each. (You may make style changes to the example as you like.)

Sample Order Form			
Quantity	Item	Unit Price	Totals
2	Apples	$5.49	10.98
3	Pears	$7.49	22.47
	Grapes	$6.49	0.00
5		Subtotal	33.45
		Tax @ 6%	2.01
Compute		Total	35.46

The form operates as follows: you type values in the left columns for quantities of apples, pears, and grapes, and then click Compute, which will calculate the following values:

- Total number of fruits (fourth input box down on left)
- Subtotal prices for apples, pears, and grapes (top three input boxes on the right)
- Sum of the subtotals, Subtotal (fourth input box down on right)
- Tax @ 6%, which is 6% of the Subtotal value
- (Final) Total, which is the sum of Subtotal and Tax @ 6%

Controls

Your form will have input boxes for the quantities to be purchased of apples, pears, and grapes, into which the user can type values. Use a stylesheet to set the width of all input boxes. There will also be "read-only" input boxes for computed fields (described above); to make an input box read-only, use the following syntax:

```
<input class="in" type="text" id="Subtotal" readonly="readonly" />
```

You will also have one button (Compute) that calls the JavaScript function that does the calculations.

Output

In order to get two decimal places after each computational field on the right side of the form, use the `toFixed()` function with a parameter of 2 (for two decimal places). Otherwise, you may get long and ugly numbers in some of the fields. (This will not be needed on the total units on the left side, though.)

Validations

In the figure above, no value was entered for the number of grapes ordered, so the computation used a value of zero for that field. To do this on your page, you will need to check the validity of the input fields by using the `isNaN()` function in `if`-statements. If the input is ever invalid, change the associated quantity or quantities to 0.

Extra Credit

For extra credit, mark each field in error (non-blank but not a number) with a red asterisk * and pop up an error message telling the user to correct his or her input. This asterisk can be placed in a `<span>` with an `id=""` property and a `class=""` property, which can then be hidden using an internal stylesheet to set the `display` property to *"none"* for the span in the same way we hid divisions. Then, place the red asterisk inside the span and set the `display` property to *"block"* when the field is in error.

Finally, note that a blank input field is valid input and means to use a quantity of zero. This means that to complete the extra credit, your testing will need to be relatively messy, because you will need to test separately for blank input (quantity 0) and invalid input (to show a red asterisk).

Implementation Strategy

Start with the `SimpleAdder.html` page (where the sum of two numbers is computed) since it shows how to fetch user input. Create your own form, making all input boxes read-only except for the three quantity boxes, and use an external or internal stylesheet to set the size of the input boxes and also right-justify the numbers. (You may also want to place a border around the input boxes so they are easier to see.) Once your form is working, add a button and make sure it calls the computation function. Then get each value one at a time in the code and show those values with an alert. The point of all this is to add changes slowly, to insure that the program works with each additional line instead of coding the whole thing at once without testing. Below is a list of steps you should be following in your JavaScript:

1. Fetch user input numbers for the quantities of each item, and store them in three separate variables with names like `apples`, `pears`, and `grapes`.
2. If the input is valid, convert the input numbers to integers with `parseInt()`. Otherwise, set the quantity (or quantities) to zero.
3. Compute the subtotals for each item by multiplying the quantity values obtained in (1) and (2) above by the appropriate prices (5.49, 7.49, 6.49), and store the results in three new variables named something like `totApples`, `totPears`, and `totGrapes`.
4. Compute the total of these subtotals in a variable like `total`.
5. Compute the total tax, which is the product of the total and 0.06 (6%), and store it in a variable like `totalTax`.
6. Compute the grand total, which is the sum of the total and the total tax. Store it in a variable with a name like `grandTotal`.
7. Put the six computed values back in the form, meaning the three subtotals from step 3, the total, the total tax, and the grand total.

CHAPTER 9 – ADVANCED JAVASCRIPT

Objectives

This chapter covers several more advanced topics in JavaScript, including arrays, objects, environment testing, and timers. The intent of this material is to give you, the student, an overview of these topics and also enough understanding to create a base from which you can do additional research. These topics will only be covered at an introductory level, though, as a full treatment is beyond the scope of this text.

The Conditional Operator

The conditional operator works exactly like an `if-else`-statement, in that the specified test condition is evaluated and one of two paths is taken. The operator is used to choose between two values or expressions based on the test condition, and then it often uses that value or expression to initialize a variable afterwards. The operator is sometimes called a *ternary* operator because it requires three operands: the test condition and two expressions to branch to. The syntax is as follows:

```
(<Test Condition>) ? <Expression 1> : <Expression 2>;
```

<Test Condition>	This is any logical expression that would be appropriate for an `if`-statement. It might be a comparison between two items using a comparison operator, or it might be a function like `isNaN()`.
<Expression 1>	This can be a constant, a variable, or an expression of any kind. The type of each expression (numeric or string) should match the other expression (see examples below).
<Expression 2>	Same as <Expression 1>.

In the example below, assume you have a variable called **age** that has a whole number obtained from the user. Say we want to display a message that says "Minor" if the age is less than 21 or "Adult" otherwise. The `if-else`-construct solution might look as shown below on the left, and the same solution using the conditional operator is shown below on the right.

```
var message;
if (age < 21)
  message = "Minor";
else
  message = "Adult";
alert(message);
```

```
var message = (age < 21) ? "Minor" : "Adult";
alert(message);
```

The conditional operator first compares **age** to 21, and if **age** is less than 21, the variable **message** is set to **"Minor"**. On the other hand, if **age** is greater than or equal to 21, **message** is set to **"Adult"** instead.

Note that the conditional operator tends to shorten the code, which is the reason it exists; in this case, five statements are reduced to two.

Since any kind of expression can be used with the conditional operator, you could use another conditional operator as one of the expressions. For example, say you have two variables, **a** and **b**, and you want to display a message that says "a < b" or "a > b" or "a = b" depending on the respective values. The solution is shown below. (The second expression in the conditional operator that tests a < b is actually another conditional operator that tests a > b.)

```
var message = (a < b) ? "a < b" : (a > b) ? "a > b" : "b = a";
alert(message);
```

Additional Replacement Operators

In chapter 5 you learned how to initialize variables using the equals sign (=) in a *replacement statement*. The following examples were given:

```
var pi = 3.14159273;
var stateName = "Michigan";
var milesPerHour;
milesPerHour = 60;
```

Later on, you learned how to update variables where the variable appeared on both sides of the equals sign. Here are some examples:

```
x = x + 1;
i = i + 2;
j = j - 4;
tableString = tableString + "</table>";
```

In all of these examples, a variable is being changed by something being added or subtracted (numeric variables) or appended (string variables), and then the result is stored back into the variable. In the first example, the variable **x** is incremented by 1; in the second example, the variable **i** is being incremented by 2; in the third example, the variable **j** is being reduced by 4; and in the final example, the variable **tableString** has additional information being appended to the end of string. To make coding these common situations easier, JavaScript defines 5 additional numeric replacement operators and 1 additional string operator, as listed in Table 23.

Numeric Replacement Operators		
Operator	**Example**	**Result**
+=	x += 1;	Same as x = x + 1; (x increases by 1)
+=	x += 5;	Same as x = x + 5; (x increases by 5)
-=	x -= 1;	Same as x = x - 1; (x decreases by 1)
-=	x -= 13;	Same as x = x - 13; (x decreases by 13)
*=	x *= 2;	Same as x = x * 2; (x is doubled)
/=	x /= 2;	Same as x = x / 2; (x is halved)
%=	x %= 7;	Same as x = x % 7; (x is set to the remainder after dividing by 7 and will be between 0 and 6)
String Replacement Operator		
Operator	**Example**	**Result**
+=	str += "World";	Same as str = str + "World" (the phrase "World" is appended to str)

Table 23. New replacement operators

These new operators will allow you to tighten up your code and improve its readability. For example, the following two lines of code are equivalent, but the second is shorter and easier to read. (This example comes from Figure 72.)

```
tableString = tableString + "<table border='2'>";
tableString += "<table border='2'>";
```

Note that you do not need to use these operators, but can always continue instead to use the equals operator and the variable name on both sides. These are shown mostly for completeness' sake, because you may encounter them in JavaScript examples you find online.

Increment/Decrement Operators

Two ways to add 1 to a variable (x = x + 1; and x += 1;) have been covered so far. Similarly, two ways to subtract 1 from a variable (x = x - 1; and x -= 1;) have been shown. In this section, we will show another way to add or subtract 1 from a variable: by using the increment or decrement operators.

The increment operator consists of two plus signs (++) and the decrement operator consists of two minus signs (--). These operators can be placed immediately before a variable or immediately after a variable, as in x++ or ++x. In both of these cases the variable x is incremented by 1. Similarly, with either x-- or --x, the variable x is decremented by one.

When x++ or ++x appears on a line by itself, it does not matter which way it is written, because x is incremented by 1 and no other variables are involved. In the same way, it would not matter whether you wrote x-- or --x if it were on a line by itself. However, if you set a variable equal to another variable with the increment or decrement operator (as in y = x++;), the way it is written *does* matter in this case (and many others). When an increment operator appears after the variable, it is called a *post-increment* operator, because the increment update occurs *after* the variable's contents have been used in the replacement statement.

On the other hand, placing the increment operator before the variable (as in y = ++x;) means that the increment step occurs *before* the value of the variable is used, and the operator is called a *pre-increment* operator. This distinction is easier to understand if you study Table 24. (The decrement operators operate in the same fashion as the increment operators, which are called the *post-decrement* operator or *pre-decrement* operator, respectively.)

A complete example that reproduces the conditions in Table 24 is given in the chapter 9 online examples under the title "Increment and Decrement Operators." To see the operators in action for yourself, copy the source to that example into your own page and try changing the numbers.

Operator	Code Segment	Result after Code Segment		
		x	y	Remarks
++	x = 4; y = x++;	5	4	The variable y is set to the initial value of x (4), and after, x is incremented by 1 to 5.
++	x = 4; y = ++x;	5	5	The variable x is incremented first and then the variable y is set equal to it. Both have a value of 5.
--	x = 4; y = x--;	3	4	The variable y is set to the initial value of x (4), and after, x is decremented by 1 to 3.
--	x = 4; y = --x;	3	3	The variable x is decremented first and then the variable y is set equal to it. Both have a value of 3.

Table 24. Increment/decrement operators

The increment and decrement operators are useful in loops, and in particular, in working with arrays. Below is a code segment that would reverse the order of the entries in an array of numbers called **nums**. Don't worry if you don't understand the code; just notice how the increment and decrement operators are used to simplify the code. In both cases, the index is used *before* it is incremented or decremented. (The complete example is included in the chapter 9 online examples under "Reverse Array Order".)

```
// Reverse the order of the array
var t = 0;                    // Index to top of the array
var b = nums.length - 1;      // Index to bottom of the array
while (t < b)                 // Continue while top index is above bottom index
{
  // Swap entries at t and b
  var temp = nums[t];         // Save current value at top
  nums[t++] = nums[b];        // Move bottom entry to top and move top index down
  nums[b--] = temp;           // Move top entry to bottom and move bottom index up
}
```

Classes and Objects

The following discussion will border on the theoretical and, as such, may confuse some. An understanding of this material is not really necessary to be able to develop web pages; however, understanding this material may help clarify some of the other material in this book, and in particular, discussions in the remainder of this chapter.

Classes and objects became popular in computer science about 15 years ago. In the simplest terms, a *class* is a blueprint for creating an *object*. Like a blueprint for a house describes how to build a house, a class is a blueprint that describes what data and functions will be included in objects created from the class. Using classes and objects in programming is called Object-Oriented Programming, or sometimes just abbreviated as OOP.

A familiar example may help you get started. In chapter 5, the concept of a string was introduced. You created a string by using the **var** keyword, a variable name, and then setting that name equal to a sequence of letters, as in:

```
var myName = "John";
```

This created a storage location named **myName** that stored a set of characters. Variables so created are **String** class objects, and the data associated with those objects are the text of the strings. Strings, however, also include a variety of functions (see Table 12) that can be used to search the strings or create variations of those strings. For example, we saw in chapter 5 that we could create a new string from an existing string that was all uppercase letters:

```
var myName = "John";
var nameUpper = myName.toUpperCase();
```

In summary, since it has functions, the variable **myName** created above is an object, and not just a memory location with some data.

> **Definition of *Class***
>
> A *class* is a blueprint that describes what types of data will be maintained in each *object* created from that class. It also usually includes functions for manipulating and/or modifying the data being stored.

Definitions

The above example that created the variable **myName** created an object which is a specific *instance* of the **String** class. This distinction is important. The *class* is the blueprint that describes the data and functions, but it is not the data. The *object* is the data. It is the same with a

> **Definition of *Object***
>
> An *object* is a specific *instance* (memory location) created from a *class*. There may be many objects created from the same class.

house plan: the house plan is not the house, it is just a description of how the house is to be built. There may be multiple houses constructed from the same plan or blueprint, in fact. Thus we have the following two definitions:

Class A blueprint that describes data to be maintained when the object is created, and lists the functions, if any, that operate on that data. The data may consist of a single piece of information, like a string, or multiple pieces of information, like the parts of a drop-down list (see The **options** Array in Drop-Down Lists below).

Object A specific memory location (variable) that is created from the class. There may be many objects created from the same class.

Up to this point you have been told that all named things in JavaScript start with a lowercase letter. However, classes start with a capital letter so as to clearly distinguish between them and other items. Core JavaScript object classes include **Array, Boolean, Date, Function, Math, Number, RegExp,** and **String**. (Note: the Math library is a class, but in this case, its data are limited to only a few constants, like PI. Mostly it is used for the many math functions in it.) Later in this chapter, you will be studying several of the core classes and the objects created from them.

Creating Objects from Classes

Now that we have the blueprint, the next step is to create objects from the blueprint. Objects are generally created from classes using the **new** keyword followed by the class name and parentheses, as if the class were a function:

```
var now = new Date();
var imgArray = new Array();
```

You will see more examples in the documents described later in the chapter. Note that, in the syntax, the class name is followed by left and right parentheses. Every time you create an object from a class, the parentheses must be included. Note also that each time **new** is used, a **new** object is created.

Sometimes, though, the class needs additional information to create the object. For example, the **Date** class can create a date in different ways using different input (see Table 26). If you want today's date, you use the example above (i.e., blank). In another case, you might want to specify the year, month, day, hour, and minute to create a specific date. In still another case, you might want to specify the date as a string. The three **Date** object creation methods are shown below:

```
var now    = new Date();                                // Use today's date/time
var jimsBD = new Date("October 29, 1984 01:08:00");     // Date from a string
var jimsBD = new Date(1984, 10, 29, 1, 8);              // Date from year/month/day/hour/min
```

Remember that a class is a blueprint for building object. Continuing our construction analogy, note that different styles of houses could be built from the same blueprint. In the computer world, we would say that different types of objects can be created from the same class, and to specify different types for the objects, different parameters can be specified when the object is "constructed," as shown above for dates.

These special values are given to what is called a *constructor*. A constructor is like a function: when parameters are used, as illustrated above, they define the specifics of the new object; when not used, that signals a different type of object, usually using some default(s) for the specifics. Furthermore, there can be different constructors that take different kinds of input. In the date example, one constructor takes a series of values for year, month, etc., whereas another constructor takes a string, and still another takes no parameters at all.

In summary, classes define how objects can be created from them by defining one or more constructors. These constructors are documented here for the **Date** class; you can search the web for additional details on the constructors for the other core classes.

Referencing Properties and Functions in an Object

You already know how to reference the various properties and functions within an object using the "dot" notation that you have already studied. Certain data items are exposed (like the **length** property of the **Array** class) to the coder, and these are referenced with just the property name and no parentheses:

```
imgArray.length
```

Likewise, functions are accessed using the "dot" notation, but this time parentheses must be given because they are functions being referenced. Here is an example from chapter 8:

```
var inBox = document.getElementById("txtName");
```

More on Strings

The `String` class is listed above as one of the core classes in JavaScript, and objects can be constructed from it using the `new` keyword, as will be shown below. However, in JavaScript (and most other object-oriented languages) strings can be defined by simply using the equal sign:

```
var name1 = "Freddie Wilson";
```

We have seen several examples of this in previous chapters. For completeness, however, the following examples show how to create `String` objects using the `new` keyword with the appropriate constructor:

```
var name1 = "Freddie Wilson";
var name2 = new String("John Smith");
var name3 = new String(name1);
```

The first example simply uses the shortcut syntax, and the second and third examples use the `new` keyword plus the class constructor, the difference between them being whether the text is passed in (the second example) or a variable is passed in (the third example). After this third example, there will be two strings (`name1` and `name3`) that have the exact same data ("Freddie Wilson").

More on the Document Object Model

After studying this text, you may have wondered about the `document` variable that you saw in previous chapters (`document.write()`, `document.getElementById()`, etc.); specifically, whether or not it was an object. The `document` variable is indeed an object, and it contains all the content of the current HTML page as data, as well as a large number of properties and functions associated with that data.

Summary

Classes allow the JavaScript developer to create and use complex data that are fully encapsulated into one place. Furthermore, there are a variety of functions associated with the data that can reduce your work when creating your scripts.

Arrays

Arrays in JavaScript are objects created from the `Array` class. The `Array` class is very useful in organizing data, specifically data that are normally all of the same type. For example, you might have a long list of numbers from which you would want to calculate some statistics, or you might have a list of names that needs to be sorted, or a list of images that are scrolling on the screen as a photo gallery, or whatever. The advantages of an array are that you have a single name for the collection and can reference items in it easily and efficiently. For example, if you had 8 ages, you could define the 8 variables `age1`, `age2` ... `age8`, and you could perform computations with those 8 different names with something like `sum = age1 + age2 + ...` which is not too bad with only 8 names. However, what if you had 10,000 numbers? Can you imagine 10,000 separate variables? With arrays, you define one variable and it contains however many entries are required. It is like a post office that has numbered boxes, with each box having something different in it.

Array Indexing

An array is an ordered list of like values that are referenced by their positions in the array. Figure 104 is a graphical depiction of an array of ages. For example, this might be a list of ages at which people first purchased a new car, and this particular array is therefore assigned the variable name **ages**. The first thing to notice is that the single variable called **ages** includes 8 whole numbers; that is, it is not a single age but a set of 8 ages.

The numbers to the left of the cells containing the ages are the *index* numbers for the cells (in our analogy, like the post office box numbers), but index numbers in JavaScript (and most programming languages) start at 0, meaning that the first age is at index 0. This also means that the last entry in the array has an index of 1 less than the number of entries in the array (7 in this example).

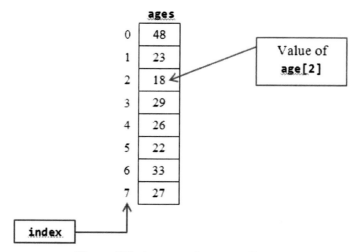

Figure 104. An example array of ages

Each age in the array has its own unique index number. Therefore, to reference a specific number in the array, you will need both the array variable's name and the number's index.

The syntax for this is to use the variable name followed by an opening bracket, followed by the index number, followed by a closing bracket. Either of the two JavaScript snippets below would place the value 18 in the variable **x**, for example. In the left snippet, the index number is given directly as a constant, while in the right snippet, the index number is given with a variable.

```
var x = ages[2];            var index = 2;
                            var x = ages[index];
```

Declaring Arrays

Since JavaScript uses the **Array** class for arrays, you declare a variable as an array using the **new** keyword. Then, after it has been created, you can initialize the entries. The following code segment would create the array shown in Figure 104 by initializing each entry one at a time:

```
var ages = new Array();
ages[0] = 48;
ages[1] = 23;
ages[2] = 18;
ages[3] = 29;
ages[4] = 26;
ages[5] = 22;
ages[6] = 33;
ages[7] = 27;
```

The first step is to declare the variable **ages** as an object of type **Array**, using the **new** keyword before the class name and parentheses after it. After the variable is created, each entry in the array is defined. This can be done one entry at a time, as shown above, or in a single step, using the following syntax:

```
var ages = new Array(48, 23, 18, 29, 26, 22, 33, 27);
var westCoastStates = new Array("California", "Washington", "Oregon");
```

The above two statements both create an array and fill in its values in one step. This syntax is useful only when you know in advance what the values in the array are and that there are only a limited numbers of entries. When you are prompting the user for each value, as in Figure 105, this syntax cannot be used.

Using Arrays

To access an entry in an array, use the variable name along with an index surrounded by brackets. This notation can appear on either side of the equals sign. In the example above, the array reference is on the left because the values are being initialized, but to reference the value of an array, use the array notation on the right side of the equals sign instead. For example, the code segment below (from Figure 105) adds up all the ages in the **ages** array:

```
var sum = 0;
for (var i = 0; i < count; i = i + 1)
    sum = sum + ages[i];
```

A variable **sum** is declared first and set to 0. Then a **for**-loop is used by defining the loop variable to be **i** and the loop step to be 1. The loop continues as long as **i** is less than the number of entries.

Note the continuation condition carefully (**i < count**). Remember that since array numbering starts with 0 in JavaScript, the last entry in the array (list) has an index equal to the count minus 1. Thus the loop continues only so long as the index variable *is less than* the count, to avoid human errors in the math for the indexes. Most loops with arrays will have a continuation condition where the index variable is less than the size of the array (instead of less than or equal to).

Arrays as Parameters and Obtaining the Size of the Array

The name of an array variable can be passed as a parameter to a function. An example of this is given in Figure 105. The function is defined as follows:

```
function showAverage(nums)
```

The function **compute()** uses **showAverage()** to show the average of the numbers fetched from the user. The array variable declaration in **compute()** and the call the **showAverage()** are shown below:

```
var numbers = new Array();        // The set of numbers
   .   .   .
showAverage(numbers);             // Have numbers; call showAverage() with array
```

The function **compute()** defines the array with the variable name **numbers** and the **showAverage()** function defines a parameter called **nums**. (These two variables will be the same data in this code, just with different names.) The **showAverage()** function adds up all the numbers in the array **nums** and afterwards computes the average.

The question then arises of how the **showAverage()** function can find out how many entries are in the array. One possibility would be to add an additional parameter to the function with the count of entries; however, the best way is to reference a property of the array variable that indicates the number of entries in it, called **length**. The segment of Figure 105 below shows how the size of the array is referenced by appending a period to the variable name and then appending the **length** property:

```
var count = nums.length;          // Get count of entries in array
```

The Average Example

Several references have already been made to Figure 105, which is a simple web page for averaging a set of user-supplied numbers. The page has some instructions and also a single compute button, which runs the function **compute()** that prompts the user for a series of numbers until the user types "Done" to indicate the end of the list. Once "Done" is typed, **compute()** calls the function **showAverage()** to display the results. Some portions of that code have been explained previously; the rest are covered here.

The numbers are prompted for inside a **do-while**-loop that ends when the user types in "Done". Note that the last value is translated to uppercase before comparing to "DONE", so that it does not matter how the word "done" is capitalized when it is typed. Note also that the **compute()** function is exited with the **return** statement when the Cancel button is clicked on the prompt box. When Cancel is clicked, the input value **inp** is null, which is the first test inside the loop after fetching **inp**.

The next test inside the loop is for the word "Done" to see if it is time for the computations. If so, the method **showAverage()** is called to show the results. If "Done" was not typed, then the new value is added to the array instead, using the following code:

```
var num = parseInt(inp);
if (isNaN(num))
  alert("Invalid; ignored");
else {
  numbers[count] = num;          // Store the new number
  count = count + 1;             // Step to the next cell
}
```

The number is first converted to a whole number and tested with **isNaN()**. If an invalid number is typed, a warning message is displayed; otherwise, the number is put at the end of the array by using the **count** variable as the index. (Remember that **count** starts at zero, which is the first entry of the array.) Then the count variable is incremented to keep an accurate count that will also point to the next entry in the array.

```html
<html>
  <head><title>Averaging Array Entries</title>
    <script type="text/javascript">
      // ** Sum numbers and compute average
      function showAverage(nums) {
        var count = nums.length;        // Get count of entries in array
        if (count === 0)                // Punt if no entries
          alert("No valid values entered; count is zero");
        else {
          // Sum numbers and compute average
          var sum = 0;
          for (var i = 0; i < count; i = i + 1)
            sum = sum + nums[i];
          var average = sum / count;
          alert("The average of the " + count + " number(s) is " + average);
        }
      }
      // ** Fetches numbers
      function compute() {
        var numbers = new Array();      // The set of numbers
        var count = 0;                  // The count of the numbers
        var inp;                        // The last input value
        do {
          inp = prompt("Enter whole number (" + (count + 1) + ") or 'Done'", "");
          if (inp === null) {
            alert("Canceled");
            return;        // Exit compute function, discarding data
          }
          if (inp.toUpperCase() === "DONE") {
            showAverage(numbers);   // Have numbers; call showAverage() with array
          }
          else {
            var num = parseInt(inp);
            if (isNaN(num))
              alert("Invalid; ignored");
            else {
              numbers[count] = num;     // Store the new number
              count = count + 1;        // Step to the next cell
            }
          }
        }
        while (inp.toUpperCase() !== "DONE");
      }
    </script>
  </head>
  <body>
    <form id="form1">
      <h1>Compute Average of Several Numbers</h1>
      <strong>
        Click the Compute button below. You will be prompted to enter a number. Type a number
        and click OK. You will then be prompted for another number. (Invalid numbers are
        ignored.) Once all the values are entered, type "Done". The average is computed and
        displayed.
      </strong><br /><br />
      <input type="button" value="Compute" onclick="compute();" />
    </form>
  </body>
```

Figure 105. Averaging a set of numbers

Array Class Properties and Functions

In addition to the **length** property previously noted, the **Array** class also includes a variety of methods that allow you to manipulate the array. With these methods, you can add elements to or remove elements from any location of the array, or use the array as a LIFO (Last In, First Out) or FIFO (First In, First Out) queue, or sort the elements, or create a larger array from two or more smaller arrays. The complete list of properties and functions is given in Table 25.

Array Class Properties and Functions	
Property	**Description**
`length`	Returns the number of entries in the array (0 if none). The size of an array is 1 more than the largest index used when adding entries to the array. For example, if index 8 is the largest index used in a statement like this: `ages[8] = 23;` then in the above example, the array size will be 9 (entries 0 through 8).
Function	**Description**
`concat(array2, array3, ... )`	Returns an **Array** which is all the arrays concatenated together, *including the array which called this function* (which is "array1"). Any number of arrays can be specified as parameters.
`join()` or `join(separator)`	Joins all elements of the calling array into a single string which is then returned. If a separator character is supplied, that character is used to join the elements; otherwise, a comma is used to separate the elements.
`pop()`	Removes and returns the last element of the array. Allows arrays to be used as a LIFO (Last In, First Out) queue (along with **push()**)..
`push(a, b, ...)`	Adds the specified elements to the end of the array and returns the new length of the array. Any number of elements can be specified.
`reverse()`	Reverses the order of elements in the array
`shift()`	Removes and returns the first element of the array. Allows arrays to be used as a FIFO (First In, First Out) queue (also known as a *stack*).
`sort()`	Reorders the original array with the elements sorted. Numbers are sorted in order of increasing size, and strings are alphabetized (see "if-Statements Comparing to Strings" in chapter 6 for more details).
`splice(index, removeCnt, a, b, ...)`	Inserts the elements specified, if any (**a, b, ...**), starting at **index**. Before the insert, it removes the number of items specified in **removeCnt**. If **removeCnt** is 0, no items are removed and only insertions take place. If **removeCnt** is the same as the number of items, then the array simply becomes the elements specified. If **removeCnt** is non-zero and no elements are specified, then items are removed without any elements being added to the array.
`toString()`	Creates and returns a string list of all elements in the array, separated by commas.
`unshift(a, b, ...)`	Adds the specified elements to the beginning of the array and returns the new length of the array. Any number of elements can be specified.

Table 25. Array class properties and functions

Missing Members in an Array

When you create an array by defining each entry, as in the ages example from earlier, then what happens if a value is skipped? Consider the web page shown in Figure 106. An array is created and entries 0 and 2 are added to it, but entry 1 is not added. It turns out that the entry at 1 in this case prints as *undefined*. To test for an undefined entry, compare the type of the value to the keyword **undefined**, as shown in the example. If you run the program, the first alert says "This is at index 1: undefined". The second alert, "Entry 1 is not defined", appears as well because the test for **undefined** is successful.

```
<html>
  <head>
    <title>Missing Member in Arrays</title>
  </head>
  <body>
    <script type="text/javascript">
      var ages = new Array();
      ages[0] = 21;
      ages[2] = 3;
      alert("This is at index 1: " + ages[1]);
      if (typeof ages[1] === "undefined")
        alert("Entry 1 is not defined");
    </script>
  </body>
</html>
```

Figure 106. Array with missing entry

Simple Image Gallery

As an example of their use, arrays can be useful in creating a simple image gallery. The example in Figure 108 shows a new picture each time a button is clicked, a technique that works by changing the properties of an image element whenever the button is clicked. Included below the image is a caption box that is also changed as a button is clicked.

The solution uses two separate arrays to store the data. The first, **imgArray**, contains the filenames of the images, and the values in this array replace the *src* attributes of the images. The second array, **capArray**, contains the alternate text for each image, and its value replaces both the *alt* and *title* attributes of the images, as well as the caption of the text box (which replaces the **innerHTML** in the **<div>** element).

The variable **imgIndex** is used for indexing through both arrays when buttons are clicked. On a next image click, 1 is added to **imgIndex** and then that value is wrapped around (if necessary) to be between 0 and the number of images minus 1. On a previous image click, 1 is subtracted from **imgIndex** and again the value is wrapped around if needed. To wrap around properly, modular arithmetic is used to set the index to the remainder after dividing by the size of the array, resulting in a range of 0 to **length** minus 1 (imgIndex = imgIndex % imgArray.length;).

The first image is shown by calling **nextImage()** when the page is first loaded. Note that the initial value for **imgIndex** is set to the length of the array minus 1, so that when it is updated by **nextImage()** during the initial load it will correctly wrap around to the first image in the list before displaying an image.

```
<html>
  <head>
    <title>Image Gallery with Two One-Dimensional Arrays</title>
    <style type="text/css">
      .gallery { border: 4px groove green; width: 250; height: 190; }
      .caption { border: 4px groove green; width: 258; height: 30;
                 font-size:larger; font-weight:bold; }
      .button  { font-size:medium; font-weight:bold; }
    </style>
    <script type="text/javascript">
      // There are two arrays, each with 4 elements: image files, and captions
      var imgArray = ["Iguacu1.jpeg", "Iguacu2.jpeg", "Iguacu3.jpeg",  "Iguacu4.jpeg"];
      var capArray = ["Top of Falls", "Panorama East", "Panorama South", "Local Flower"];

      var imgIndex = imgArray.length -1;       // Current image index; set to end of list

      function showImage(index) {
        // Updates <img> element; note caption used for title and alt
        document.getElementById('imgGallery').src      = imgArray[index];
        document.getElementById('imgGallery').alt      = capArray[index];
        document.getElementById('imgGallery').title    = capArray[index];
        document.getElementById('imgCaption').innerHTML = capArray[index];
      }

      function nextImage() {
        imgIndex++;
        imgIndex = imgIndex % imgArray.length;
        showImage(imgIndex);
      }

      function prevImage() {
        imgIndex--;
        if (imgIndex < 0) { imgIndex = imgArray.length - 1; }
        imgIndex = imgIndex % imgArray.length;
        showImage(imgIndex);
      }
    </script>
  </head>
  <body onload="nextImage();">
    <div style="text-align: center">
      <div class="caption">Pictures from Iguacu Falls</div>
      <img src="" id="imgGallery" alt="" class="gallery" />
      <div id="imgCaption" class="caption"></div>
      <br /><br />
      <input type="button" onclick="prevImage();" value="<===" class="button" />
      <input type="button" onclick="nextImage();" value="===>" class="button" />
    </div>
  </body>
</html>
```

Figure 107. Image gallery scrolled with buttons

Defining Arrays as Elements inside Arrays

Any kind of object can be an element in an array, including another array. The previous example can be simplified with this technique by changing the code to use only one array. Just the changes to Figure 107 are shown in Figure 108.

```
        // imgArray is an array with four elements.
        // Each of these elements is another array with two string elements:
        //       - The name of the image file
        //       - The caption for the image (also for title and src properties)
        var imgArray = [
                        ["Iguacu1.jpeg", "Top of Falls"],
                        ["Iguacu2.jpeg", "Panorama East"],
                        ["Iguacu3.jpeg", "Panorama South"],
                        ["Iguacu4.jpeg", "Local Flower"]
                       ];

        var imgIndex = imgArray.length - 1;        // Image index; set to last

        function showImage(index) {
          document.getElementById('imgGallery').src       = imgArray[index][0];
          document.getElementById('imgGallery').alt       = imgArray[index][1];
          document.getElementById('imgGallery').title     = imgArray[index][1];
          document.getElementById('imgCaption').innerHTML = imgArray[index][1];
        }
```

Figure 108. Arrays as elements in an array

Now there is only one array, **imgArray**, and it contains both the filenames and the captions. The main array has four elements, one for each image, and the element that defines an image is now an array with two elements (see below). The first element of this inner array is the name of the image file, and the second element is the caption/alternate text. Since there is one array inside another here, this array is a *two-dimensional array*. It can be visualized as shown in Figure 109.

0	0	"Iguacu1.jpeg",
	1	"Top of Falls"
1	0	"Iguacu2.jpeg",
	1	"Panorama East"
2	0	"Iguacu3.jpeg",
	1	"Panorama South"
3	0	"Iguacu4.jpeg",
	1	"Local Flower"

Figure 109. Four two-dimensional arrays

Notice how the array is actually declared in Figure 108. The **imgArray** is started with the left bracket and later closed with the right bracket, and between this are four elements separated by commas. However, instead of numbers or strings between the commas, there are other arrays, defined by their own left and right brackets.

Accessing Elements in a Two-Dimensional Array

Accessing elements in a two-dimensional array is fairly easy to understand. Look at the **showImage()** function in Figure 108 and note how the values are obtained. The array name, **imgArray**, is followed by two sets of brackets. The first set of brackets accesses the main array and should have an index between 0 and 3. Once an index is supplied inside this set of brackets, you have picked a particular image, and you now need to specify the element of the array of the image that you want (name or caption). Thus the second index would need to be either 0 or 1. For example, **imgArray[2][1]** would reference the third image's array and then the second part of that array, which is the string **"Panorama South"**.

Creating Arrays in Code

At the beginning of this material on arrays, the **ages** array was created with each entry specified one at a time. This same technique could be used to create the **imgArray** of Figure 108; it requires a lot more code, though, as shown in Figure 110.

```
    var imgArray;      // Image array initialized in pageInit()
    var imgIndex;      // Current image index

    function pageInit() {
      imgArray = new Array();
      // Create four rows and set each equal to an array
      for (var i = 0; i < 4; i = i + 1)
        imgArray[i] = new Array();
      imgArray[0][0] = "Iguacu1.jpeg";    // Image 1 data
      imgArray[0][1] = "Top of Falls";
      imgArray[1][0] = "Iguacu2.jpeg";    // Image 2 data
      imgArray[1][1] = "Panorama East";
      imgArray[2][0] = "Iguacu3.jpeg";    // Image 3 data
      imgArray[2][1] = "Panorama South";
      imgArray[3][0] = "Iguacu4.jpeg";    // Image 4 data
      imgArray[3][1] = "Local Flower";
      imgIndex = imgArray.length - 1;     // Point to last image
      nextImage();                        // Show first image
    }
```

Figure 110. Creating two-dimensional array in code

A new function called **pageInit()** is created that is called instead of **nextImage()** in the *onLoad* event for the **<body>** element. This function first defines the main array and uses a loop to create all the image arrays that are the elements of the main array. (Note that you cannot reference an array element without first creating the array.) Next, each entry of the image arrays is initialized for all four images. Compare Figure 108 and Figure 110 carefully to make sure you understand how the indexing is used in Figure 110.

Arrays of HTML Objects

In web pages, all *id* attributes must be unique so that the **document.getElementById()** function will find only one element with that *id* during an ID search. However, multiple elements in a document can have the same *name* attribute. (In fact, it is the *name* attribute that is used to group radio buttons into a set, which you may remember from our discussion in chapter 8.) Therefore, if you asked for a list of elements with a particular name, you might get multiple elements. This is what the JavaScript library function **document.getElementsByName()** actually does. It looks for all the elements in the HTML that have that name specified and places those elements into an array. Even if no element, or only one element, is found, the object returned by **getElementsByName()** is always an array (if no element is found, the **length** property of the returned array will be zero).

Being able to get a list of elements with the same name gives a lot of flexibility to the JavaScript programmer, and it can even simplify some code. To illustrate, the radio button example in Figure 97 will be rewritten using **getElementsByName()** and arrays. Instead of having to trap the *onclick* event for each radio button to capture information about the selection, the whole list of buttons is tested to see which one is clicked. The complete solution is shown in Figure 111 with the explanation following.

```html
<html>
  <head>
    <title>Radio Button Example Using Arrays</title>
    <script type="text/javascript">
      // ** Using the name attribute of the buttons, it tests all buttons found
      //    with that name. It then returns the index of the button in the set
      //    that is selected. If no button is selected, -1 is returned. If the
      //    name is invalid (no buttons with that name), -2 is returned.
      function getButtonIndex(buttonName) {
        var buttons = document.getElementsByName(buttonName);
        if (buttons === null  ||  buttons.length === 0)
          return -2;                             // No buttons; return -2
        for (var i = 0; i < buttons.length; i = i + 1)
          if (buttons[i].checked)
            return i;                            // Button selected; return index
        return -1;                               // None selected; return -1
      }

      // ** Display user's choice
      function displayChoice() {
        var engineType = ["3.5L", "3.7L", "5.0L"];
        var engineIndex = getButtonIndex("Engine");
        if (engineIndex < 0  ||  engineIndex >= engineType.length)
          alert("Engine has not yet been selected.");
        else
          alert("Engine: " + engineType[engineIndex]);
      }
    </script>
  </head>
  <body>
    <h1>Ford F150 Options <a href="http://www.ford.com/trucks/f150/trim/"
      style="font-size:medium; color:Blue;">(Ford site)</a></h1>
    <h2>Select Engine Type</h2>
    <form id="form1">
      <input type="radio" name="Engine" /><strong>3.5L V6 EcoBoost™ Engine</strong><br />
      <input type="radio" name="Engine" /><strong>3.7L V6 FFV Engine</strong><br />
      <input type="radio" name="Engine" /><strong>5.0L V8 FFV Engine</strong><br /><br />
      <input type="button" value="Display Choice" onclick="displayChoice();" />
    </form>
  </body>
</html>
```

Figure 111. Testing radio buttons using arrays

Compare Figure 111 to Figure 97 for the following discussion. Note first that in the HTML the **onclick** events have been removed from each of the buttons. Next, the function **setEngine()** is removed since it is no longer needed. Then, the variables **engineIndex** and **engineType** that were defined at the top of the script block have been moved to a new function called **displayChoice()**.

The **getButtonIndex()** function is the workhorse of the new solution. This function searches for radio buttons with the name specified: if no buttons are found with that name, -2 is returned, but if radio buttons are found, **getButtonIndex()** searches the buttons one at a time to find out if one of them is checked. If it finds a checked radio button, the index of that button is returned, and if none of the buttons are checked, the function returns -1.

The variable **engineIndex** is now set to the return value from **getButtonIndex()**, and this variable is used as an index into an array of engine descriptions to build the alert box message.

You may well want to save the code to **getButtonIndex()** and use it in your web pages. It includes error testing, so it will also work properly with invalid names and names of things that are not radio buttons.

The options Array in Drop-Down Lists

Sometimes you may need to reference the displayed text that is part of a drop-down list. Alternately, you might want to change something about the options – or even add options to the list – within code. Figure 112 is a revision to the drop-down list example of chapter 8 (seen in Figure 96).

```html
<html>
  <head>
    <title>Drop-Down List with Arrays</title>
    <script type="text/javascript">
      function displayChoice() {
        var index = form1.lstEngine.selectedIndex;
        if (form1.lstEngine.selectedIndex === 0)
          alert("Engine has not yet been selected.");
        else {
          alert("Engine Value:\t" + form1.lstEngine.value + "\n" +
               " Engine Text:\t" + form1.lstEngine.options[index].text);
        }
      }

      // ** Adds a dummy new option to the list. Multiple clicks add duplicates.
      function addOption() {
        var options = form1.lstEngine.options;
        var newOption = document.createElement("option");
        newOption.text = "8.0L V8 Dual Overhead Cam Hemi";
        newOption.value = "8.0L";
        options.add(newOption);
      }
    </script>
  </head>
  <body>
    <h1>Ford F150 Options <a href="http://www.ford.com/trucks/f150/trim/"
      style="font-size:medium; color:Blue;">(Ford site)</a></h1>
    <h2>Select Engine Type</h2>
    <form id="form1">
      <select id="lstEngine">
        <option value="Not SelectedL" selected="selected">Select engine below</option>
        <option value="3.5L">3.5L V6 EcoBoost™ Engine</option>
        <option value="3.7L">3.7L V6 FFV Engine</option>
        <option value="5.0L">5.0L V8 FFV Engine</option>
      </select><br />
      <input type="button" value="Display Choice" onclick="displayChoice();" /><br />
      <input type="button" value="Add New Choice" onclick="addOption();" /><br />
    </form>
  </body>
</html>
```

Figure 112. Referencing and updating options in drop-down list

The first change is to show the user both the value of the selected option and the text that was displayed in the list. This is done by accessing the **options** property of the list control. The **options** property is an array of option objects – with one object for each option in the list – and the option object at each location has two significant properties: **value** and **text**. The **value** property is the *value* attribute that could be obtained directly from the **<option>** element, and the **text** property is the text between the opening and closing tags of the `<option>` element. In addition, the `displayChoice()` function has been modified to show both of these pieces of information when an option is selected.

A new button has also been added that will allow a new entry to be added to the list of options, and this button calls the `addOption()` function. Since the `options` property of the list is an `Array` object, all the functions for arrays shown in Table 25 can be used on it, so the `addOption()` function uses the `Array` class `add()` function to add the new entry to the options list. (This function adds entries to the end of the list; by using other `Array` class functions, you could locate the new option anywhere in the list.)

What is actually being added to the `options` array is a new `<option>` element, which is created in code using the `document.createElement()` function. This function takes as its input parameter the type of HTML element being created, and after this element is created, the same two properties of `text` and `value` we saw earlier are set in the element before it is added to the list.

```
var newOption = document.createElement("option");
newOption.text = "8.0L Dual Overhead Cam Hemi";
newOption.value = "8.0L";
options.add(newOption);
```

Timing Things and the Date Class

In this section, you will learn how to have JavaScript call your functions at regular intervals. Two examples will be created: a clock program and an automatic scrolling image gallery. The code for these examples is well documented, so you can cut and paste from them into your own web pages.

The Date Class

One of the JavaScript core classes is the `Date` class, which is used for storing dates and manipulating dates in your scripts. A partial list of the constructors and functions for this class is given in Table 26. One limitation of the `Date` class that you need to be aware of is that a few of its functions require a date on or after January 1, 1970 (known in programming as the "epoch").

The `Date` class includes four different constructors, which you can choose from depending on how you want to specify the date to be used: use today's date; use the passed-in date encoded as a string; use the passed-in date specified by separate numbers for year, month, day, etc.; or use the date specified by the number of milliseconds since January 1, 1970. Choose the constructor that best suits your needs.

Date Class Constructors and Functions (Partial List)	
Constructor	**Description**
`Date()`	Creates a new `Date` object initialized with today's date.
`Date(milliseconds)`	Creates a new `Date` object whose date is determined by the number of milliseconds since midnight of January 1, 1970 (the "epoch", in programming terms).
`Date(dateString)`	Creates a new `Date` object whose date is calculated by parsing the input string. For example: `var jimsBD = new Date("October 29, 1984 01:08:00");`

`Date(year, month, day, hour, minute, second, millisecond)`	Creates a new `Date` object from the values passed in. Parameters are optional and 0 will be used if any are omitted. Note the order of the parameters, and especially that **year** is the first parameter. In the example below, the seconds and milliseconds are omitted, so 0 is used for those values.
	`var jimsBD = new Date(1984, 10, 29, 1, 8);`
	If you just want a date and not a time, just use the date information only:
	`var jimsBD = new Date(1984, 10, 29);`

Function	**Description**
`getDate()`	Gets the day of the month (1 to 31).
`getDay()`	Gets the day of the week (0=Sun 1=Mon 2=Tue 3=Wed 4=Thu 5=Fri 6=Sat).
`getFullYear()`	Gets the year (four-digit format, as in "1984").
`getHours()`	Gets the hour in a 24-hour format (0 to 23).
`getMilliseconds()`	Gets the milliseconds (0 to 999).
`getMinutes()`	Gets the minutes (0 to 59).
`getMonth()`	Gets the month (0=Jan, 1=Feb, ... 10=Nov, 11=Dec).
`getSeconds()`	Gets the seconds (0 to 59).
`getTime()`	Gets the milliseconds since midnight of Jan 1, 1970 (the "epoch").
`getTimezoneOffset()`	Gets the time difference between your local time and GMT (in minutes).
`parse()`	Scans a date string and computes the number of milliseconds between it and midnight of January 1, 1970 (the "epoch").
`setDate()`	Sets the day of the month (1 to 31).
`setFullYear()`	Sets the year from a four-digit number (for example, 1984).
`setHours()`	Sets the hour from a 24-hour format (0 to 23).
`setMilliseconds()`	Sets the milliseconds (0 to 999).
`setMinutes()`	Sets the minutes (0 to 59).
`setMonth()`	Sets the month (0=Jan, 1=Feb, ... 10=Nov. 11=Dec).
`setSeconds()`	Sets the seconds (0 to 59).
`setTime()`	Sets a date and time by adding or subtracting a specified number of milliseconds to/from midnight of January 1, 1970 (the "epoch").
`toDateString()`	Converts the date portion of a `Date` object into a human-readable string.
`toLocaleDateString()`	Converts the date portion of a `Date` object into a human-readable string, using locale conventions.
`toLocaleTimeString()`	Converts the time portion of a `Date` object into a human-readable string, using locale conventions.
`toLocaleString()`	Converts a `Date` object into a human-readable string, using locale conventions.
`toString()`	Converts a `Date` object into an abbreviated human-readable string. For example: `Thu Nov 29 01:08:00 EST 1984`
`toTimeString()`	Converts the time portion of a `Date` object into a human-readable string.

Table 26. Date class constructors and functions

Adding Days and Months to Dates

You can add days or months to a given date using the following technique. In the example, the `setDate()` function sets the day of the month and creates a new date, and the `setMonth()` function sets the month of the year and creates a new date. The `Date` class can handle a day out of range (less than 1 or greater than the number of days in the current month) or a month out of range (larger than 12 or less than 1) by updating the day, month, and year as needed.

```
theDate.setDate (theDate.getDate()  + daysToAdd);
theDate.setMonth(theDate.getMonth() + monthsToAdd);
```

Calculating Days between Dates

The `Date` class does not include any function for calculating the number of days between two dates. This function can, however, be created by using the number of milliseconds since January 1, 1970 for both dates and subtracting those numbers. This generates a number of milliseconds between the dates, which is then converted to days by dividing it by the number of milliseconds in one day. The complete code is shown in Figure 113.

```html
<html>
  <head>
    <title>Subtracting Dates</title>
    <script type="text/javascript">
      // ** Computes difference in days between two Date objects
      //    Subtracts date1 from date2, so a negative difference is possible
      function dateDif(date1, date2) {
        var MS_PER_DAY = 1000 * 60 * 60 * 24;     // Milliseconds in one day
        var dif = date2.getTime() - date1.getTime();  // Difference in milliseconds
        var days = Math.round(dif / MS_PER_DAY);   // Compute days from milliseconds
        return days;
      }
    </script>
  </head>
  <body>
    <script type="text/javascript">
      var dt1 = new Date(2010, 1, 11);
      var dt2 = new Date(2010, 3, 4);
      var dif = dateDif(dt1, dt2);
      alert("There are " + dif + " days between " +
        dt1.toDateString() + " and " + dt2.toDateString());
    </script>
  </body>
</html>
```

Figure 113. Computing days between dates

Clock Application Overview

The complete clock application example has been broken into three figures here. Figure 114 is the HTML, including the clock form and the internal stylesheet; Figure 115 is the first part of the JavaScript; and Figure 116 is the rest of the JavaScript. The application uses a table inside a form to display a short date and long date, and the display is updated every second. Buttons are included to stop and start the clock.

Clock Application HTML

The table that shows the dates is nested within a division for centering purposes. After the time and dates are calculated from the **Date** object, they are stored in the table by referencing the *id*s of the cells (**clock**, **shortDate** and **longDate**). An internal stylesheet is used to center the table (**center** and **centerFF**) and format the buttons (**btn**).

Finally, a timer is used to update the clock every 1,000 milliseconds (that is, every second), and arrays are used to store the strings for the days of the week and the months of the year.

```html
<html>
  <head>
    <title>JavaScript Clock and Dates</title>
    <style type="text/css">
      .btn { width:150px; }
      .center { text-align: center; }
      .centerFF { margin-left: auto; margin-right: auto; }
    </style>
    <script type="text/javascript">
      // JavaScript in next figure
    </script>
  </head>
<body onload="initPage();">
  <div class="center">
    <table border="2" class="centerFF">
      <tr><th colspan="2">Timer and Date Data Types</th></tr>
      <tr><th>Clock</th><td id="clock" class="center">??</td></tr>
      <tr><th>Short Date</th><td id="shortDate" class="center">??</td></tr>
      <tr><th>Long Date</th><td id="longDate" class="center">??</td></tr>
      <tr><th colspan="2">
        <input type="button" class="btn" value="Start Clock" onclick="startClock();" />
      </th></tr>
      <tr><th colspan="2">
        <input type="button" class="btn" value="Stop Clock" onclick="stopClock();" />
      </th></tr>
    </table>
  </div>
</body>
</html>
```

Figure 114. Clock application HTML

Setting and Clearing Timers

Figure 115 illustrates how a timer can be used to make something happen at regular intervals. The concept is this: a function (**updateClock()** in this case) is defined that will be called whenever a specified interval of time has elapsed. (This is a regular JavaScript function, but without any parameters.) To start this process, the library function **setInterval()** is called with two parameters: (1) the name of the function as a string (**"updateClock()"**) and (2) the number of milliseconds to wait between calls to the function (1000 in our case, or 1 second).

The timer is created in the **startClock()** function, which is called by both the Start Clock button and by the **pageInit()** function. Since it is called by **pageInit()**, the clock is started when the page is first loaded.

When the `setInterval()` function is called, it returns a timer ID variable for the interval that was started, which needs to be saved so that the interval timing can be stopped later. The code below saves this ID in the variable `timerId` that is placed at the top of the script, so it can be available to all functions.

When the function `stopClock()` is called, it in turn calls the library function `clearInterval()` and passes it the ID obtained earlier from `setInterval()`. To keep the button from trying to clear the interval timer multiple times, the `timerId` variable is set to *null* after the timer is stopped. Note that `stopClock()` first checks for a *null* value for `timerId` before trying to clear the interval, to avoid errors.

```javascript
// Interval timer object
var timerID = null;

// Page initialization: start interval timer and show data
function initPage() {
  startClock();
}

// ** Start Timer:
//   The interval timer is started with the function setInterval().
//   This function takes two mandatory parameters:
//     1) The name of the function to call each time the interval expires,
//        entered as a string
//     2) The number of milliseconds to delay between calls to the function;
//        to wait one second, set the second parameter to 1000, as shown here
//   Note that the setInterval() function returns a value, which is the ID for
//   the timer. This value is stored in a variable at the top of the script
//   and then referenced later by stopClock().
//   You may start as many timers as your script needs, but to stop them, you
//   will need to save the ID of each timer, as shown here.
function startClock() {
  if (timerID != null)  // Only start timer if it does not already exist
    timerID = setInterval("updateClock()", 1000);
    updateClock();
}

// ** Stop Timer
function stopClock() {
  if (timerID)                    // Only stop timer if it exists
    clearInterval(timerID);
    timerID = null;               // Not running so clear ID
}
```

Figure 115. Clock application JavaScript part 1

Creating the Time String

The function `showTime()` first creates a new `Date` object using the current date (which means no parameters are passed to the constructor). Then the individual values for hours, minutes, and seconds for the current time are obtained by using the `getHours()`, `getMinutes()`, and `getSeconds()` functions, respectively. The code then pads all minute and second numbers with a leading zero if the values are only one-digit numbers, and the time of day (AM or PM) is computed from the hour of the 24-hour clock (hours range from 0 to 23). Finally, all this is put together into a string and set as the `innerHTML` on the `clock` cell.

Creating the Date Strings

The function **showDate()** first defines two arrays, for the possible days of the week (**dayArray**) and for the possible months (**monthArray**). This is followed by getting and checking the date's year, and obtaining the day of the week, using **getDay()**. (This will be used as an index into **dayArray**.) Then the month and day of the month are obtained, using **getMonth()** for the month (which will be used as an index into **monthArray**) and **getDate()** for the day of the month, which is formatted as a two-digit value. Finally, the short and long dates are formatted and returned to the table.

```javascript
// ** Show Time: Makes the minutes and seconds into two-digit numbers,
//    uses a 12-hour clock, and shows AM or PM.
function showTime() {
  var now = new Date();                  // Get current date and time
  var hours = now.getHours();            // Split off the hours,
  var minutes = now.getMinutes();        //    minutes, and
  var seconds = now.getSeconds();        //    seconds
  if (minutes < 10)                      // Pad the mins and secs with zeros, if required
    minutes = "0" + minutes;
  if (seconds < 10)
    seconds = "0" + seconds;
  var timeOfDay;                         // Choose either "AM" or "PM" as appropriate
  if (hours < 12)
    timeOfDay = "AM";
  else
    timeOfDay = "PM";
  if (hours > 12)                        // Convert the hours component to 12-hour
    hours = hours - 12;
  if (hours === 0)                       // Convert an hour of 0 to "12"
    hours = 12;
  // Compose the string for display
  var nowString = hours + ":" + minutes + ":" + seconds + " " + timeOfDay;
  // Update the time display
  document.getElementById("clock").innerHTML = nowString;
}
// ** Show Date
function showDate() {
  // Labels for days and months
  var dayArray = new Array(
      "Sunday", "Monday", "Tuesday", "Wednesday", "Thursday", "Friday", "Saturday");
  var montharray = new Array("January", "February", "March", "April", "May", "June",
      "July", "August", "September", "October", "November", "December");
  // Get current date and time
  var now = new Date();
  var year = now.getFullYear();
  var day = now.getDay();                // Day of week: 0=Sun, 1=Mon, ... 6=Sat
  var month = now.getMonth();            // Month: 0=Jan, 1=Feb, ... 11=Dec
  var daym = now.getDate();              // Day of month: 1 ... 31
  if (daym < 10)                         // Force day of month to be two digits long by
    daym = "0" + daym;                   //    adding leading zero when < 10
  var monthLabel = montharray[month];    // Get month label
  var dayLabel = dayArray[day];          // Get day label
  // Generate labels
  var shortLabel = "" + (month + 1) + "/" + daym + "/" + year;
  var longLabel = dayArray[day] + ", " + montharray[month] + " " + daym + ", " + year;
  // Add dates to table
  document.getElementById("shortDate").innerHTML = shortLabel;
  document.getElementById("longDate").innerHTML = longLabel;
}
// ** Show time and date: called by timer
function updateClock() {
  showTime();
  showDate();
}
```

Figure 116: Clock application JavaScript part 2

Scrolling Image Gallery

Using the timer object as described above, a version of the image gallery from earlier in the chapter can be created that automatically scrolls through pictures at specified time intervals. The complete code is shown in Figure 117. The major change is that the function **startClock()** calls the function **nextImage()** after every clock interval. (Also, the function **startClock()** is called when the page first loads.)

```html
<html>
  <head>
    <title>Image Gallery with Two-Dimensional Array</title>
    <style type="text/css">
      .gallery { border: 4px groove green; width: 250; height: 190; }
      .caption { border: 4px groove green; width: 258; height: 30;
                 font-size:larger; font-weight:bold; }
      .button  { font-size:medium; font-weight:bold; }
    </style>
    <script type="text/javascript">
      var imgArray = [["Iguacu1.jpeg", "Top of Falls"],   ["Iguacu2.jpeg", "Panorama East"],
                      ["Iguacu3.jpeg", "Panorama South"], ["Iguacu4.jpeg", "Local Flower"] ];
      var curImage = imgArray.length - 1;      // Current image; set to end of list
      var timerID = null;                       // Interval timer object
      function showImage(index) {
        document.getElementById('imgGallery').src       = imgArray[index][0];
        document.getElementById('imgGallery').alt       = imgArray[index][1];
        document.getElementById('imgGallery').title     = imgArray[index][1];
        document.getElementById('imgCaption').innerHTML = imgArray[index][1];
      }
      function nextImage() {
        curImage++;
        curImage = curImage % imgArray.length;
        showImage(curImage);
      }
      function startClock() {
        if (timerID != null)   // Only start timer if it does not already exist
          timerID = setInterval('nextImage()', 1500);   // 1.5 seconds between photos
        nextImage();
      }        function stopClock() {
        if (timerID)                // Only stop timer if it exists
          clearInterval(timerID);
        timerID = null;             // Not running, so clear ID
      }
    </script>
  </head>
  <body onload="startClock();">
    <div style="text-align: center">
      <div class="caption">Pictures from Iguacu Falls</div>
      <img src="" id="imgGallery" alt="" class="gallery" />
      <div id="imgCaption" class="caption"></div>
      <input type="button" class="btn" value="Start Clock" onclick="startClock();" />
      <input type="button" class="btn" value="Stop Clock" onclick="stopClock();" />
    </div>
  </body>
</html>
```

Figure 117. Automatic-scrolling image gallery

Using the Image Gallery

If you wish to incorporate an image gallery in your code, start with the `ImageGalleryClock.html` example shown above and then change the `imgArray` array by adding rows of images inside the basic array. Use your names for the images and your captions for the captions. Also, adjust the time delay to your needs in the call to `setInterval()` inside the function `startClock()`.

Obtaining Environmental and Browser Details

Three objects that are useful when you work with the screen or need to determine your current environment are `screen`, `window`, and `location`. These objects are always available in JavaScript, just as the `document` object is. International standards list various properties and functions for these objects, but some of the properties differ from browser to browser. Therefore, this section will only document those properties that work with all browsers, or, for those that differ, document how to handle the differences. The reader should note that using these objects can be fairly complicated; because of this, you should plan on researching the Web as you develop pages with these objects.

The `screen` Object

The `screen` object describes the size and color depth/resolution of the screen, as shown in Table 27.

Screen Object Properties	
Property	**Description**
availHeight	Height of screen excluding the taskbar (returns full height in some browsers)
availWidth	Width of screen excluding the taskbar (returns full width in some browsers)
colorDepth	The color bit depth (typically 24)
height	The total height of the screen
pixelDepth	Color resolution in bits per pixel (typically 24)
width	The total width of the screen

Table 27. Screen object properties

The `window` Object

The `window` object, as documented on the Web, is not fully supported by all browsers. As a result, only one of its properties will be described here. That property is the `location` object, which has information about the page itself and also the server hosting the page. (The `location` object is covered in the next section.)

The `location` Object

The `location` object is available directly in JavaScript, just like the other objects we have discussed (`document`, `screen`, etc.) Alternately, this information is also available by referencing `window.location`. A partial list of the properties and functions of the `location` object are given in Table 27. Note especially the ability to see host information and the complete URL of the current page. Also note the functions that can be used for page navigation within JavaScript in the second part of the table.

Finally, note the difference between the `assign()` and `replace()` functions. The `assign()` function allows the browser user to click the back button and return to the current page. In contrast, the `replace()` function does not save the current location in the history and the back button goes to the page prior to the current page.

Location Object Properties and Functions (Partial List)	
Property	**Description**
`host`	The host server name and port
`hostname`	The host server name
`href`	The full URL to the page
`pathname`	The path name of the URL (that is, directory structure + filename)
`port`	The port number used on the server
`protocol`	The current protocol (usually `http:`)
`search`	The query string associated with the URL (if any)
Function	**Description**
`assign(pageName)`	Loads the specified page but allows a return back to the current page
`reload()`	Reloads the current document
`replace(pageName)`	Replaces the current page with the specified page, with no history or ability to go back to the current page

Table 27. Location object properties and functions

Review Questions and Exercises

Since this chapter presents optional topics for advanced students, there are no review questions or exercises.

CSS Style Guide Appendix

Specifying Styles

<u>Styles can be specified in one of three ways:</u>

1. *Inline* using the `style=` attribute, as shown below. Inline styles are used to change the display attributes of just one element. If multiple elements need to use the same style, that style should be specified as an internal or external style instead.

   ```
   <p style="text-align:center; font-weight:bold;"> . . . </p>
   ```

2. As an *internal* stylesheet, in the `<head>` section between `<style>` and `</style>`. Internal styles are used to specify styles that are particular to just that page. If multiple pages use the same styles, place those styles in an external stylesheet instead.

   ```
   <head>
     <style type="text/css">
       p { text-align:center; font-weight:bold; }
     </style>
   </head>
   ```

3. As an *external* stylesheet, with the link specified in the `<head>` section. Multiple `<link>` commands can be used and will be cascaded into one sheet, with the lower sheets redefining styles from sheets listed above.

   ```
   <head>
     <link rel="stylesheet" type="text/css" href="mystyle.css" />
   </head>
   ```

   Notes:
   a. The syntax between quotes in an inline style is identical to the syntax between braces in an internal or external stylesheet.
   b. If you specify both an external and an internal stylesheet, be sure to place the external `<link>` element *before* the internal `<style>` element.
   c. If a single element has a lot of style associated with it (like several lines of styles), don't place them in an inline style; instead, give the element an *id* and use the # notation in an internal stylesheet (see Three Ways of Defining Styles in an Internal or External Stylesheet below).

Design Issues

The external stylesheet defines the look and feel of the entire site (or for just selected portions of the site). As a website designer, you would plan the overall appearance of the site first and then place the style definitions in an external stylesheet (or stylesheets) that would achieve that appearance. Then, when specific pages need to vary from the overall style, place those changes in an internal stylesheet for each of those pages. Finally, if individual elements need to have changed appearances, these can be styled inline.

Three Ways of Defining Styles in an Internal or External Stylesheet

1. Use the element's tag type in the CSS to define attributes for that element type. Then, when an element is used in an HTML page that has that stylesheet included, the element will have that appearance defined. This method of defining style will occur in both *external* and *internal* stylesheets. Within the HTML there is no need to reference anything in the CSS file, though. All pages that reference the stylesheet in the example below will have `<h1>` centered. (Note that the `<link>` command shown below is assumed to be in all HTML pages shown here.)

   ```
   h1 { text-align: center; }
   ```

2. Define a class name (you pick the name) and use that class name in the HTML. The advantage over using the element's tag (method (1) above) is that the style can be applied to multiple types of elements. The class name can be defined globally (for all selectors/elements) or just for a single element. The element is defined in a CSS section, while class names tend to be more global in nature and affect multiple HTML elements; as a result, class names will more often be found in an *external* stylesheet.

   CSS Page: `.setCenter { text-align: center; } /* Global */`
   `p.setCenter { ... } /* Applies only to p */`
   HTML Page: `<h1 class = "setCenter" > ...`

   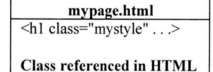 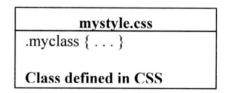

3. Reference the CSS class ID defined for the element. Here the element in one or more HTML pages is assigned a unique name (unique for any one page, that is). This name's style is then defined in a CSS section. The ID selector technique applies style to only one element on a given page; as a result, you will frequently find the ID selector in an *internal* stylesheet.

   CSS Page: `#h1Center { text-align: center; }`
   HTML Page: `<h1 id="h1Center" > ...`

   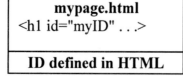 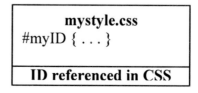

Note: in tables below, possible values for each property are in *italics*, and default values are in **bold**.

Backgrounds	
CSS Property	**Description**
background	Define all the background properties of an element at one time (in this order: color image repeat attachment position); values separated by spaces
background-attachment	Define whether background image is fixed or scrolls with page: *scroll, fixed, inherit*
background-color	Define background color of an element
background-image	Define background image
background-position	Position background image using pairs from *left, right, center* and *top, center, bottom*. Alternately: x% y% or x and y in pixels. Ex.: left top, right center, center bottom, 8% 2%, 20px 40px
background-repeat	Define if and how background image repeats: **repeat** (repeat horizontal and vertical), *repeat-x, repeat-y, no-repeat, inherit*

Borders and Outlines (see box model)	
CSS Property	**Description**
border	Define all border properties of an element at one time (in this order: width style color); values separated by spaces
border-bottom	Define all bottom border properties of an element at one time (in this order: width style color); values separated by spaces
border-bottom-color	Define bottom border color°
border-bottom-style	Define bottom border style: *none, hidden, dotted, dashed, solid, double, groove, ridge, inset, outset, inherit*
border-bottom-width	Define bottom border width: *thin,* **medium**, *thick,* length*, *inherit*
border-color	Define colors° of the four borders (in this order: top right bottom left); values separated by spaces
border-left	Define all left border properties of an element at one time (in this order: width style color); values separated by spaces
border-left-color	Define left border color°
border-left-style	Define left border style: *none, hidden, dotted, dashed, solid, double, groove, ridge, inset, outset, inherit*
border-left-width	Define left border width: *thin,* **medium**, *thick,* length*, *inherit*
border-right	Define all right border properties of an element at one time (in this order: width style color); values separated by spaces
border-right-color	Define right border color°
border-right-style	Define right border style: *none, hidden, dotted, dashed, solid, double, groove, ridge, inset, outset, inherit*
border-right-width	Define right border width: *thin,* **medium**, *thick,* length*, *inherit*
border-style	Define styles for all four borders, separated by spaces (in this order: top right bottom left): *none, hidden, dotted, dashed, solid, double, groove, ridge, inset, outset, inherit*
border-top	Define all top border properties of an element at one time (in this order: width style color); values separated by spaces
border-top-color	Define top border color°
border-top-style	Define top border style: *none, hidden, dotted, dashed, solid, double, groove, ridge, inset, outset, inherit*
border-top-width	Define top border width: *thin,* **medium**, *thick,* length*, *inherit*
border-width	Define widths for all four borders, separated by spaces (in this order: top right bottom left): *thin,* **medium**, *thick,* length*, *inherit*
outline	Define all outline properties of an element at one time (in this order: color style width); values separated by spaces
outline-color	Define outline color°
outline-style	Define outline style: *none, dotted, dashed, solid, double, groove, ridge, inset, outset, inherit*
outline-width	Define outline width: *thin,* **medium**, *thick,* length*, *inherit*

* **Size Options:** Sizes can be specified as numeric values with optional decimal places, followed by the dimensions in **cm** (centimeters), **em** (height of that element's font), **mm** (millimeters), **in** (inches), **pt** (points, where 1 pt = 1/72 inch), **pc** (picas, where 1 pc = 12 pt), **px** (pixels), or **%** (percentage). **pt** and **pc** are *not* recommended.

◊ **Color Options:** Colors can be chosen from *aqua, black, blue, fuchsia, gray, green, lime, maroon, navy, olive, purple, red, silver, teal, transparent, white,* and *yellow,* or entered as red/green/blue values using #rrggbb, where rr, gg, and bb are two-digit hex values, as in rgb(rr, gg, bb), or rgb(rr%, gg%, bb%), where rr%, gg%, and bb% are 0–100.

Dimensions and Size

CSS Property	Description (NOTE: does not include padding/borders/margins)
height	Define height of an element
max-height	Define maximum height of an element
max-width	Define maximum width of an element
min-height	Define minimum height of an element
min-width	Define minimum width of an element
width	Define width of an element

Fonts

CSS Property	Description
font	Define all the font properties of an element at one time (in this order: style variant weight size family); values separated by spaces
font-family	Define font family (text only)
font-size	Define font size: *xx-small, x-small, small,* **medium***, large, x-large, xx-large, smaller, larger, inherit*; also, percentages, points, and other units can be used
font-style	Define font style: **normal**, *italic, oblique, inherit*
font-variant	Define whether font is normal or small-caps: **normal**, *small-caps, inherit*
font-weight	Define font weight: **normal**, *bold, bolder, lighter, 100-900* (where *700* = bold), *inherit*

Generated Content Properties

CSS Property	Description
content	Combine with *:before* or *:after* pseudo-elements to insert content
counter-increment	Add 1 to one or more counters
counter-reset	Define or clear one or more counters
quotes	Define quotation mark type for quotes

List Properties

CSS Property	Description
list-style	Define all style properties of an element at one time (in order: type position image)
list-style-image	Define image to be used to mark list items
list-style-position	Define whether the list-item symbols are inside or outside the content flow: *inside,* **outside**, *inherit*
list-style-type	Define the type of list item marker: *none, circle, disc, square, decimal, lower-alpha, lower-latin, lower-roman, upper-alpha, upper-latin, upper-roman, inherit* (no Greek)

Margins (see box model)

CSS Property	Description
margin	Define margin properties for all four sides of an element at one time (in this order: top right bottom left); values separated by spaces
margin-bottom	Define bottom margin: *auto*, length*, *inherit*
margin-left	Define left margin: *auto*, length*, *inherit*
margin-right	Define right margin: *auto*, length*, *inherit*
margin-top	Define top margin: *auto*, length*, *inherit*

\multicolumn{2}{c}{**Padding** (see box model)}
CSS Property	**Description**
padding	Define padding properties for all four sides of an element at one time (in this order: top right bottom left); values separated by spaces
padding-bottom	Define bottom padding: *auto*, *length**, *inherit*
padding-left	Define left padding: *auto*, *length**, *inherit*
padding-right	Define right padding: *auto*, *length**, *inherit*
padding-top	Define top padding: *auto*, *length**, *inherit*

\multicolumn{2}{c}{**Positioning Block Elements**}
CSS Property	**Description**
bottom	Define the bottom margin for a positioned box: *auto*, *length**, *inherit*
clear	Define which floating elements are no longer floating: *left*, *right*, *both*, **none**, *inherit*
clip	Clips an absolutely positioned element (clips sides in this order: top right bottom left): **auto**, *inherit*
cursor	Define cursor type (many properties available)
display	Define how an element is to be displayed; choose from the following, depending upon the type of the element: *none*, *block*, **inline**, *inline-block*, *inline-table*, *list-item*, *run-in*, *table*, *table-caption*, *table-cell*, *table-column*, *table-column-group*, *table-footer-group*, *table-header-group*, *table-row*, *table-row-group*, *inherit*
float	Define how a box should float: *left*, *right*, **none**, *inherit*
left	Define the left margin for a positioned box: *auto*, *length**, *inherit*
overflow	Define how to display content that overflows its specified box: **visible**, *hidden*, *scroll*, *auto*, *inherit*
position	Define how to position a block element: *absolute*, *fixed*, *relative*, **static**, *inherit*
right	Define the right margin for a positioned box: *auto*, *length**, *inherit*
top	Define the top margin for a positioned box: *auto*, *length**, *inherit*
visibility	Define whether an element is visible or not: **visible**, *hidden*, *collapse*, *inherit*
z-index	Define stack order for overlapping elements: **auto**, *number* (can be negative), *inherit*

\multicolumn{2}{c}{**Print Properties**}
CSS Property	**Description**
orphans	Define minimum number of lines to remain at the bottom of a page when a page break splits an element; used when targeting a printer
page-break-after	Define how a page break is to occur after an element: **auto**, *always*, *avoid*, *left*, *right*, *inherit*
page-break-before	Define how a page break is to occur before an element: **auto**, *always*, *avoid*, *left*, *right*, *inherit*
page-break-inside	Define how a page break is to occur inside an element: **auto**, *avoid*, *inherit*
widows	Define minimum number of lines to remain at the top of a page when a page break splits an element; used when targeting a printer

Table Properties	
CSS Property	**Description**
`border-collapse`	Define how to show adjacent table borders: *collapse*, **separate**, *inherit*
`border-spacing`	Define spacing between borders of adjacent cells
`caption-side`	Define location of table caption: **top**, *bottom*, *inherit*
`empty-cells`	Define how to show borders and background on empty cells in a table: *hide*, **show**, *inherit* (NOTE: not handled uniformly by all browsers)
`table-layout`	Define how table is to be laid out: **auto**, *fixed* (based on cell sizes), *inherit*

Text Properties	
CSS Property	**Description**
`color`	Define text color for an element◊
`direction`	Define text direction for an element: *ltr* (left to right), **rtl** (right to left), *inherit*
`letter-spacing`	Define amount of increase (+value) or decrease (-value) in space between characters in a text element
`line-height`	Define line height for an element: **normal**, *inherit*, number, length*, or % (percentage value)
`text-align`	Define horizontal alignment for an element: *left, right, center, justify, inherit*
`text-decoration`	Define text decoration to be added to an element: **none**, *underline, overline, line-through, blink, inherit*
`text-indent`	Define amount of indentation for the first line in a text block (0 is default)
`text-transform`	Define capitalization of an element: **none**, *capitalize, uppercase, lowercase, inherit*
`vertical-align`	Define vertical alignment of a text element: length*, *baseline, sub, super, top, text-top, middle, bottom, text-bottom, inherit* (NOTE: a positive or negative length can be given to move up or down)
`white-space`	Define how to process whitespace within an element: **normal**, *nowrap, pre, pre-line, pre-wrap, inherit*
`word-spacing`	Define amount of increase or decrease in space between words in a text element: **normal**, length*, *inherit*; length can be positive or negative value

Pseudo-Classes / Elements (internal or external stylesheets only, not inline)	
Pseudo-Class	**Description**
`:active`	Adds a style to an element that is activated
`:after`	Adds content after an element
`:before`	Adds content before an element
`:first-child`	Adds a style to an element that is the first child of another element
`:first-letter`	Adds a style to the first character of a text element
`:first-line`	Adds a style to the first line of a text element
`:focus`	Adds a style to an element that has keyboard input focus
`:hover`	Adds a style to an element when you mouse over it
`:lang`	Adds a style to an element with a specific *lang* attribute
`:link`	Adds a style to an unvisited link
`:visited`	Adds a style to a visited link

CPSIA information can be obtained at www.ICGtesting.com
Printed in the USA
BVOW03*1138010914

364857BV00005B/7/P